"Lost" Causes

D1569907

"Lost" Causes

*Agenda Vetting in Global Issue Networks
and the Shaping of Human Security*

Charli Carpenter

Cornell University Press
Ithaca and London

Cornell University Press gratefully acknowledges receipt of a grant from the University of Massachusetts Amherst, which helped in the publication of this book.

First published 2014 by Cornell University Press
First printing, Cornell Paperbacks, 2014
Printed in the United States of America

Library of Congress Cataloging-in-Publication Data

Carpenter, R. Charli, author.
　Lost causes : agenda vetting in global issue networks and the shaping of human security / Charli Carpenter.
　　　pages cm
　Includes bibliographical references and index.
　ISBN 978-0-8014-4885-0 (cloth : alk. paper)
　ISBN 978-0-8014-7604-4 (pbk. : alk. paper)
　1. Human rights advocacy.　2. Globalization and human rights.
3. Human rights movements.　I. Title.
　JC571.C319　2014
　361.2'6—dc23　　　　　2013050932

Cornell University Press strives to use environmentally responsible suppliers and materials to the fullest extent possible in the publishing of its books. Such materials include vegetable-based, low-VOC inks and acid-free papers that are recycled, totally chlorine-free, or partly composed of nonwood fibers. For further information, visit our website at www.cornellpress.cornell.edu.

Cloth printing　　　　　10　9　8　7　6　5　4　3　2　1
Paperback printing　　　10　9　8　7　6　5　4　3　2　1

Contents

Plates follow page 30

PREFACE

In early December 2006, as part of my work on the human rights of children born of war rape, I sat in a meeting in Cologne, Germany, where human rights activists from several countries discussed strategies for addressing the social problems faced after armed conflicts by children fathered by foreign soldiers.[1] The meeting had been organized by social scientists at the University of Cologne and a Norwegian nongovernmental organization (NGO) concerned with adult "war children." The event drew together researchers from eastern Europe, the United States, and Africa to "consolidate the evidence base" on "children born of war" and develop a strategy for policy changes to address the needs of this population.

Present also at the meeting was a representative from the United Nations Children's Fund (UNICEF), and much discussion centered on whether the United Nations, and UNICEF in particular, should pay attention to the "war child" population. Over the course of the two days, the UNICEF representative consistently argued against this idea, stressing a variety of organizational, conceptual, and logistical issues. Toward the end of the conference, despite case data, statistical evidence, and eloquent rights-based arguments by several of the activists at the conference, the UNICEF representative stated, "I remain to be convinced of the merit of UNICEF treating these children as a specific group."[2]

What struck me about this interaction was the power dynamic between an elite bureaucrat from a highly influential node in the child rights network—UNICEF—and the less powerful, less well-connected entrepreneurs championing the cause of an overlooked group. I dwelt on this at some length in a chapter of my subsequent book, *Forgetting Children Born of War*. That book did not focus on advocacy networks specifically but rather on the entire set of institutions involved in constructing narratives of women and children in postwar Bosnia. Still, the question of how issues come to the attention of global advocacy organizations—and the significance of *certain* organizations in promoting or blocking such emergent ideas—caught my attention, given a general optimism at the time about the power of "transnational advocacy networks" in global norm-building. If advocacy networks were such an obvious force for good and a natural vehicle for individuals to mobilize pressure for social change from recalcitrant states, then how could we explain why so many causes got overlooked, even when norm entrepreneurs went to great lengths to format and present new ideas to these very networks?

Actually, why certain issues, ideas, and vulnerable groups fall through the cracks in global issue networks had fascinated me since early in my academic career, and I had long sensed that this was not a dynamic limited to the human rights network. In my dissertation on humanitarian affairs, I had documented how the gendered structure of both international norms and advocacy discourse produced a general inattention to the vulnerability of civilian men in conflict zones.[3] In my master's-level work on sovereignty and international space policy, I noticed how issues straddling seemingly disconnected policy arenas—such as environmentally friendly efforts to achieve interstellar travel—failed to achieve resonance or policy significance.

In thinking about these broader issues around 2007, I found little scholarly attention to the dynamics of issue neglect in international relations scholarship, and I found my own work on the subject matter limited by a small-N problem: like so much scholarship on successful advocacy campaigns, my research on issue neglect tended to draw on data from only one issue at a time. I could offer a detailed explanation of how one specific group fell off the global advocacy radar, but to what extent could I assume the factors that mattered in that case could explain other cases or could be generalized to other issue areas?

I wanted to study this in a more rigorous way. In 2007, several colleagues and I applied for and received an award from the National Science Foundation (NSF), which enabled us to develop models for studying global issue emergence empirically (any opinions, findings, and conclusions or recommendations expressed in this material are those of the author[s] and do not necessarily reflect the views of the NSF). The first year was spent developing, testing, and refining a methodology for tracking advocacy networks and issues online, and for identifying and exploring the nonemergence of neglected issues. The project enabled us to employ and train thirty-seven students, build and launch a sophisticated website, advance conceptual understandings of what is on the human security issue agenda and what is not, and build a theory explaining this variation by integrating domestic agenda-setting models into the study of transnational politics. For data on the issue agenda we drew on surveys and web content; for data on the preferences of human security elites, we drew on focus groups with human security practitioners; and for an understanding of how this process panned out over time on existing issues, I tracked the work of three emerging campaigns in three different issue areas: humanitarian affairs, security, and human rights.

The picture that emerges is profound: lots of issues get overlooked in international politics, and the survival or salience of issues is not determined by the merit of the issues themselves or the receptivity of the external environment. Rather, *relationships within the network* make all the difference—relationships between issues, between actors, between individuals, and between subnetworks themselves. The density of network ties, the nature of network ties, and individuals' judgments about the affiliations of others all influence perceptions about the credibility of messengers and the value of ideas in global networks. In this book, I show how and why this is the case.

Since my key method for understanding global networks was to talk to people located within them, this book would not have been possible without the willing engagement of practitioners. Numerous individuals embedded in and around the human security network allowed me to enter their spaces as an observer (and sometimes participant), and invested valuable time joining me in conversational settings of my own making—interviews, focus groups, and informal discussions. It is hard to express enough gratitude for these interactions: they are the legs this project stands on, the backbone of my data, and the key source of my insights. I am indebted to all those at the International Committee of the Red Cross, Human Rights Watch, Amnesty International, and the UN Office for the Coordination of Humanitarian Affairs, and myriad other NGOs, think tanks, UN agencies, and academic institutions for their time and insights about these global processes. I am especially indebted to those informants like Richard Moyes who went well beyond formal involvement as research subjects by engaging candidly in long exchanges on the dynamics of global agenda setting in a reflective, theoretically informed, and iterated way throughout the life of the study.

No study of this breadth could be completed without considerable institutional, intellectual, financial, and staff support. On the institutional side, the School of New Media Studies at the University of Amsterdam incubated these ideas at the New Network Theory conference in 2007; the Political Networks Section of the American Political Science Association fed and watered them throughout subsequent years. Simon Reich at the University of Pittsburgh's Ford Institute of Human Security provided personnel and office space during the early data collection phase. Brian Job at the University of British Columbia's Liu Institute for Global Issues shared his human security mailing list for my snowball sample. The NGO Equitas in Montreal provided access and logistical coordination to interview global South activists participating in their International Human Rights Training Program. Peter Uvin of the Institute for Human Security at Tufts University's Fletcher School provided facilities space and staff for the focus groups. The Department of Political Science and Center for Public Policy and Administration at the University of Massachusetts at Amherst provided the most supportive research environment imaginable including small grants, the opportunity to present our research at multiple workshops, and the freedom to build innovative classes integrating the research. And I am grateful to the fine folks at Amherst Coffee for allowing me to use their whiskey/wine bar as a work space for five straight years.

Four senior personnel on the NSF grant were indispensable to the project as it was conceived, developed, and implemented. Richard Rogers designed, built, and provided assistance with the online tools with which we gathered and visualized our data, including the Issuecrawler. Alex Montgomery worked painstakingly to create, tweak, and retweak the network visualizations in these pages, patiently corrected my many erroneous early interpretations of network data, and kept me laughing. James Ron picked apart my research design, supplemented it by sharing his own data on global South networks and embedding my questions in his surveys carried out in collaboration with Equitas, and provided critique, encouragement, and inspiration as a social scientist, issue entrepreneur, and great friend.

Finally, Stuart Shulman pioneered a unique approach to coding used in this project as founder and director of the Qualitative Data Analysis Program (QDAP), first at the University of Pittsburgh and then at the University of Massachusetts, where he and I traveled in 2008. The technical, analytical, and personnel support he and his coders provided shaped the feasibility and sophistication of this research and made it educational and fun. As an academic ally, Stu contributed numerous insights helpful to the overall ecology of the project: about grant writing, pedagogy, text analytics, the care and feeding of research assistants and research subjects, and the importance of leaving work behind sometimes and heading to the garlic patch, soccer pitch, or climbing wall.

Beyond these four, I also owe thanks to countless individuals for feedback, for sometimes no-holds-barred critique, and other intellectual contributions over the years. A few of the most important are Clifford Bob, who pioneered the "gatekeeper" model of global agenda setting that I expand on in this book; Daniel Nexon, who taught me to see power in terms of networks; Daniel Drezner, who got me thinking about relationships between online and offline social worlds; Robert Keohane, whose warm-hearted mentorship and a course-correcting early deep read were invaluable; Patrick Jackson for push-back on methodologies; Marty Finnemore, Susan Sell, and Debbi Avant, whose collaborative projects on governance and networks provided crucial opportunities for synergistic engagement as these ideas formed; and Kathryn Sikkink, for a riveting artillery barrage of helpful feedback just in time for final revisions.

Other important sources of insight and inspiration include Michael Barnett, Don Hubert, Peter Haas, Roland Paris, M. J. Peterson, Richard Price, and Wendy Wong. Participants and discussants at research presentations provided useful feedback at the University of Massachusetts, the University of British Columbia, the University of Southern California, the University of California at Irvine, Georgetown, George Washington

University, the University of Chicago, Columbia University, the University of Nebraska, Stanford University, and the University of Pittsburgh. My graduate student discussants at these forums deserve special praise, particularly Dawood Ahmed, Andrew Cockrell, Kerry Crawford, Rebecca Gibbons, and Michelle Jurkovich. Also, blog commenters at the Duck of Minerva, Current Intelligence, and Lawyers Guns and Money taught me a thing or two, deconstructing and refining early articulations of my findings.

Funding was crucial. I was lucky to receive support from the National Science Foundation's Human and Social Dynamics program and Law and Social Science programs, as well as internal grants from both the University of Pittsburgh and the University of Massachusetts. This money made possible field research in places such as Washington, New York, London, Geneva, Oslo, and Helsinki, where interviews were conducted and participant-observation at transnational sites occurred. It also covered the cost of flying human security practitioners to focus groups at Tufts University, of meetings with a team of collaborators from three countries and two continents, and of training students in web-sphere analysis and qualitative coding. The incredible staff at both Pitt and UMass (especially Michelle Goncalves, Trish Bachand, Laurel Person, and Sandy Monteverde) provided indispensable help administering the grant money and making sure I didn't break any rules. In addition I benefited from the kindhearted advice of multiple program officers at the NSF who shepherded me through the grant-writing/grant-getting process.

It was the student research assistance these grants provided that enabled me to collect, process, and analyze the data on which this book is based. I am honored to have worked with many gifted graduate students. Betcy Jose-Thota, Peace Medie, Ben Rubin, and Rebecca Wall oversaw the coding and assisted with conceptual development in the early phases of the project at the University of Pittsburgh, and other grad students did significant legwork in those early days: Luke Gerdes, Rachel Helwig, Vanja Lundell, Chris Moran, Marianne Nichols, Justin Reed, and Abbie Zahler. Carleton University students Sarah Peek, Phillipe Martin, and Maria Derks, and Kathleen Rodgers of McGill University assisted my colleague James Ron with interviewing global South activists, from whose experiences I derive my understanding of the human security network and agenda as seen from the developing world. At the University of Massachusetts, the focus groups could not have come together without the help of Sirin Duygulu and Anna Rapp; Sirin also helped build a medium-N dataset of campaigns on which I drew. Several doctoral students at Tufts University assisted with the focus groups: Zinaida A. Miller, Elizabeth McClintock, and Noel Twagiramungu. Kyle Brownlie oversaw the coding of the focus group data during a grueling yet memorable summer in the QDAP lab. Minako Koike, Jason Wilson, Ardeshir Pezeshk, and Katie Boom helped collect and visualize data on my case studies. Aparna Bagri built the project website; Nathaniel Develder provided additional digital support. The graduate students in my class on Global Agenda Setting also provided significant insight through their work testing this model against multiple emerging cases.

As I integrated my research into my human security classes at UMass, many brilliant undergraduates joined my research team, either implicitly through their engagement in the classroom or directly by helping put my case studies in order or working laboriously as coders, assisting me in making inferences from web content and focus group transcripts. In the latter category are Meghan Boesch, Olivia Faulkner, Dan Glaun, Gabrielle Griffis, Solomon Heifets, Emily Jacobs, Kendell Johnson, Nicholas Losso, Brian Quadrozzi, Casey Reinhardt, Lisa Shaikhouni, and Eric White. Solomon Heifets deserves special thanks for his past and ongoing engagement with the project as a student, research assistant, and intellectual peer.

In advising doctoral students, I tell them to enjoy the process of dissertation writing, because it is the only book they'll ever write where they will get constant mentorship while it is in progress. My experience with book editors since I left graduate school is that most manuscripts benefit from an editor's touch once they are written, but very few owe so much to the firm hand of a gifted, engaged editor throughout the process. So it has been a distinct pleasure to work with Roger Haydon of Cornell University Press given his uniquely engaged approach to not only the style of the work but to its substance. Roger served as a sounding board for these ideas long before they materialized on the page, encouraged me to see my earlier projects as leading logically toward this one, and provided the sort of lengthy, extensive, and probing written commentary on several early and untested drafts that one normally expects only from a dissertation advisor. Most important, he validated my work on cases at which many others raised eyebrows, encouraging me to ask the very questions and adopt the very reflective style that my training and institutional incentives encouraged me to avoid. Much of the final shape of this project is owed to Roger's vision and critical edge. I am also thankful to Cornell's editorial staff for working patiently with me on the production process, particularly the fairly tricky and unusual inclusion of color graphs.

Though it is too rarely recognized, work of this nature requires time away from hearth and home, and when raising children this in turn necessitates a particularly supportive and dynamic kind of family system. My children, Haley and Liam, both accompanied me politely on research forays at times, and patiently carried on in my absence at others. A skilled co-parent, a vast tribe of siblings, two grandmothers, irreplaceable neighbors, and gifted house sitters also filled in for me during gaps. I am especially grateful for the feats of surrogate parenting by Maryann Barakso, Ami and Renee Carpenter, Ruth Hutton, Brian Schaffner, Larry and Sheila Shulman, and Caitlyn Shatford at crucial junctures of this project.

However, of all the contributors to the creation of this book, the deepest gratitude goes to the norm entrepreneurs, those individuals pioneering innovative ideas in advocacy networks, often against great odds and at great personal cost, out of a sense of personal concern to make the world better for vulnerable populations. I thank the Campaign for Innocent Victims in Conflict directors and staff (especially Sarah Holewinski and Scott Paul); the experts associated with the International Association on Robot Arms Control (especially Noel Sharkey, Peter Asaro, and Mark Avrum Gubrud) and with the Consortium on Emerging Technologies, Military Operations and National Security (especially Ron Arkin); and the numerous members of the movement to ban infant male circumcision (especially Marilyn Milos, J. Steven Swoboda, and Georgeanne Chapin) for their time, confidence, and trust as I chronicled their activities.

I hope that the story I tell in these pages rings true to their experience and honors their efforts and achievements. What ties these various political entrepreneurs together is their unflagging vision and determination in the face of initial pitfalls and pushback from global policy networks. For some, it turned out to be a story of sudden success against all odds; for some it has been a story of slow but ever more heartening baby steps on the way to social change; for others it remains a story of diligence, fortitude, and persistence in the face of ongoing and sometimes incomprehensible silence from the very global organizations they most need as allies to achieve their goals. Understanding how network politics affects these outcomes will, I hope, provide new insights to these social change agents and to others who follow in their footsteps in pressing for new normative standards in global politics.

Acronyms

AI	Amnesty International
AWS	autonomous weapons systems
AWTG	Autonomous Weapons Thrust Group
CETMONS	Consortium on Emerging Technologies, Military Operations and National Security
CIVIC	Campaign for Innocent Victims in Conflict
DU	depleted uranium
ECOSOC	United Nations Economic and Social Council
FGM	female genital mutilation
HRW	Human Rights Watch
ICRAC	International Committee on Robot Arms Control

ICRC	International Committee of the Red Cross
IHL	international humanitarian law
IO	international organization
MAC	Making Amends Campaign
NATO	North Atlantic Treaty Organization
NGO	nongovernmental organization
NOCIRC	National Organization of Circumcision Resource Centers
NOHARMM	National Organization to Halt the Abuse and Routine Mutilation of Males
NORM	National Organization for Restoring Men
NSF	National Science Foundation
OCHA	Office for the Coordination of Humanitarian Affairs
OXFAM	Oxford Committee for Famine Relief
POC	protection of civilians
QDAP	Qualitative Data Analysis Program
TAN	transnational advocacy network

"Lost" Causes

1

Agenda Vetting and Agenda Setting in Global Governance

In April 2013, outside the steps of Parliament in London, a group of nongovernmental organizations (NGOs) launched a new campaign to ban the use of fully autonomous weapons. Concern over this issue had been raised since 2004 by political entrepreneurs from the academic community, but their calls for an anti-"killer-robot" norm had been virtually ignored by the advocacy community for over seven years. When asked about the issue in 2009, many advocacy elites in mainstream humanitarian disarmament organizations expressed bemusement. They pointed out that there were far more serious threats to human security in conflict zones, and that these weapons had not yet been developed or deployed. As one of them said, "You don't need a norm for science fiction." These heavyweights of human security refused opportunities to join calls for a ban. As late as spring 2011, no NGO had autonomous weapons formally on its agenda.[1]

Things began to change in late 2011 when the president of the International Committee of the Red Cross (ICRC) acknowledged the problem of fully autonomous weapons in a keynote address on emerging technologies.[2]

And they changed even more dramatically when another well-known NGO, Human Rights Watch (HRW), published a report the following year calling for a ban. [3] Within a month, nine well-known human security organizations had joined the steering committee for a new campaign. In April 2013, thirty NGOs showed up to a London conference on the topic prior to the launch of what was widely hailed as the "next landmine ban campaign." By mid-May, twenty-nine organizations had officially joined a growing list of signatories. "Killer robots" were suddenly creating the biggest "human security" buzz since cluster munitions.

What happened between 2004 and late 2012? Why did well-known organizations such as Human Rights Watch pay so little attention to autonomous weapons for so long, despite considerable lobbying from norm entrepreneurs, and why did this change so suddenly? Why did other human security organizations avoid the issue for so long, but join the campaign so readily once the ICRC acknowledged the issue and Human Rights Watch took the lead? And why did humanitarian disarmament campaigners set their sights on a category of weapons that didn't yet exist? Why not (for example) a campaign against depleted uranium weapons, said to harm the health of thousands in conflict zones, which had an even longer and more widespread history of concern by political entrepreneurs?

A rash of literature in the past two decades has hailed the significance of transnational advocacy networks in global norm development and governance. But much less research has focused on why such networks gravitate toward certain issues and reject or dismiss others at any particular time. And as this example suggests, the construction of new transnational issues clearly requires more than dedicated norm entrepreneurs. [4] For a new issue to be taken seriously, entrepreneurs must successfully market their issues within global political structures, and doing so is no simple task. Indeed, the story of the killer robot campaign suggests two truths about global advocacy work and raises two equally important questions.

The first of these truths is that new normative ideas do not float freely in global networks. It matters very much who is promoting them. Whereas entrepreneurs are always necessary, they are rarely sufficient or sufficiently skilled to effectively promote their ideas: new global norms are born or stillborn not merely due to entrepreneurs' dedication or persistence but by the grace and acquiescence of powerful organizations with access to global policy stakeholders. Professionals in these organizations, facing a menu of competing claims, must make strategic choices about where to place their attention. Only if these advocacy elites legitimize a new issue is it likely to proliferate. Like the killer robot ban campaign, other powerful human security norms—against child soldiering, conflict diamonds, landmines—hit the global agenda not when a norm entrepreneur raised the issue, however tirelessly, but when a mainstream human security organization eventually "adopted" it, throwing its institutional weight behind the idea. Causes that never get legitimized in this way seldom skyrocket to global prominence; those that never achieve prominence among global policy elites seldom result in meaningful global governance.[5]

Indeed, it is often easy to forget that transnational social problems with which we are now familiar were not preordained to succeed on their merits but are instead simply the lucky survivors of such a selection process. For example, Raphael Lemkin pitched the concept of "genocide" to a number of governments and celebrities before his idea found a home at the United Nations in 1948.[6] Women's rights groups worked unsuccessfully to mainstream their concerns into the human rights movement until Charlotte Bunch constructed the issue of "violence against women" and brought leading human rights NGOs on board.[7] But many other issue entrepreneurs are not so lucky, and find their causes dismissed, rejected, blocked, or simply ignored by advocacy elites. When this happens, their chances of achieving global resonance drop significantly. These elites do not just "set" the agenda: sometimes they actively "vet" the agenda as well.

This leads to the second truth: despite all the optimism about the power of global civil society, the media spotlight on successful campaigns blinds observers to myriad issues that never rise to the top of the global advocacy agenda.[8] In the disarmament area, many problematic weapons receive less advocacy attention than landmines, cluster bombs, small arms, or now robots: depleted uranium, fuel-air explosives, and pain weapons, to name a few.[9] The same variation holds true in other issue areas. Internal wars are an important concern for conflict prevention analysts but gangs and urban violence are on the margins of the global security agenda.[10] HIV/AIDS and severe acute respiratory syndrome (SARS) are championed as health issues while other communicable diseases such as pneumonia and Type 1 diabetes get only limited attention; nondisease health issues such as maternal mortality and the right to pain relief get even less.[11]

Figure 1. Human security issues according to survey respondents. Issue content from advocacy websites combined with survey responses to the question, "Name *three* or more specific issues that come to your mind when you think of human security today. An issue means something that human security specialists are actively concerned about." Font size corresponds to issue frequency in dataset, averaged across both data sources. Visualized by Many Eyes.

These twin observations lead us to three questions addressed in this book through a discussion of several neglected causes. First, what gives a few organizations such disproportionate influence over the advocacy agenda? Second, what determines how they choose to use this power? That is, given the agenda-setting (and agenda-vetting) power of global advocacy elites, how do they decide what to work on and what to ignore? What distinguishes the issues that they eventually "adopt" and launch to prominence from those that they ignore or dismiss, and which continue to fall through the cracks? And third, given these dynamics, how can issue entrepreneurs championing neglected issues successfully press their claims on the global stage?

In this book I show that the answer to all three questions is to be found in the structure of global networks themselves. Expanding on Clifford Bob's influential study of human rights organizations, I argue that "agenda vetting" constitutes a powerful form of global governance. But unlike earlier studies, I show the power to set or "vet" the advocacy agenda is not an intrinsic attribute of organizations but rather a function of their structural position within networks. Indeed, the logic of network relations not only confers special agenda-setting and agenda-vetting power on certain organizations but also plays a crucial role in determining the answer to the second question: how they decide when to invest resources and attention, and when to withhold it. My research shows that advocacy elites choose issues not just based on their merits, or mandate, or the wider political context, but partly on calculations about the structure of their institutional relationships—to other actors, to other issues, and to networks themselves. Therefore, understanding how to use network ties strategically is a key ingredient in any recipe for successful global norm entrepreneurship.

I arrived at this conclusion by analyzing agenda setting in a "network of networks"—the transnational advocacy network associated with the concept "human security." Although the language of "human security" is on the decline,[12] the concept continues to be useful to describe and bound what Roland Paris has called "the glue that holds together a jumbled coalition of 'middle power' states, development agencies and NGOs seek[ing] to shift attention away from conventional security issues and toward goals that have traditionally fallen under the rubric of international development."[13]

Indeed, my research shows that aside from conceptual debates about the term's meaning, a human security network exists as an empirical fact.[14] It is composed of several subnetworks and includes organizations working in the areas of human rights, humanitarian affairs, arms control or disarmament, environmental security, conflict prevention, and development. It also includes many "hybrid" organizations that do work in more than one of these areas and many initiatives that cut across these specific communities of practice.[15] This broad "human security" network (like others) includes not only nongovernmental organizations but also international organizations (IOs) such as the United Nations (UN), international specialized agencies such as the World Health Organization (WHO), governments, academics, regional bodies, foundations, and think tanks.[16]

Of these, organizations vary in terms of their centrality to or connectedness with the rest of the network and to specific subnetworks. My central claim is that for any given issue network within this space, the most important agenda-setting and agenda-vetting power is held by the organizations most centrally connected to that subnetwork, and most connected to the entire network. I develop a theory of how such "hubs" construct their preferences over which issues to select or avoid—focusing not only on the political economy of ideas and moral altruism but also on how structural relations within networks affect actor preferences.

In developing and testing this model, this book fills four important gaps in the literature on transnational advocacy networks. First, it focuses on how advocacy networks determine their own agenda, rather than how effectively they influence the practices of states. Even though the relationship between advocacy networks and global policymaking has been established,[17] very little empirical research currently exists explaining why transnational activists themselves mobilize around certain kinds of problem and not others at specific points in history. Some hypotheses are implicit in the literature, yet rarely tested.[18] Yet understanding why issues emerge at all is very important, since absent effective problem construction within global civil society, changes in state behavior are unlikely.

Second, this analysis advances theories of global "issue creation" by distinguishing between issue definition by local activists and issue adoption by powerful civil society actors at the center of advocacy networks. Much of the earlier literature on issue creation focused on the role of issue entrepreneurs, but the examples above suggest there is considerable variation in the ability of issue entrepreneurs to convert their ideas into global norms.[19] A permissive or inhibiting role is also played in issue creation by actors with the ability to disseminate and promote new issues but who pick and choose among the range of possible emerging claims, launching some issues to prominence and sidelining others. Understanding the relationship between problem definition by entrepreneurs, issue adoption by advocacy elites, and issue diffusion throughout a network is vital for grasping the construction of global norms.

Third, in so doing, the project "unpacks" the concept of the "transnational advocacy network." Earlier literature on advocacy networks has tended to view them as a monolithic force in a uniform dialectic with the state system. Jutta Joachim's book on agenda setting, for example, posits an NGO sector in contradistinction to a UN sector, but does not examine hierarchies, conflict, and power differentials among NGOs themselves.[20] Clifford Bob looks at NGOs as "gatekeepers" but neglects other actors that also inhabit advocacy networks and exert influence over the global agenda: epistemic communities, donors, celebrities, IOs, governments, and individual citizens with particular forms of expertise.[21] By opening the black box of the "transnational advocacy network" through both network analysis and in-depth case studies, I contribute a critical view of power relations *within* global civil society, as well as between civil society and states.

Finally, in contrast to existing studies of advocacy campaigns, this book focuses primarily on cases during the period *before* agenda setting has succeeded. The limited work explicitly tracing the emergence of new issues on the international agenda is generally based on case studies of issues that *have* emerged, making it difficult to test hypotheses for issue creation against negative cases. In focusing on the political power involved in agenda vetting, I aim to understand the selection process whereby certain ideas are precluded from gaining a foothold on the transnational advocacy agenda. These "negative events" are as significant as visible campaigns in constituting global issues, norms, and standards and reshaping state behavior; and the process of agenda denial, while examined in the domestic policy literature, has been drastically understudied by international relations scholars. By comparing dogs that didn't bark (or have barely started barking) to the rich empirical literature on issues that have successfully emerged in the past, I illustrate the politics of agenda vetting in practice.

"Entrepreneurs" and "Advocacy Elites": Issue Creation in Advocacy Networks

This book focuses on the dialectic between norm entrepreneurs and authorities in specific transnational issue domains in converting global social problems into "issues."[22] A large scholarly literature has, since the late 1990s, documented the power of transnational advocacy networks (TANs) in global civil society.[23] As the literature has demonstrated, networks such as these do a great many things, including lobbying, standard setting, monitoring of compliance with standards, and shaming norm violators;[24] and much of the emphasis has been on demonstrating that their efforts actually make a difference when it comes to what states do. But two of the most pivotal yet understudied aspects of transnational network politics are the construction and acceptance of specific problems as international issues in the first place.[25] These twin steps, together constituting what I call *issue creation*, are logically prior to building campaigns, negotiating treaties, and holding states accountable to new norms.

Understanding the dynamics of issue creation is crucial to assessing the power of TANs in world politics. Not all global social issues become codified as international norms: once an issue has emerged within a TAN issue pool, it may or may not elicit a campaign or concerted action. But if an issue never enters the agenda, effective advocacy is rarely possible, since all subsequent advocacy politics depend on an issue being defined as such by a norm entrepreneur and accepted as such by a critical mass of activists and gatekeepers. In short, issue creation is the conceptual link between the myriad bad things out there and the persuasive machinery of advocacy politics in world affairs. Everything, in a sense, depends in the first place on the advocacy agenda.[26]

So the key question motivating this book is how to explain variation in the issue creation stage: How do global social problems become transnational issues, and why do some issues end up on TAN agenda space while others fall by the wayside? Although existing TAN literature tends to talk only vaguely about "norm entrepreneurship" as a permissive condition driving campaigns, it is useful to distinguish at least two necessary phases of transnational issue creation, either of which may fail to occur: *issue definition* by an entrepreneur and *issue adoption* by one or more major advocacy organizations.[27] The distinction is vital for understanding issue creation, because an issue may be defined by an entrepreneur but not adopted into the mainstream TAN discourse by advocacy gatekeepers.

Issue definition is the first step in the global policy cycle.[28] It involves both identifying a problem and linking it to some official platform. Problem definition is the process of demonstrating "that a given state of affairs is neither natural nor accidental, identify[ing] the responsible party or parties, and propos[ing] credible solutions."[29] Problems are defined when actors articulate the case that existing conditions are wrong and are changeable. But problem definition by any one individual does not ensure that an issue will be constructed as such on anyone's policy agenda. To go from being a "problem" to an "issue" requires some organizational platform or official agenda. This could be an academic institution, a small NGO, an individual, or a group that goes beyond complaining about a problem to mobilizing institutionally to solve it.[30]

By contrast, issue adoption occurs when an entrepreneur convinces at least one major player in a broader network, associated with the issue cluster in which the new issue is conceptually embedded, to incorporate the

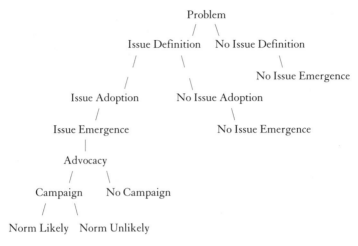

Figure 2. Issue emergence in global civil society.

new issue into its formal agenda. This moment has enormous conceptual and political significance. According to Clifford Bob, the formal adoption of an issue by at least one powerful player within an advocacy network is a defining moment in the construction of new issues on the global stage. It is a hurdle that must be passed for an idea to move from nascent to politically salient within global civil society; and a prerequisite for the development of a campaign that might result in new international norms.

This effect is so powerful because of the structure of issue networks in global civil society. For any global issue area, a handful of actors possess the largest budgets, the greatest name recognition, the most access, and the densest network with the other core actors as well as with advocacy targets and stakeholders. They are the ones that will come to mind when people think of a particular issue area. Beyond these "hubs" are a cluster of "core" organizations enjoying a modicum of recognition by the hubs that can play matchmaking roles with other core or hub organizations in the network. They enjoy connections to and relationships with the hubs. Beyond those are many small or "no-name" NGOs whom very few people could name if asked. Their ties to the core of the network tend to be unidirectional and aspirational. Their agendas matter much less in defining the overall issue pool for the intersubjectively understood "human rights" or "environmental" or "arms control" issue areas.

The best issue adopter for a new cause will depend on the issue and the specific thematic issue area. For actors pitching "disability rights" to the United Nations, the endorsement of human rights for disabled people by Amnesty International (AI) constituted an important moment of legitimation for the movement; as Janet Lord has documented, Human Rights Watch's unwillingness to adopt the issue had previously posed an obstacle.[31] That is because AI and HRW are the two most widely recognized human rights NGOs. For the network advocating against infant male circumcision, the denial of such legitimation by the same players compromises the entrepreneurs' ability to use rights-based rationales when they take their cause to the media, the public, or the United Nations. On the other hand, for entrepreneurs concerned with little-known environmental issues, such as the export of waste products to developing countries, it is acknowledgment not by AI but by an environmental leader such as Greenpeace or the World Wildlife Fund that will catapult their issue into global notoriety. For advocates of fair trade in particular commodities, it is recognition by organizations concerned with socially responsible consumerism and social justice that matter.

This is why, as I show in chapter 2 and the case studies, that what Bob calls "gatekeeper" status is best understood as a relational construct, not an attribute of specific organizations. The flow of information, ideas, and frames throughout an advocacy network involves many points of contact, with each organization or individual convinced of the worth of an idea pitching it tactically to players on the chain with greater credibility, legitimacy, or access than they themselves possess. At any point in this process, agenda vetting may occur, altering the potential of the idea to reach policymakers, and changing how it is formulated.

Though Bob's pathbreaking analysis was focused on insurgent movements within states pitching their grievances to international NGOs, the same logic applies to many current thematic issues in global society and many different types of organizations. Indigenous movements may vary in the extent to which they can get international attention; but the thematic concept of indigenous rights as a global issue area itself was also an idea that required adoption by key players within the human rights movement before it began to receive policy attention at the United Nations. Other thematic issues claimed as "rights"—like the right to bear arms or the right to water—have had less success on the international agenda because they have had less legitimation from the human rights mainstream. The same dynamic holds true in other areas such as global health.[32]

This rise of issues on the global agenda and their conversion to international normative standards is not necessarily a linear or one-time process. The campaign to end child recruitment, for example, went through several iterations of issue creation and re-creation. Yet in each case, the agenda cycle looked much like the model visualized above.[33] Norm development may also stall for a time even once an issue is on the formal advocacy agenda. It rarely occurs at all, however, without concerted attention to a problem and resources from the players in advocacy networks with the greatest name recognition, resources, access, and clout.

There are of course exceptions to this rule. Sometimes, actors are able to take their ideas directly to their targets of influence with some success and enact policy changes without global campaigns for norm change. For example, as described in chapter 4, the Campaign for Innocent Victims in Conflict (CIVIC) managed to convince certain governments to provide condolence payments to civilians in the absence of a global norm, and only later set their sights on creating an expectation of such action.[34] In other cases, global norms themselves emerge in the absence of widespread transnational campaigns, usually when powerful states themselves are the entrepreneurs.[35] Moreover, in cases where the targets of influence are highly motivated for strategic or normative reasons to preempt a campaign before it mobilizes, governance around a newly defined problem can emerge so quickly that the issue adoption process within advocacy networks, though it may still unfold, exerts little decisive effect on the policy process. In the case of conflict diamonds or the UN's scandal over sexual exploitation by peacekeepers, policy change was facilitated and hastened by the extreme sensitivity of the perpetrators—the diamond industry and the UN—to public embarrassment, triggering a swift desire to be seen to do something.

In many cases, however, advocacy campaigns precede international norm change. A flourishing international relations literature documents myriad cases where international normative understandings would not have been altered but for the political imagination and concerted action by coalitions of activists. This is usually the case where the targets of influence are opposed or indifferent to the idea of the new norm.[36] My argument is that under conditions when transnational advocacy campaigns *do* matter, issue adoption by at least one powerful actor within a preexisting network is a crucial prerequisite for successful agenda setting. Although political entrepreneurs outside the system are often the best source of new normative ideas, governments take these ideas much more seriously when they come from United Nations agencies or NGOs with whom they are familiar and have a historical working relationship than from political entrepreneurs outside this formal system. According to Don Hubert, "The message may be the same, the evidence may be the same, but official 'letterhead' matters to governments."[37] Absent this legitimation by a hub within a network, issues can sometimes succeed, but they are likelier to stall or remain marginal to the global agenda; and unless championed by states rather than global civil society actors, they are unlikely to result in global "norms."

Agenda Vetting and Political Power in Advocacy Networks

The point of all this is to emphasize that a significant amount of understudied effort by political entrepreneurs goes not into teaching or persuading states, but rather into selling their ideas to the advocacy elites who can carry their message to governments. Because of this dynamic, a significant power relationship exists between issue entrepreneurs and global governors who control the advocacy agenda, one with crucial yet poorly understood implications for the normative structure of global politics.[38]

This bears some foregrounding given that many individuals working in the most influential advocacy organizations do not see themselves as powerful because they are comparing themselves to the states whose behavior they hope to change. But in wielding such an influence over what enters or is excluded from the global agenda, these leading advocacy organizations determine the ideational content and reinforce or strategically alter the structure of global civil society, contributing to the regulation or nonregulation of political outcomes affecting the lives and security of individuals. Defining what counts as a legitimate advocacy claim within an issue domain constitutes an exercise of at least three of the types of power outlined by Barnett and Duvall in their pathbreaking study.[39]

First, it offers or denies *institutional* power to claimants on the material resources and ideational influence of respected advocacy organizations in global civil society. Within advocacy networks, constituent parts' authority and influence is based on moral legitimacy and persuasive power.[40] As Lake and Wong have demonstrated, in transnational advocacy networks "nodes in networks are not equal": that is, some entities have much greater influence than others.[41] Their analysis describes the contagion effect on the human rights community when leading NGOs such as Human Rights Watch or Amnesty International begin referencing new issues; correspondingly, many problems never get defined or, once defined, never spread because they are not endorsed by powerful gatekeepers, whose "choices have powerful demonstration effects, signaling that certain causes are important."[42] By articulating a new problem as an "issue," a network hub legitimizes that problem and defines it in a particular way, thus triggering donor attention and material resources, and affecting the visibility of that issue within the informational content of the issue network to which it is associated.

Second, this agenda-setting/agenda-vetting process does not simply channel the soft power of global civil society, relative to states, toward some issues and away from others: it is also in itself an expression of *structural* relations of power *within* advocacy networks. The asymmetrical influence of powerful organizations in a network stems from factors such as relative connectivity to the rest of the network; name recognition; financial capacity; linguistic, diplomatic, and technological mastery; and access to states and global policymakers. In a global sector defined by its ability to invest symbolic meanings with legitimacy and to disseminate information effectively, these are coveted resources.[43] Granting or denying access to such resources is itself an expression of power that reproduces the central place of such gatekeepers within the structural hierarchy of a transnational network. The creation of rules and procedures by which such requests are considered is itself a form of governance.[44]

Third, selecting issues for adoption constitutes a form of *productive* power.[45] The construction of "child soldiers" or "HIV-AIDS orphans" as specific categories of concern signals a need for policies to address such populations, and produces new claims on the governance activities of states, NGOs, and international organizations.[46] Conversely, to determine which voices shall not be given credibility in such forums constitutes an exercise of power that decisively shapes the global agenda. As Holzscheiter writes, "The subjugation of minority voices originates in a manipulation of the issues that are talked about, in the limitation of legitimate participants in the discussion and of the ways of talking about the issues."[47]

Such a practice of "non-decision-making," to draw on Bachrach and Baratz's famous articulation of the process, constitutes an exercise of what these authors refer to as the "second face of power": "When the dominant values, the accepted rules of the game, the existing power relations among groups, and the instruments of force, singly or in combination, effectively prevent certain grievances from developing into full-fledged issues which call for decisions...a non-decision-making situation exists. To pass over this is to neglect one whole face of power."[48]

Limiting the scope of decision making to "safe" or politically "acceptable" issues is an act of power.[49] Thus, actors in a position to determine which issues their leading organization shall formally adopt govern the global agenda by influencing definitions of what constitutes a public good.[50] When Amnesty International and Human Rights Watch acknowledged women's rights as part of their global human rights agenda, it lent strength to women's mobilization by signaling the fundamental, rather than subsidiary, importance of gender issues, by situating women's concerns within rather than as separate from the broader movement, and by committing their own advocacy influence to the movement.[51] By contrast, institutionalized violence and discrimination under India's caste system was tolerated for decades until Indian activists convinced human rights gatekeepers to address their concerns under the rubric of "work-based discrimination."[52]

The decisions of network hubs nested in different issue domains also have an important effect on *how* issues are framed. It is one kind of political act to deal with the protection of civilians within the humanitarian arena; it is a different political act to begin treating this as a security problem at the level of the UN Security Council. Similarly, landmines were once treated primarily as an arms control problem; reframing them as a humanitarian concern required the mobilization of prominent civil society organizations, and this reframing had consequences for eventual governance in this area, as well on the chances of related problems (such as cluster munitions) themselves receiving attention.[53] In Africa, lead organizations and donors often ask whether an issue is security or development related, given that these are the current master frames driving the human security issue agenda.[54] Thus, agenda-vetters place conditions on the way in which a problem can be articulated in order to receive their endorsement, and issue entrepreneurs must often resist having their problem definition watered down.[55]

Because of their power and their role in the global agenda-setting process, it thus becomes crucial for scholars of civil society and activists pressing new claims on states to understand the decision-making practices and preferences of these global advocacy elites or "gatekeepers." The rest of this book offers precisely such a road map, drawing on the insights of numerous practitioners within lead advocacy organizations. It combines an overall theory of agenda vetting with a set of illustrative cases that expose the complexity of intranetwork politics in global civil society.

Methodolog(ies) and Outline of the Book

In the next two chapters, I first demonstrate the power of agenda vetting, detailing how structural position as a network hub confers authority within networks, and correlating the absence of "hub organization" support to a variety of failed campaigns. I then propose a theory of "advocacy elite" preferences, describing what authorities positioned in hub organizations want, why they gravitate toward certain issues and not others, and the strategies they use for exercising agenda denial in certain cases, or issue appropriation in others. The empirical grounding for this general argument is comparative case analysis, focus groups, surveys, in-depth interviews, and website analysis of the cluster of actors (including NGOs, governments, think tanks, and IOs) most centrally associated with the advocacy network around "human security."[56]

Any general study of elite decision making in constructing global issues requires three key steps: measuring the existing issue agenda for a particular network, capturing problems that have been identified by activists but are not yet on a network's issue agenda, and gathering insights from actual practitioners that can explain this variation. I briefly discuss each of my data sources below; a more detailed description of how the data were collected, coded, and analyzed appears in the appendix.

Measuring the issue agenda. In this book, I combine three sources to gauge the salience of issues on the global agenda for the period of this study: advocacy websites, surveys, and focus groups with individuals associated with the human security network. Websites within the human security network were identified using co-link analysis tools, and text data from the "mission statements" and "issues" sections of organizational home pages were captured and coded to identify the most and least salient issues on the human security agenda. I triangulated this with an online survey of practitioners associated with the actual network around "human security," disseminated to those on the University of British Columbia's Liu Institute for Global Issues mailing list and then by snowball method. Although it is impossible to get a representative sample of a transnational network, survey responses to questions such as "which organizations come to mind when you think about human security?" and "which issues come to mind when you think about human security?" enabled me to corroborate the findings of the web-based analysis.

Capturing nonissues. The selection of negative cases constitutes an important problem for agenda-setting theory. First, it is impossible to know the total population of negative cases and, as with advocacy networks themselves, representative sampling of "nonissues" is therefore infeasible. A tempting solution is to gravitate toward cases known to the researcher, but this introduces an unacceptable amount of researcher bias into the study. I developed a population of candidate cases by asking survey, interview, and focus group respondents to tell me which human security problems they knew of that had received too little attention from advocacy organizations.

Studying advocacy elite preferences. I gathered data on the decision-making process of advocacy gatekeepers in organizational hubs from three sources. First, I conducted a series of focus groups with practitioners drawn from organizations identified as belonging to the human security network, to talk broadly about agenda-setting politics within the network.[57] Second, I conducted in-depth interviews around this broad question with representatives of three influential organizations particularly relevant to my case studies: Human Rights Watch, the International Committee of the Red Cross, and the United Nations Office for the Coordination of Humanitarian Affairs.[58] Third, in both interviews and focus groups, I asked respondents to think hypothetically about specific "nonissues" drawn from responses to the survey, or relevant to the cases I was studying, and explain whether their organization would consider joining a campaign for that issue, and why or why not. These various methods and data are used to develop the arguments laid out in chapter 2, and are explained in further detail in the appendix.

Case selection. Chapters 4–6 consist of detailed case studies illustrating the dialectic between issue entrepreneurs (who define a global "problem" and pitch it to powerful players in existing advocacy networks) and network gatekeepers who decide whether and how to "adopt" a new problem into an existing advocacy agenda; or whether and how to block it altogether. In each chapter, I highlight the variation that exists within the specific issue area in terms of issues on the agenda and candidate issues; and, within that context, I examine a particular case for insight into the moment when an issue is stalled in the agenda-setting process and why.

Chapter 4 tracks emerging advocacy in favor of a right to compensation for civilians harmed by legitimate military operations, an issue that is now gaining ground but had previously been opposed by antiwar groups and some humanitarian organizations. Chapter 5 documents the efforts of epistemic communities to promote a precautionary principle governing the deployment of autonomous robots in conflict zones; the initial resistance encountered by leading organizations advocating for weapons bans, such as the International Committee of the Red Cross; and how this changed. Chapter 6 examines the efforts of issue entrepreneurs to define infant male circumcision as a human rights violation, and explains the ongoing agenda denial exercised by leading human rights NGOs and the United Nations. The cases were developed through a combination of content analysis, process tracing, participant-observation, and elite interviews with both seasoned advocacy elites in organizational hubs and with issue entrepreneurs.

In selecting these illustrative cases, I sought out cases in which (a) an issue entrepreneur had already identified the problem and a platform for defining the issue, and was engaged in a process of dialogue with gatekeepers on how to move forward, and (b) at the time of the research the issue had not yet become salient on the human security agenda. From the range of cases available that I might have followed, my selection of these three cases was influenced by ethical, conceptual, and logistical concerns.

First, because the process of researching nonissues inevitably constitutes a notable, if modest, agenda-setting enterprise in itself, researchers cannot afford to be sanguine about the types of conversations they have with practitioners. This means case selection is a question of ethics as well as methodology. When one asks a policy practitioner to explain his or her organization's inattention to a specific social problem, one inadvertently becomes a de facto spokesperson for "problems" identified by social change agents.[59] Therefore, raising new or unknown issues in conversational settings with practitioners can come close to a form of action research, even where that is not the intent. To address this, while I did not go into the research process with the goal of promoting any particular cause, nor did I actively participate in advocacy on any of these campaigns during the period of field research,[60] I did choose issues that I felt had a plausible chance of contributing to the general goal of human security if attended to by global policymakers.[61]

Second, this choice served a helpful conceptual purpose in guiding the study: it meant that I limited my analysis to "hard cases," where the logic for issue creation can be clearly articulated from a human security perspective, and where therefore the absence of the issue from the agenda is theoretically most puzzling. In other words, while several interview respondents in this study told me, "You know a lot of ideas out there just aren't very good ideas," in this study I have focused only on ideas that are at least as plausible from a human rights/human security perspective as many others already on the global agenda.

Finally, I focused on issues where I was easily able to gather real-time data in a continuous manner over the life of the study through frequent iterated contacts with activists. My choice to follow the CIVIC campaign, for example, stemmed partly from easy proximity to Washington, DC, which facilitated case study work, interviews, and participant-observation in meetings. Because of the way logistical preference and chance influenced my case selection, it should be stressed that this set of cases, while illustrative of the dynamic I describe, is neither exhaustive nor necessarily representative of the range of issues being pitched by activists to advocacy gatekeepers in many parts of the world.[62] The cases that do appear cover health and human rights, humanitarian affairs, and weapons norms, spanning several prominent issue areas in the broader human security agenda under study. Each documents a social problem at a different stage of issue creation and with a different cluster of attributes, but all are examples of contested claims in global society that have been put forth by proponents and—crucially—*not* yet accepted by network elites at the time the data were gathered. Together they offer a detailed analysis of the politics of global agenda setting and agenda vetting *within* networks—a politics that determines the shape and extent of global norms and plays a decisive role in global governance.

2

Networks, Centrality, and Global Issue Creation

Why do some global social problems become prominent "issues" around which advocacy networks campaign while others get neglected? Standard answers to this question overemphasize factors exogenous to the structure of advocacy networks themselves. Issue creation is usually explained by the attributes, behavior, and interests of specific agents (entrepreneurs or "gatekeepers") or by factors external to and beyond the control of the activist networks (the intrinsic nature of issues, of targets of influence, or of the broader political environment).[1] Much less attention has been paid to how the internal structural relations within the networks themselves enable or foreclose advocacy around specific issues. In this book I show that these kinds of intranetwork relations provide a crucial answer to the question of why some issues get noticed and others get neglected.

Focusing on what happens inside advocacy networks provides a fresh view of the politics of transnational spaces. For too long international relations scholars have accepted a conceptualization of advocacy networks popularized in the early literature—one that posits advocates as an altruistic, nonhierarchical, sovereignty-free alternative to the hierarchical states system. Instead, to properly explore our big question, we need to carefully unpack the terms "issue," "transnational," and especially the concept of "networks" as applied to global policymaking. In doing so, it becomes clear that advocacy networks are not simply the loci of people power vis-á-vis hierarchical states. Rather, they are sociopolitical structures with their own kinds of hierarchies, power relations, and governing mechanisms.

These network structures impact the nature of the political agendas their members espouse, helping answer my question about issue selection. But to understand how, a discussion of "networks" themselves is warranted. In this chapter, I draw on insights from social network theory to sharpen our understanding of advocacy networks and show why it matters to the question of how activists select issues for attention. I begin by discussing ways in which the concept of a "transnational advocacy network" as originally articulated by Margaret Keck and Kathryn Sikkink might be sharpened and operationalized, giving examples from my study of the human security network. I argue that these networks are *global*, not transnational; are *issue* networks, not advocacy networks; and in particular that they are *structures*, not organizational types. In particular, I distinguish four types of relevant structural relations that deserve closer scrutiny by international relations scholars: relations among *actors*, relations among *issues*, relations among *individuals*, and relations among *networks*. I then show how these intranetwork relationships matter causally in determining which issues become salient within advocacy networks and which get overlooked.

The Network Structure of Global Civil Society

In their landmark study of transnational advocacy networks, Margaret Keck and Kathryn Sikkink defined them as "those relevant actors working internationally on an issue, bound together by shared values, a common discourse, and dense exchanges of information and services.... Networks are forms of organization characterized by voluntary, reciprocal and horizontal patterns of communication and exchange.... Their goal is to change the behavior of states and of international organizations."[2] Much of the wider literature on advocacy networks has uncritically adopted this view: presumably advocacy networks are actors vis-à-vis the state system, they are constituted by common values, and they are relevant primarily because they alter state preferences. Of course, some of the newer literature questions old assumptions: Sharon Hertel and Cliff Bob have shown, for example, that the values within advocacy networks can actually be quite contested,[3] and James Ron, Alexander Cooley, Susan Sell, and Aseem Prakash have challenged the association of advocacy networks with altruism.[4] However, even these works treat advocacy networks as forms of organization distinguished from the hierarchical state system by their horizontal ties, and generally aim at documenting how these "networks" (often identified through assertion) affect states through single case studies, rather than examining them using the tools and theories of network analysis.[5]

As Hafner-Burton, Kahler, and Montgomery have pointed out, a view of advocacy networks as agents vis-à-vis states offers a very limited understanding of how they operate by abstracting away from a discussion of how they are constituted structurally, and how these structural relations affect both their own behavior and their significance to the wider international system.[6] Rather than see advocacy networks as alternative forms of governance, we should view networks as empirically measurable "relationships defined by links among nodes"; patterns of links (or "ties") create structures that enable or constrain constituent nodes, conferring power on some at the expense of others.[7] Indeed, network structures, understood in this way, have been shown to affect states' trading relationships, the effects of international organizations on interstate conflict, and the political capital of transnational criminals.[8]

Thinking about networks as relational ties of some analytically relevant type between politically salient entities, rather than as simply a metaphor for nonstate political activity, leads to fresh insights about what scholars have referred to as "transnational advocacy networks" as well. For one thing, many of these networks are perhaps best described as "global" rather than "transnational": their aims are often to affect global norms and policymaking processes, rather than the behaviors of specific states; they often involve both champions and claimants from numerous countries around the globe, rather than the "boomerang effect" as originally articulated; and their modes of advocacy draw on global norms and make use of global institutions, technologies, and information flows.

Second, while this book (like many) focuses specifically on the advocacy component of their work, organizations in these networks are involved in many functional activities besides advocacy, including research and service delivery, so distinguishing the networks themselves according to the advocacy component may not be conceptually helpful.[9] Indeed, many global civil servants in such networks resist or avoid describing themselves primarily as "advocates," preferring to think of themselves as "experts" in global public policy sectors.

What is unique about such a global network is not the functional activity (advocacy) but the extent to which a particular issue area ("environment" or "human rights" or "arms control") is a salient form of categorical identity around which the actors in that network cohere. This has led some scholars to refer to such networks as "issue networks" rather than "advocacy networks."[10] According to Richard Rogers, who has developed tools for mapping "issue networks" on the web, an issue network is "a heterogeneous set of entities (actors, documents, slogans) that have configured around an issue (a claim formatted in such a way that it circulates and attracts actors to a network around it)."[11] Indeed, this definition comes closer to describing the phenomena on which scholars of "advocacy networks" tend to focus. In this book I use the term "global issue network" interchangeably with "transnational advocacy network" to describe patterns of globally oriented political activity around specific categorical domains.

But before proceeding, the concept of "network" itself must be unpacked: however we label them, an emphasis on the structure of ties among nodes in networks, rather than on networks as forms of organization, suggests a different approach to what networks themselves *are* and therefore how to measure and study them. For example, politically salient nodes in global issue networks can be of several different types. The most common use of the term "network" in the literature on campaigns, and indeed in the international relations literature generally, is to describe patterns of social ties among *networks of actors*.[12] Indeed, whether the emphasis is on international organizations, transnational criminals, business networks, or intergovernmental agencies, the focus of empirical international relations scholarship has tended to be *actor* networks, with distinctions drawn primarily among the organizational type and functional activities of the actors involved.[13]

Moreover, scholars of global civil society have tended to focus on *certain* actors. In particular, such work regularly conflates advocacy networks with "NGO networks."[14] An empirical look at advocacy networks around a specific issue, however, yields a more complicated picture. Aside from the fact that the definition of NGOs is rather contested itself, effective global issue networks rarely involve only, or even primarily, such organizations. Instead, they often draw engagement from collections of different political entities: NGOs to be sure, but also UN agencies,[15] think tanks,[16] donors, communities of academic experts, media organizations, powerful individuals such as certain celebrities, government agencies, and in some cases private firms.[17] Moreover, rather than advocacy networks being distinct from the state system, they are intimately entangled with it as specific states often constitute vital network nodes. Canada, Norway, and Japan, for example, have been crucial players in the human security network and entrepreneurs on key campaigns such as landmines and cluster munitions.

Rather than assume that the relevant actors driving the advocacy train are "NGO networks," a more rigorous approach to advocacy networks is to begin with the "issue" in question and from there identify the actors most closely associated with the "issue" network.[18] As Schrad writes, "Inclusion in a transnational advocacy network is based more upon the extent to which an actor shares similar values...than through some external, objective categorization."[19] Consider the human security network, which I mapped out by examining hyperlinks among websites linked to those appearing in a Google search for the concept "human security."[20] As plate 1 shows, the network around the concept of "human security" includes certain United Nations agencies,[21] key states that have championed the concept or are known for funding human security projects,[22] academic institutions,[23] and a few large, well-funded NGOs.[24] What distinguishes these actors (and binds them together) is not their organizational type or their functional activity but rather their conceptual and transactional ties to the category "human security" and to one another through this ideational frame.[25]

This implies a second insight: it is a mistake to think of issue networks *as simply* networks of actors. As White has pointed out, ultimately all networks are *networks of ideas*.[26] Keck and Sikkink's original definition posited that networks were constituted and bound together by ideas—common values and discourses—as much as by information exchange. And in fact, the meanings around which actors in these networks organize—both discrete issues and categorical clusters of meanings with which practitioners identify—also exhibit a network structure.[27]

Plates 1 and 2 demonstrate this thematic clustering within the core human security network by actors and by issue. Although the network is characterized by much synergy and interaction across thematic categories, with many types of issues sharing space on specific organizational agendas, specific issues tend to cluster in one of several thematic subcategories within the broader network. These can broadly be described as "peace and security," "arms control," "environment," "development," "human rights," and "humanitarian affairs." The relational ties between these concepts are politically important because they shape the discursive landscape in which new advocacy claims may arise and take root. In this book, I will show that the structure of ideas within the network affects the likelihood that new concepts, pitched to specific actors associated with specific themes, will resonate sufficiently to gain a foothold in the wider ideational pool. This is because certain of these ideas are more closely related structurally than others.

Networks of individuals can also be carriers or nodes for categorical ideas. This means that empirically examining individuals as nodes and the social ties between them should be as important for scholars of issue networks as examining ties among organizations.[28] Individual global public servants circulate through networks of organizational affiliations. The professional and interpersonal ties between them—and between each of them and the thematic categories with which they are associated—affect the circulation of ideas within and among issue networks.

In the human security network, these dynamics were also reflected in the self-reporting of focus group participants about their professional networks (see plate 3). Most of my respondents reported expertise in more than one thematic issue area within human security, and most reported significant contacts with colleagues in other issue areas besides the one in which they had expertise. But certain types of thematic expertise seem more closely related than others. For example, those reporting thematic expertise in "human rights" report significant connections to colleagues in "development" but weaker connections to those in "conflict prevention" or "arms control." However, this self-reporting may also be the result of specific institutional cultures within specific organizations embedded in these wider networks.

Thus issue networks exhibit the properties associated with Daniel Nexon's concept of embedded relationalism, or a *"networks of networks."* Nexon points out that international social structures are constituted by different types of nested network relations. The ideal-type anarchical state system, for example, is composed of both dense and categorically similar ties among subunits *within* relevant social sites (e.g., states) but relatively sparse and categorically distinct ties among the sites. However, even at the international level, density of ties ("netness") and categorical homogeneity ("cat-ness") vary measurably among states, leading to the variation in the consequences of anarchy identified by Alexander Wendt and demonstrated empirically by Zeev Maov.[29] For Nexon then, the interesting question is how shifts in the nature of embedded ties correlate to shifts in international governing orders, such as the emergence of the Westphalian system from the dustbin of empires.[30]

Applied to global issue networks, a similar nested structure can be documented, whether between organizations or issues themselves. As Wendy Wong's work demonstrates, one way to think about this is to recognize that global advocacy organizations themselves are networks of organizational nodes and of professionals: many NGOs are structured internally as advocacy networks, with a headquarters and many national-level chapters.[31] The same is true of many international secretariats.[32] Yet these organizations, as global entities, are also embedded in wider networks (such as "human rights" or "development") around specific concepts; and hubs from those issue areas may also collectively comprise interlocking subclusters in supernetworks, such as the network around "human security." Within these master networks, actors or issues with a high degree of "cat-ness" cluster more densely than do those perceived to be more categorically dissimilar, and this structures professional relations and ideational creativity within networks. All this can be mapped out empirically, as visualized in figure 2 and plate 1.

Finally, whether the relevant nodes are organizations, issues, individuals or subnetworks, network theory provides a set of tools for understanding power relations *among* network nodes (as opposed to between networked and hierarchical political entities), and suggests that the nature of those relations will be dependent on the structural characteristics of particular networks. Such an approach would treat Keck and Sikkink's characterization of advocacy network relations as "horizontal and reciprocal" as a hypothesis rather than an assumption. That earlier characterization of advocacy networks, for example, imagined them as distributed networks, analogous to U.S. roadways, whereby nodes (towns and cities) were linked together through bidirectional roadways allowing many different pathways between any two nodes. But newer studies of advocacy networks suggest that they function not as flat, distributed networks but as scale-free networks in which a few major hubs dominate, and pathways between peripheral nodes are dependent on these hubs.[33] The same appears to be true in global issue networks: some nodes have a disproportionate influence based on their *centrality* within a network.[34]

However one thinks about the relevant networks, the key central insight of social network theory is that patterns of ties among nodes yield specific structural and ideational constraints and opportunities that affect political outcomes. Network structure can vary widely, as can the structural position of nodes—be they individuals, organizations, issues, or master frames. Some nodes may be highly central to specific networks but peripheral to others. Others may be less central in a specific network but may occupy a strategic location between other important nodes. These relations can be measured according to different metrics and, as my elite interviews and focus groups with global human security practitioners will show, they are acknowledged by participants in these networks as powerful influences on decision-making processes. In the rest of this chapter, I discuss ways in which these network analytical concepts—especially connectedness and betweenness as relational properties of nodes—can help us understand the agenda-setting power of specific actors in global issue networks.

Network Centrality and Issue Emergence

Keck and Sikkink argued that network density, important to activist success, was a function of *quality* as well as quantity: "ability to disseminate information, credibility with targets, ability to speak to and for other social networks."[35] In network analytical terms this claim is imprecise, but the authors are alluding to an important insight: nodes in networks vary in these crucial attributes for advocacy success, and networks around specific issues vary in the extent to which they attract nodes with these attributes. Issue networks that include nodes with the characteristics listed above are likelier to become politically salient. Therefore, the readiness of *certain* organizations to join emerging issue networks—to "adopt" emerging issues—is an important reason why some issues become politically salient in specific issue areas and others do not.

Indeed, several later studies have found that the organizational agenda of the most powerful actors in an actor network around an issue area have an important impact on the issue agenda for that issue area, suggesting that any new issue being "formatted" to that issue area requires the legitimation of the most powerful nodes. In the context of the human rights network, Clifford Bob posits that such organizations function as network "gate-keepers," legitimizing certain new ideas and not others. He defines human rights gatekeepers as "entities at the core of the human rights movement, whose support for a claim can boost it substantially.... The choices of 'gate-keepers' signal the worthiness of certain issues and, by implication, the dubiousness of others."[36] The case studies in his book bear this out.

More recent work has extended this finding beyond human rights advocacy to show that it holds in other advocacy networks. Sirin Duygulu and I examined seventeen campaigns across human security issue areas, expanding on a dataset compiled by Joshua Busby at the University of Texas–Austin. Our findings broadly confirmed this general pattern.[37] Whether in health, peace and security, humanitarian affairs, arms control, or human rights, the overall pattern of campaign development closely fits our model: entrepreneurs are typically drawn from small NGOs or from the academic community, but norm campaigns proliferate throughout global policy networks and eventually reach states after they are adopted by one or more organizations central to the issue network in question.

In 94 percent of the cases examined, global agenda-setting success occurred only after adoption by central hubs in the issue area. Moreover, adoption by hubs produces commitments by governments within an average of five years, whereas the same issues had been neglected for on average of seventeen years in the absence of hub support (see plate 4).[38] In short, network structure exerts a causal effect on issue selection. Whether the most powerful nodes are governments, NGOs, UN agencies, or think tanks, their organizational agenda will carry disproportionate weight within the broader issue network or networks in which they are embedded. Once these advocacy "superpowers" have adopted it, an issue is not only likelier to attract policy interventions from states but likelier to proliferate within advocacy networks.

Before turning to a discussion of how such "superpowers" construct their preferences, the rest of this chapter explores and expands on the sources and nature of this agenda-setting (and agenda-vetting) power. Although

Bob and his collaborators originally stressed organizational power in material terms, I develop Keck and Sikkink's original brief discussion to show it is actually relational position within networks that confers this influence. In the sections below, I detail how the access of network brokers (the "ability to disseminate information") and the authority of network hubs (the "credibility with targets" that gives them the power to legitimate claims) is derived from their network position rather than their material resources.

Structural Position and Influence in Networks

Two particular measures of centrality are crucial to the power of organizations in advocacy networks. First, *connectedness* (known in social network analysis jargon as "in-degree centrality") is a measure of how prominent an organization is within a network, measured in the number of organizations that establish or attempt to establish links with that node.[39] According to Hafner-Burton, Kahler, and Montgomery, "A network node with a high 'in-degree centrality' (strong links from many other nodes) may possess social power, easily accessing resources and information from other nodes because of its central position."[40] This heightened degree of what I term "connectedness" translates into influence when actors within and outside the network look to the organizational agenda of these players as an indicator of the network agenda.

For example, Murdie's quantitative analysis of citations among human rights organizations listed in the Union of International Associations Yearbook demonstrates that "the human rights network is comprised mainly of a few central players who are seen as prestigious within the network and others trying to link themselves to these players."[41] Wong has demonstrated how this privileged position allowed Amnesty International to control international understandings of human rights for much of the second half of the twentieth century.

Organizations can also exercise disproportionate influence on issue emergence within the network as a function of their *betweenness*—a measure of their brokerage power. A node's betweenness (or "betweenness centrality" in social network analysis jargon) is high when it "possesses exclusive ties to otherwise marginalized or weakly connected nodes or groups of nodes.... Social capital can be turned into social power by a node that bridges structural holes in the network."[42] Stacie Goddard postulates that nodes with a high degree of betweenness are able to serve as "brokers" by "maintaining ties with actors who would otherwise remain unconnected."[43] As I show in chapter 5, for example, the presence of such a broker was important in promoting attention to autonomous weapons as a disarmament issue.

Two kinds of betweenness place certain organizations in a more influential position relative to others in transnational advocacy networks. First, some organizations possess relatively greater ties to global policy stakeholders, including governments, or access to international forums. This makes these organizations themselves targets of influence for those who would like to access such stakeholders. Because so many NGOs lack these connections, alliances with those who have them constitute resources for newcomers to the international scene.[44] If an issue entrepreneur without such access attracts the support of such an organization, it enhances its chances of being heard by governments. For these reasons, such leading organizations themselves constitute coveted access points for newcomers or issue entrepreneurs with an idea to pitch in global civil society. This in turn enhances their connectedness, credibility, and authority.

In the human rights network, for example, Murdie found that more central organizations engage in the bulk of all international advocacy activities with governments; for players on the margins of the network, the dominant strategy is to attempt to get the attention of the network hubs in order to exploit their brokerage role vis-à-vis governments.[45] Similarly, the ICRC occupies a position of betweenness relative to global civil society and governments in its quasi-NGO status as guardian of the Geneva Conventions.[46] It can thus either block new ideas, as with depleted uranium, or create new ones, as with blinding lasers.[47]

Second, organizations may occupy an ideational space at the interstices of networks of meaning. The human security network consists of a variety of categorical issue networks including human rights, humanitarian affairs, development, environment, conflict prevention, and arms control. Certain organizations are most prominent in each of these areas; individual professionals within these networks use these frameworks to organize their own identities and frameworks vis-à-vis one another. Organizations whose work spans several issue clusters are valued resources for issue entrepreneurs aiming to frame their issue in such a way as to attract a broad coalition, not simply because they provide information bridges between networks, as Murdie and Davis show, but also because they are embedded conceptually in the space spanning issue areas, thereby linking adopted issues to multivocal frames.[48]

For example, Human Rights Watch's position at the intersection of the human rights and humanitarian law issue clusters has given it an influence over not only human rights agenda setting but also over arms control campaigns. Its categorical *betweenness* enables it to play a role in reframing issues from security to human rights, though its overall *connectedness* is lower than either Amnesty International or the International Committee of the Red Cross in the wider human security network. Similarly, the World Food Program is closely connected to both the humanitarian affairs and development clusters in the human security area. By extension, such organizations are connected to the networks of issues that are associated with those categorical clusters, conferring particular meanings on new issues that they adopt. As one interview respondent explained as she described the determinants of successful coalition building:

> Multi-issue organizations are key, organizations doing many things, connected to many sectors, who could prioritize anything but choose to do *this*: picking landmines over something else for a period and putting your energy to it. Big organizations that have some wherewithal and the attention you can finally catch to say "this matters."[49]

The respondent above is describing an effect noted by Daniel Nexon in his study of network relations and structural change in early modern Europe.[50] Nexon argues that collective mobilization is easier or harder depending on the network structure of relevant actors, with mobilization easiest in structural relations characterized not only by high network density (in Tilly's words, "net-ness") but also by high levels of categorical homogeneity ("cat-ness.") Network hubs and brokers encourage the proliferation of issues through contagion, thus enhancing the "net-ness" of issues. But as brokers, they also help create issue frames that transcend multiple categorical identities within advocacy clusters, increasing an issue's "cat-ness" as well.

The Recursive Relationship between Centrality and Authority in Specific Issue Domains

So far, I have argued that the defining attribute of "advocacy superpowers" is their structural position as hubs and brokers within advocacy networks. An alternative argument is that such power instead inheres in organizations'

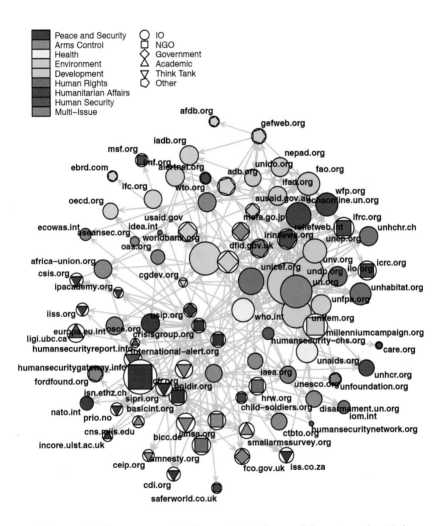

Hyperlink network of human security hubs by organizational type and thematic mandate. Nodes represent websites; ties represent hyperlinks. Data rendered by Issuecrawler captures organizations with two incoming links from the network around the top ten Google search results for the term "human security" in October 2007. Visualized by Alexander Montgomery using R.

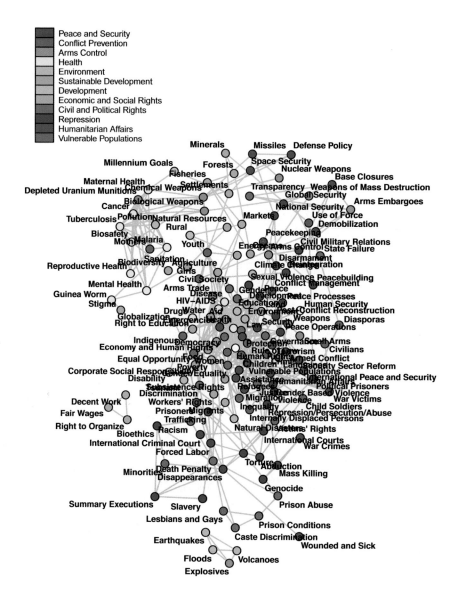

Network structure of human security issues. Co-occurrences of issues on human security organization websites, 2008. Visualized by Alexander Montgomery using R.

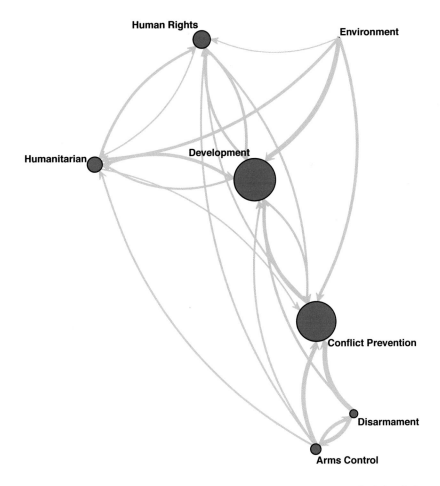

Strength of reported ties between participants and thematic issue areas. Participants had identified themselves as having expertise in specific thematic clusters. They were then asked to respond to the following question: "Please describe the number of professional or personal connections you have to people working in different thematic clusters within the human security network. For each cluster, write whether you have 'a great many, some, very few or almost no' contacts in those areas. Please check only one category for each cluster." The visualization demonstrates the strength of reported ties from self-identified thematic clusters to other clusters. In this graph, only ties occurring more often than the median are visible. Visualization created by Alexander Montgomery using R.

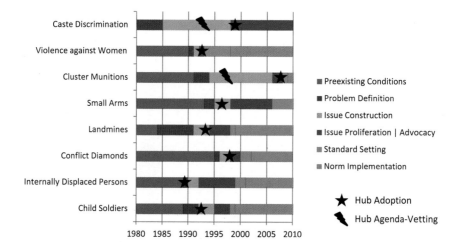

Impact of network hub issue adoption on issue life cycle.

Perpetrator Attributes Magnitude Issue Simplicity/Complexity Feasibility/Solvability Victim Attributes Ripeness Attributes Powerful Interests Government Demand Emotional Appeal Toxicity/Sensitivity Donor Demand Chance Claimant Demand Trigger Events Measurability/Data/Evidence Legal Framework Forum Broader Linkability State of the Economy Media Attention Network Context Celebrity Influence Academics/Experts Agenda-Space Issue Conflicts/Competition Strategic Linkages/Issue Turf Intra-Network Dynamics Entrepreneur Access to Funding Effects Beneficiary Buy-in Attributes Advocacy Skills Bandwagoning Fit / Value Added Adopter Marketability Interests Senior Leadership Prestige Funding Resources/Cost-Benefit Influential Allies Credentials Unlikely Leader Language Fluency

Reported factors affecting issue salience. Tag cloud lists analytical codes used to describe and group substantive patterns in practitioner discourse on correlates of global issue salience from the "brainstorming" section of the transcripts. Tag size corresponds to code frequency across all focus groups.

Abolition 2000
Explosives
Landmines
Cluster Munitions
Nuclear Weapons
Small Arms
Arms Trade
Depleted Uranium

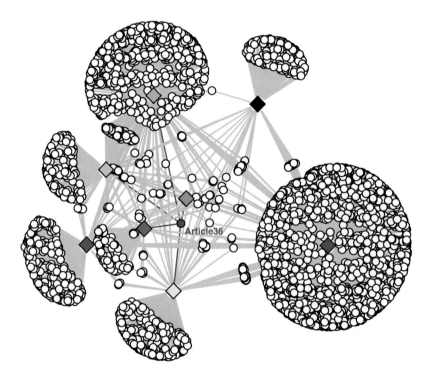

Affiliation ties between organizations and disarmament campaigns, as represented on the World Wide Web, 2012. Colored nodes represent campaigns; transparent nodes represent organizations; ties represent membership in campaigns. Data was taken from the campaign websites in summer 2012. Visualization created by Alexander Montgomery using R.

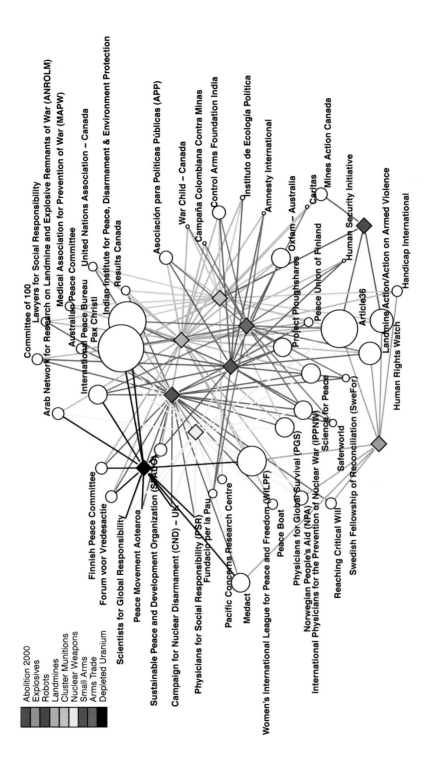

High-centrality affiliation ties between organizations and disarmament campaigns. Nodes are included only if they share three or more affiliations. Node size varies by number of affiliations to campaigns. Visualization created by Alexander Montgomery using R.

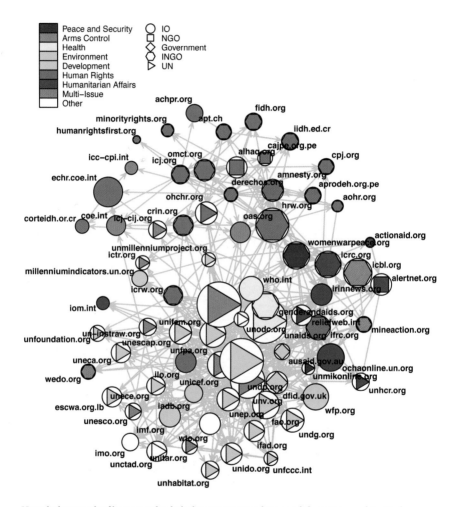

Hyperlink network of human rights hubs by organizational type and thematic mandate. Nodes represent websites; links represent hyperlinks. Data generated by IssueCrawler in 2008. Graph triangulates crawls using Amnesty International directory, the Choike Human Rights Directory, and the UDHR60 NGO web links as starting points. Node size represents in-degree centrality within the network. Graph created by Alexander Montgomery using R.

relative material resources: in Clifford Bob's formulation, "these are the organizations with the largest budgets, best staff and greatest credibility."[51]

Although it is true that credibility in networks often coincides with material resources, it is network centrality that confers both. There are numerous examples of low-resource organizations that have risen to prominence in a particular issue area by positioning themselves strategically within networks of organizations and ideas. Wong's study of Amnesty International, for example, demonstrated that Amnesty was long underfunded relative to other international NGOs, yet came to exercise a disproportionate influence in the human rights network due to the way it organized itself transnationally.[52]

Material resources do help, as do organizational attributes such as age. In any given issue area, the central hubs are often the oldest and most well-established NGOs.[53] In the issue area of "women, peace, and security," the Women's International League for Peace and Freedom has a century of historical experience on the international stage. This translates into overwhelming recognition by activists in the area of women and peace.[54] As Anna Snyder has detailed, WILPF's relatively greater power within the women's network gave it and other northern organizations an advantage, relative to women's groups from the developing world, in framing the women's agenda at the 1995 Beijing Conference.[55] However, not all well-established organizations can maintain their influence. Anti-Slavery International, for example, no longer occupies a preeminent space in the human rights network despite its earlier prominence as a leader in the nineteenth century anti-chattel networks.

What matters most is centrality. This is why resource-poor organizations new to the scene can compensate by positioning themselves as hubs in new networks. Consider Global Witness, the first organization to brand itself in the new issue area of "conflict resources," focusing originally on diamonds—an issue that became salient once large human rights NGOs such as Amnesty International adopted it[56]—but more recently on timber, oil, water, and other natural resources that can be said to contribute to the political economy of armed conflict. In so doing, Global Witness has not only constructed a new advocacy arena in which a variety of issues will surface over time but has situated itself as the lead player in this area. It has gone from being an issue entrepreneur pitching new problems to global civil society NGOs to being an authority in a newly defined issue area. NGOs interested in launching a campaign against the trade in coltan or in exposing the links between coffee companies and human rights abuses will therefore likely attempt to solicit the assistance, publicity, and networking opportunities that an alliance with Global Witness can provide.[57] This example underscores the point that agenda-setting/agenda-vetting power inheres not in a specific organizational size or type but in its relative centrality within a specific issue arena at a specific time: entrepreneurial actors can construct entirely new issue arenas and then control access to them (turning themselves into gatekeepers).

These are recursive processes, such that organizations that gain early notoriety in an issue area become more central over time relative to newcomers and thus occupy a disproportionately influential role within a given network.[58] Professional experience confers not only recognition but also the skill sets and attributes requisite for effective multilateral diplomacy, such as expertise in diplomatic protocols and treaty-making procedures, or what Joachim calls "procedural expertise."[59] This expertise is an important resource in itself, and also places the organization in a position to garner additional mobilizing resources and political opportunities unavailable to more marginal players. As Merry writes, "Attending UN meetings is expensive, but it facilitates fundraising. Since funding comes primarily from the global North, NGOs in consultative status that come to New York or Geneva have the opportunity to meet with funders, find out what the current hot topics are, learn the appropriate language in which to phrase funding proposals, and hear what other groups are doing."[60]

So the right organizational policies and profiles help explain centrality; and centrality also confers an advantage in garnering the very organizational resources and attributes Bob identifies as important to network influence.[61] Ultimately, however, it is an organization's visibility in a particular network, not its resources per se, that enable certain organizations disproportionate influence over the network issue agenda.

This is why, as I will show, many norm entrepreneurs will ask for nothing more of a hub organization than to lend its name to their coalition or mention the new issue on their website. Resources and expertise may matter in the advocacy and monitoring phase of norm development when, for example, a fact-finding study must be funded and carried out. But the expenditure of such resources is not necessary for high-centrality organizations to have an impact on issue proliferation within networks. At the issue creation stage, because of their status as thought leaders in networks, merely *acknowledging* a new issue has this effect. Accordingly, as I detail in the next sections, choice by network hubs *not* to adopt new issues has an equally dampening effect on some advocacy claims.

How Network Position Confers Agenda-Vetting Power

When a few organizations possess either or both types of centrality (relative to the many lesser-connected organizations of which a network is composed) it gives them disproportionate power over the network agenda irrespective of the resources or expertise they bring to an issue, because simply adopting an issue as an organizational priority is likely to raise its salience within the network as a whole.

The organizational agendas of network hubs influence third parties' social perceptions of what constitutes a particular transnational issue area and a legitimate claim within it. Since most outsiders will be drawn first to the hubs—imagine a journalist, educator, or policymaker Googling "children and armed conflict" to get a sense of the players and issues in that area—it is hub organizations' issue agendas that are perceived to be most constitutive of a given issue network's agenda. Adoption by such an organization signals the issue's importance to a particular network of meaning, be it human rights or development or the environment.

Relatedly, adoption by central organizations confers not only visibility but also legitimacy on new issues as perceived by targets of influence. Promotion of a new issue by an organization unknown to most stakeholders has lesser political meaning than adoption of that issue by an organization strongly associated with the issue area. Knowing this, other organizations within a network will look to the network hubs for signals as to whether new issues are perceived to constitute legitimate activity within the issue area, and take this into account in their assessments of whether their own advocacy on an issue is likely to succeed. Thus organizations are likelier to risk committing resources to an issue if central actors are also on board, creating a bandwagoning effect in coalitions once one or two key players join and dampening issue proliferation if they do not.[62] As one campaigner told me:

> There are a huge number of factors that bear on [advocacy NGOs], but where we devote time and resources on a particular issue is conditioned by our sense of what other organizations are likely to be interested in doing on that issue.[63]

Human Security "Non-Issues" Identified by Practitioners

Issues identified through survey / focus group responses to the question, "Sometimes problems exist in the world that get little or no attention from transnational activists. What human security problems can you think of that are not very prominent as issues in the human security movement?"

Aging of northern populations	Language extinction
Civilian men	Leprosy
Climate refugees	Literacy
Collateral damage	Male circumcision
Coltan	Megacities
Conscription	Mercenaries
Consumerism	Militarism
Corporate resource plunder	Nonlethal weapons
Cyberterrorism	Nuclear weapons
Developed world poverty	Opthalmic care
Familization of governance	Persecution propaganda
Family integrity	Piracy
Fetal rights	Recycling exports
Fighting women	Resource extraction
Food prices	Right to emigrate
Forced marriage	Robotic weapons
Fundamentalism	Safe child-bearing
Genetically modified organisms	Safe passage for IDPs
Global social welfare system	Sexual orientation
High sex ratios	Slums
Hijackings	Social esteem needs
Hostage taking	Social exclusion
Improvised explosive devices	Traffic accidents
Impunity for world leaders	Urban insecurity
Indigenous land rights	U.S. military budget
Infant circumcision	Worker's rights

These two pathways converge to confer great political significance to the issue adoption or nonadoption decisions of network hubs. In the human security network, for example, peripheral organizations' perspective on what constitutes a human security issue matters less than press releases issued by the Human Security Report Project in drawing in-network and out-network attention to new issues. When asked to name "issues that come to mind when you think of human security," practitioners will generally name the same issues that dominate the websites and promotional materials of human security hubs.[64] Correspondingly, absence of attention to an issue by network hubs can reduce that issue's chance of being adopted by other organizations within a network.[65]

Because of their disproportionate agenda-setting power, acknowledgement of a new issue by a hub organization constitutes a valued resource for more peripheral organizations aiming to pitch their issue to a wider network or to the world. This puts the hubs in a position to pick and choose between a range of potential new ideas, bestowing legitimacy on some and denying it to others: agenda-setting power implies agenda-vetting power. Any central organization's decision to adopt or ignore a particular problem within their issue pool or their decision as to how to frame it constitute acts of power that shape the types of governance that become possible in international society while reinforcing their position in the transnational hierarchy.[66]

But this model requires two caveats. First, as noted, what constitutes a "superpower" in a network depends not on an organization's absolute power but on its centrality both to the thematic issue and to the issue network, *relative* to the entrepreneur.[67] In other words, network theory tells us that the ability to vet the agenda is a relational construct dependent on particular configurations of relative resources, power, and interests between established players in a network and issue entrepreneurs within or outside the network. So, the term "gatekeeper NGO" may be a misnomer—gatekeeping is a verb rather than a noun. What matters is the relative connectivity between those players in a position to construct new ideas and those in a position to block their proliferation to a wider network. No one organizational actor or type of actor always plays either role. Powerful NGOs may "gatekeep" but international organizations and governments can also play this role, and a particular organization's structural position changes with the context.

Additionally, structural position does not *determine* an organization's role in agenda setting. Rather, it determines an organization's relative capacity for achieving its goals. Thus, while Bob refers to "NGO superpowers" (hubs) as "gatekeeper organizations," the very same structural position enables such players to function as entrepreneurs when they choose to do so.[68] Similarly, while Goddard sees a brokerage role as a necessary attribute of political entrepreneurs,[69] an organization situated as a "broker" (that is, with a high degree of ideational or organizational betweenness in the network) can choose to play the role of entrepreneur, gatekeeper, or "matchmaker,"[70] depending on their structural position at the interstices of different network players and their organizational interests in a particular context.

In sum, the ability to vet the advocacy agenda is not an attribute of particular organizations per se, but a relational construct dependent on relative network positions—between players most central to a particular issue network and issue entrepreneurs within or outside the network—in a given thematic area. Modified thus, this model explains not only human rights advocacy, where this model was pioneered, but transnational agenda setting and agenda vetting more generally.

So far, I have advanced three claims. First, significant and puzzling variation exists in the pool of issues that transnational advocacy networks take up at any given time. Since global norm development is at least partly a consequence of transnational advocacy movements, explaining internal advocacy network agenda setting should be an important concern for scholars of global norm development.

Second, I join earlier scholars in arguing that variation in the advocacy network agenda within a given issue area is largely explained by the organizational agendas of the most powerful nodes in that network. Third, I argue that this can be explained, however, not by material resources but by network position: claims arising from transnational networks (as opposed to those arising from states' own interests) are taken seriously by governments when *certain* members of global civil society press those claims. Agenda vetting is thus a tool of influence used by organizations whose agenda matters most for constructing intersubjective understandings of an issue area. This suggests that the likelihood of global norm entrepreneurship paying off with widespread coalitions resulting in norm change hinges on convincing neither states nor massive numbers of NGOs, but rather on convincing powerful central hubs at the interstices of networks around specific issue areas related to the new norm.

This means norm entrepreneurs must make their arguments in a manner that will speak to the preferences of network hubs if they are to increase their chances of being heard and acknowledged by governments. So how do central organizations in transnational issue networks construct their preferences? In the next chapter, I develop a theory of those preferences to assist both analysts and activists in understanding the conditions under which new campaigns for global norms are likely to emerge and succeed in different issue areas, before turning to case studies that explore the efforts of norm entrepreneurs to maneuver in the context of these constraints.

3

A Network Theory of Advocacy "Gatekeeper" Decision Making

So far I have argued that privileged network positions constitute certain organizations as authorities within issue networks; and that such transnational advocacy elites in these hubs govern the global advocacy agenda. But what do these authorities in global policy networks want? Why do they gravitate toward certain issues while exercising agenda denial around others? What do savvy issue entrepreneurs need to know about their preference structure in order to have the best possible chance of "selling" their cause in the global arena?

Although very few studies address this question explicitly, several explanations are implicit in the literature. One relates to the intrinsic aspects of issues (or people's perceptions of those aspects) that make them likelier or less likely to be selected for advocacy. Examples of *issue attributes* drawn from the literature include the nature of the victims (are they, or are they likely to be perceived as, innocent or vulnerable?),[1] the nature of the harm caused (bodily integrity rights violations versus social harms),[2] the nature of the perpetrators (some are more politically acceptable to target with advocacy claims than others),[3] the nature of the causal chain between victim and perpetrator,[4] and whether or not the issue is culturally sensitive in nature.[5]

2. Another strand of research emphasizes the attributes of norm entrepreneurs, many of whom come from outside gatekeeping organizations.[6] Busby calls this dynamic "messenger effects," arguing that *entrepreneur attributes*—credentials, celebrity, or similarity to gatekeepers—help ensure access and enhance credibility.[7] Bob also suggests that marketing savvy makes all the difference: entrepreneurs with the skills to package their issues so as to match potential adopters' mandates will have an edge.[8] In either case, as Busby puts it, "the attributes of advocates can be as important—if not more so—than the content of the message."[9]

3. A third line of thinking sees these preferences as related more to *adopter interests* than to the qualities of issues or entrepreneurs themselves. Perhaps advocacy organizations pick and choose among possible issues according to how well they mesh with the organization's need to survive and thrive.[10] In this sense, transnational organizations are said to function much like domestic interest groups.[11] In considering where to place their advocacy attention, organizations consider whether or not there is space on their agenda for an additional issue, whether or not an issue fits the mandate and programming culture of the organization, and whether it will be marketable and enhance organizational resources and prestige.[12]

4. Other authors stress the *broader context* in which advocacy attempts occur or, as Cooley and Ron put it, "the incentives and constraints produced by the transnational sector's institutional environment."[13] Similarly, theorists of political opportunity structures assign explanatory value to "the broader institutional context that provides opportunities for or imposes constraints on NGOs"[14] and which are crucial to "understanding a movement's emergence and to gauging its success."[15] This context primarily includes factors outside the advocacy network itself: the preferences of governments, the mood of donors and of the media, and trigger events beyond the control of actors inside the network.[16]

5. By contrast, a final strand of literature focuses on relationships within advocacy networks, or *intranetwork relations*. Rather than examining the individual characteristics of adopting organizations or of entrepreneurs, the intrinsic attributes of issues, or the nature of the external environment, this set of explanations focuses on relationships among advocacy organizations

within a specific issue area or across issue areas. In the human rights area, Hertel and Bob have found that significant contestation may exist among advocacy groups either opposing one another's causes or opposing specific framings of those causes.[17] Hadden's work on climate politics found that organizations mobilized around a specific cause may disagree on tactics, altering the nature of the agenda-setting process.[18] My earlier work on civilian protection and gender-based violence shows how these kinds of relationships, as well as intersubjective understandings about how issue turf is compartmentalized across networks, affect advocates' understandings of whether and how to adopt new issues.[19]

How might we know which of these patterns holds best across cases? Until now, very little has been done in the way of testing which combination of the preceding explanations most closely structures practitioners' decisions, and most of those look only at positive cases. The best general study is Bob's *The Marketing of Rebellion*, but he stresses "substantive, tactical and organizational matching" between issues and organizations, without exploring precisely *how* agents in these organizations *judge* the substantive, tactical, or organizational "fit" of issues.

My team and I explored what "advocacy superpowers" want by studying the reactions of multilateral practitioners in a conversational setting.[20] This chapter draws on the experiences and insights of forty-three senior officials drawn from organizations central to the human security network.[21] Our goal was to spearhead a discussion about why some issues gain attention within this network of networks, and why others do not; and to compare the narratives presented by practitioners to scholarly understandings of these dynamics. Six focus groups were completed by University of Massachusetts Amherst researchers at Tufts University's Fletcher School of Law and Diplomacy in fall 2009. Each began with a brainstorming session on issues missing from the network. Participants were asked to list as many issues as they could think of that are not getting enough attention from human security specialists. The brainstorming session led into a larger discussion of why certain issues make it onto the advocacy agenda and others do not.

After a coffee break, the final segment of the focus groups centered on thought experiments where the moderator presented issues that have not yet garnered international attention, drawn from a pool of candidate issues in our database, and the participants were asked to analyze why these issues lack saliency.[22] At the end of the focus group sessions there was time for a more general discussion and for comments on the research methods.

Responses from the discussions fell into five broad categories roughly mapping onto a typology of relevant factors described in the literature (see plate 5): *broader context, issue attributes, entrepreneur attributes, adopter attributes*, and *intranetwork relations*.[23] However, the significance of these different claims appeared to depend on whether practitioners were thinking in the abstract or considering specific cases of low-salience issues. In particular, broader context factors beyond the control of practitioners— what scholars would refer to as the "political opportunity structure"— were frequently mentioned as constraints in the abstract, but carried much less weight when practitioners were asked to consider concrete "candidate issues." The same was true of some actor effects: practitioners discussed the characteristics of entrepreneurs in the abstract but stressed them less in evaluating candidate issues (although the importance of adopter organizational interests remained constant). However, two other sets of factors—the attributes of issues themselves and (importantly) relational effects between issues and actors—mattered *far more* in the concrete than in the abstract, suggesting these factors are prominent in practitioners' minds when they consider the merit of specific issues (see figure 3).

These findings are detailed in this chapter. I suggest that while a culture exists among transnational advocates of downplaying their own agency relative to that of external forces, practitioners' judgments about the merit of specific issues hinge less on the constraints posed by these broader factors and more on (a) an issue's attributes and (b) its connection to the wider advocacy landscape. This confirms and refines much of what is known about the importance of issue attributes. But it suggests that much more attention should be paid to the way in which *perceived relational ties*—between issues, between issue areas, between organizations, and between activists themselves vis-à-vis others—structures how those attributes, and thus their "fit" to specific organizational agendas, are understood. In short, network structure does not merely position some organizations as "gatekeepers": it also helps to constitute gatekeepers' preferences, and thus the advocacy agenda. Below, after describing the overall findings in more detail, I expand on what this tells us about the role of networks ties in issue adoption decisions.

Issue Selection: What Human Security
Elites Say and What They Do

Unsurprisingly, given that many hypotheses about issue selection have been derived from case studies built on elite interviews with practitioners in advocacy networks, support for all five of these causal hypotheses was evident to some extent in the narratives of practitioners. However, some of these explanations were more frequent across the dataset than others; and within each category of responses, some specific causal claims were mentioned more often than others. Moreover, my team discovered that the factors human security elites stressed when thinking in the abstract were very different from their evaluations of specific candidate issues.

Although we found only limited references to it, respondents placed some emphasis on the importance of a skilled and dedicated sponsor who initially advocates for new ideas, echoing the insights of scholars who emphasize political entrepreneurs as drivers of global policy processes. We found indeed that personal charisma, credentials, an extensive personal network, Internet and social media skills, advocacy skills, and a mastery of the English language were all discussed as attributes of a successful entrepreneur.[24] Repeatedly, participants argued that access to funding is one of the most critical aspects of successful entrepreneurship. A few comments suggested that entrepreneurship or championing by an "unlikely leader" provides additional likelihood of success; the promotion of the cause of nuclear disarmament by former Cold War hawks was mentioned as an example.[25]

We also found support for the notion that legitimation by network hubs helps ideas proliferate among organizations in advocacy networks.[26] As one participant said, "I think that some of the larger NGOs have quite a bit of power with regard to being able to set the agenda in their field." We found low but consistent evidence that organizations see themselves as constrained by unit-level concerns: in weighing candidate issues, organizations do consider their mandate, resources, and organizational prestige. This thematic concern was constant across both sections of the focus groups, constituting roughly 14 percent of the overall discussion in each.

There was also some commentary about the importance of *issue attributes*. It was mentioned several times that an issue is more likely to succeed if there is an obviously vulnerable victim and an obviously guilty perpetrator.[27] Participants suggested that issues that are "too complex" are thought to be less likely to gain advocacy attention, as are issues that seem to have impossible or unachievable solutions. Respondents also stressed the subjective, emotional side of agenda setting: issues that are "scary" or that "tug at heartstrings" are more likely to be picked up by advocates—not because advocates care more, but because it is assumed that emotional appeals are often helpful when marketing issues to other NGOs or to a given constituency. But respondents also confirmed that systematic, quantifiable evidence to supplement the shocking testimonies is crucial in communicating the severity of the problem to advocacy gatekeepers, many of whom pride themselves on their objective technical expertise.[28] Relatedly, advocates emphasized the inherent *measurability* of the problem—a function of the issue itself as well as the tools available to advocates.[29] About 15 percent of all responses in the dataset centered on issue attributes such as these.

Though these issue-and-actor-level explanations were frequent, we heard far *more* talk about how the advocacy agenda is driven by events and interests *outside* the advocacy network. Our respondents described how historical shifts create or shrink space for advocacy, affecting organizations' sense that specific issues may succeed.[30] Advocates seize windows of opportunity presented by "focusing events" such as international conferences, reports, or legislative debates, but these factors are often beyond their direct control. It was also mentioned that issues have "life cycles": "Often ideas will percolate for decades before the moment arrives." This "moment" might be caused by a "trigger event" such as a natural disaster, genocide, or an industrial accident. The case literature suggests such events have a "cognitive punch effect"[31] that provides an opportunity for the advocates to "push for their pet solutions."[32] Some participants argued that donors set the agenda, handpicking which issues will be funded and which will not.[33] Others argued that governments play a leading role in setting the global advocacy agenda, and that the most powerful states play the most powerful roles.[34] Expert, media, and celebrity attention to an issue were also regularly mentioned as important contributing factors.[35]

Overall, these "broader context" factors beyond the control of practitioners—what scholars would refer to as the "political opportunity structure"—were by far the most frequently mentioned as constraints in the overall dataset, featuring in 45 percent of all comments. However, this appears to be due to their overrepresentation in the "abstract brainstorming" section: the broader context carried much less weight when practitioners were asked to asked to evaluate the neglect of specific issues (figure 3).[36] In other words, practitioners overwhelmingly stressed the broader political context when asked open-ended questions such as "why do some issues get attention and others don't?" But when asked to comment about the absence of international advocacy around *specific* low-salience issues (collateral damage control, autonomous weapons, infant male circumcision, forced conscription, and military basing) broader context explanations dropped from 45 percent to 26 percent, while the emphasis placed on *issue attributes* jumped significantly, from 16 percent to 33 percent of the total. Similarly, the *intranetwork relations* category was far more salient in the "thought experiments" section than in the earlier, more abstract discussion: when evaluating candidate issues, practitioners often stressed the issue's relationship to other issues, their own relationships with other partner organizations, and the issue's or entrepreneur's relationship with other organizations inside or outside the human security network in approximately 21 percent of these comments.

To some extent, this greater emphasis on the "political environment" when thinking abstractly is consistent with attribution theory, which suggests both that actors are likelier to attribute outcomes they like to their own agency and outcomes they dislike to the broader environment, but

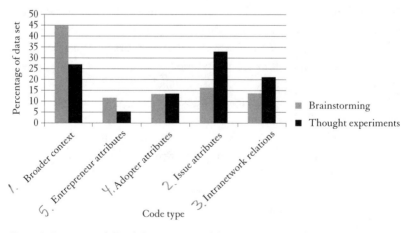

Figure 3. Percentage of all coded passages in total dataset receiving specific code type.

also that this relationship is reversed when it comes to their assumptions about others.[37] Indeed, by disaggregating causal claims in the evaluative section according to the speaker's relative enthusiasm for or skepticism about the issue in question one discovers an almost inverse relationship between the emphasis on the broader environment and an emphasis on organizational interests (see figure 4). Those who favored the status quo (neglect of these particular issues) were likelier to attribute the issue's absence from the agenda to organizational agency, rather than to the factors beyond activists' control; those who disliked the status quo (preferring that the issue in question get attention by activists) were likelier to blame constraints in a broader political environment (such as donors or governments).

However, evaluative arguments stressing the attributes of issues themselves and intranetwork relations remained very high in the evaluative section relative to the more abstract discussion, and did *not* vary significantly with respondents' affect for the issue in question. This suggests that these variables, operating in tandem, are particularly important in practitioners' evaluations of candidate issues, controlling for how sympathetic they are to an issue. This is especially interesting since scholars have paid relatively less attention to how practitioners come to believe that an issue has specific attributes. Based on the prominence of intranetwork relationships as a cross-cutting explanation in the dataset, I conclude that a

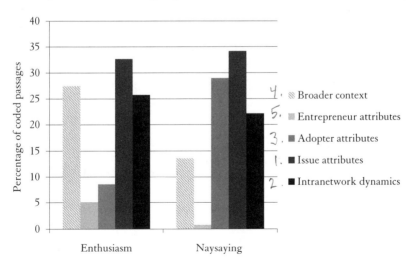

Figure 4. Explanations of issue neglect based on affect.

significant and mostly overlooked factor affecting practitioner judgment on which issues are "worthy" of advocacy is dynamics within networks, rather than the intrinsic attributes of either issues or actors.

Intranetwork Relationships: Constituting Practitioner Preferences

Respondents spent much time describing the social dynamics within and across advocacy networks, or "intranetwork relations." By this I mean connections between organizations and perceived or actual relationships among issues on existing agendas. Intranetwork relations were the third most frequently cited explanation for issue salience in the dataset overall, and one of the two explanations cited significantly more in the thought experiment sections. In addition to practitioners' specific explanations, I show in this section that several of the more novel responses about issue and actor attributes are comprehensible partly through the concept of intranetwork relations, and that it is only by considering these network effects that actor or issue attributes such as "credibility," "fit," and "do-ability" are given meaning by practitioners.

When coding the focus group transcripts, my team looked for references to ties among organizations and among issues as constraints on or facilitators of issue adoption or proliferation. Although early TAN literature assumed that dense networks constitute a resource for activists, practitioner narratives suggest that the trend can work the other way: ties between issues, issue areas, and organizations can result in conflict or competition among issues, and the way that issues are packaged structurally and mapped onto different organizations' issue "turf" affects the receptivity of the network to certain new ideas.

The concept of intranetwork relations also answers some remaining puzzles about issue attributes and actor attributes. Many issue attributes described above are actually subjective. Given that X issue attribute "matters," how do transnational advocates determine that an issue has that quality or not? Entrepreneur "credibility," for example, appears to be based as much on the entrepreneur's credentials, choice of allies, and relationship to the claimant population as on their actual expertise, advocacy skills, or the merit of the cause they champion. Adopters make guesses about these attributes based on what they know about the entrepreneur's social context. These types of concerns form a crucial part of their estimate as to whether an issue "fits" their organizational culture. I describe each of these patterns below.

Ties among issues.   One set of questions practitioners ask themselves is about the nature of the relationship between the emerging issue and their existing issue agenda. As Bob's notion of "substantive matching" predicts, respondents spoke of issue attributes in relational terms, claiming there was only so much space for advocacy, both within an organization and in the broader networks: participants described a zero-sum relationship between new issues and existing issues. A new issue must be different enough from the current issue agenda to merit inclusion, but also similar enough not to conflict with or undermine an organization's existing issue pool:

> We don't want more issues. We've got enough to work on already. We will only take them on if we see the possibility of them helping the issues that we already have, rather than seeing them as competing issues that draws away from our pet issues that we've been working on.[38]

> An issue "takes" much quicker if it can be related to an existing issue or set of issues that groups are already campaigning on because they've taken a lot of effort to construct them.

Sometimes issues are perceived as being in competition with one another; sometimes they are seen as conflicting entirely. Issue conflicts were cited across several of our "thought experiments" as a reason for avoiding advocacy. As I show in the case study chapters, advocacy elites perceived that infant male circumcision might draw resources away from the campaign against female genital mutilation, seen as a worse evil; but it might also conflict directly with issues they cared about, such as religious freedom or HIV-AIDS prevention. Similarly, while some practitioners were sympathetic to the campaign for collateral damage compensation, representatives from humanitarian organizations voiced concerns that the idea—for militaries to directly provide payments to civilians—would compromise humanitarian space by militarizing a role that depends on neutrality.

Ties among organizations.   Additionally, participants suggested that organizations often consider their existing coalitions when determining whether or not to sign on to a new campaign or adopt a new issue, as they would not want to compromise alliances with other organizations. For that reason, they feel the need to "negotiate" their various involvements in calculating the interest they have in supporting an issue:[39]

Not all issues are equal. Not all organizations and partnerships are equal. Complementarity is very essential on this question why certain issues are more prominent than others.

I think to some extent each organization is reactive to discussions that are going on in other institutions.

So judgments about an issue's likelihood of success, and therefore of whether it would be a good investment for an organization, are partly related to whether other organizations in the same issue space or organizational niche, or with whom they have strong partnerships on other issues, are also amenable to taking them up. This is partly pragmatic, but partly symbolic:

Talking strictly from a think tank perspective—we're always seeking funds. And so issues that kind of have saliency with other think tanks are going to be able to attract money more, because you can show more easily that it is a salient issue, because of people taking it seriously.

Thus, intranetwork relations can facilitate diffusion of an issue (or issue fragment) once it is adopted by a network hub: practitioners reported a bandwagoning effect when issues quickly proliferate within the network most closely associated with the organization that legitimized it:

Not many people were doing climate change a few years ago. Now everybody's got it somewhere in their agenda because it's the talk of the day, the buzzword.

There is this groupthink idea, that think tank is doing a security and development program—*we* have to do security and development. And you know in a few years it will be something else.

I think one thing that's really interesting is to see how issues from one organization influence another and how they have this ripple effect.

Indeed, some practitioners acknowledge that an expectation of creating just such a ripple effect sometimes drives their own issue-adoption decisions:

One of the big projects that we're working on right now is actually around maternal mortality. And the reason we picked that is because if you look at all the Millennium Development Goals, this is the one that has made the least amount of progress. We did an assessment that we could make an impact in this area, that if we began working on it, it would receive a wave of attention from governments, NGOs, others in the public.

In addition to network composition, perceptions of *network density* also matter. It is not necessarily believed that denser networks equal greater likelihood of issue adoption: practitioners report that this effect hits a tipping point after a short initial bout of issue proliferation. Potential adopters must gauge whether an issue is still at an early enough stage that they can be seen to be making a significant contribution rather than simply bandwagoning:

> You're not going to be able to attract the funds if already too many people are doing it. So, there is a tipping point, the kind of bell curve where at the bottom there's not enough money yet, because there's not enough interest. And then as interest gains, you can get more money. But then once you hit the top, if there's too many people doing it, then funders are going to be like, well, what's the point? So, there's that sweet spot that you have to kind of hit.

Ties among issue areas.   Issues in the human security network cluster into a set of "issue areas," which are identifiable both in terms of issue ties and organization ties. In short, an "issue area" might be defined as the package of organizations and issues tied together structurally in a certain sphere of advocacy space. The perceived and actual ties between these issue clusters, however, also make a difference in practitioner's judgments about issue adoption.

As noted in the previous chapter, the issue agenda within and across organizations itself has a network structure, with some issues closely related to one another and some barely connected at all. An issue's *perceived* relationship to the existing issue area helps shape adopters' judgments about whether it is a "fit" for them relative to some other organization. Depleted uranium munitions, for example, have long been ignored by hubs in the weapons and arms control area, primarily because the issue is strongly associated in their minds with the antinuclear and environmental lobby.[40] Similarly, our respondents raised the same concern with respect to the idea of a campaign against forced conscription: although issue entrepreneurs have framed this as a form of forced labor, many of our respondents perceived the issue to be associated instead with the peace movement and therefore a nonstarter for human security organizations:

> Conscription is just simply not one that so many organizations would embrace. A lot of them aren't pacifists. They are human security organizations, but they are not pacifists. So that puts them in a different camp, really.

Categorical heterogeneity within networks also leads to buck-passing. The disaggregation of the human security network into subnetworks, and the increasingly cross-cutting nature of issues, allows some issues to fall between the cracks. This dynamic arises from the compartmentalization of issue turf within the network, or what respondents referred to as the "problem of the silos":

> [Their organizational] mandates are giving us problems right now.... They make us work in silos and the communications are not very good. There was a food conference recently. Not one word about climate or environmental change was mentioned in the food conference. And the people who are going to meet over the climate are not going to talk about food prices and oil prices and all these things, yet increasingly they impact forced migration. And what we are not finding right now is the right form to start putting the dots in between these silos.

In short, there may be a sense of which organization, or which type of organization, an issue "belongs" to, and other organizations may not pick up an issue if they feel it has a better "home" elsewhere:[41]

> The real problem in terms of what gets attention and what doesn't, a particular *strand* gets attention because the real solution is so complex, if you're going to get funding (and that's a relevant concern) you simplify it. So we end up taking the piece where we think we can get the best bang for the buck, and we're fully aware that we're leaving off all kinds of critical shavings because we can't advance the agenda as a whole.

Ties Among Individuals   Finally, some respondents argued that interpersonal networks between individuals across various different organizations in a network may matter most of all:

> Usually there is a small network of people in these organizations that are really moving things.... People move around and they have their networks and they work together regardless of the organization they're in. I think

L→ who are these indv ?

that works sort of across the issue spaces and geographically as well. I think the interpersonal nature of these networks is a lot more important than the abstract calculations like who's in power.

This suggests that studies of advocacy networks need to play close attention not only to which organizations join a coalition but to which individuals' social connections are driving issue formation. Stacy Goddard argues that it is precisely individuals intersecting different communities of ideas that tend to be key sources of innovation in a network.[42] One observation from our focus groups was that professional ties reported by our participants were somewhat segmented into discrete subnetworks, even as they include synergies that cut across issue areas. To the extent that interpersonal relationships grease the wheels of innovation in networks, this segmentation provides a clue as to why some issues get more attention than others—those that fall between communities of practice that rarely interface may have a harder time gaining a foothold.

Actors' personal, intellectual, and professional histories may also have a potential to affect their decision to prioritize certain issues over others.[43] During the thought experiment and conclusion sections of the focus group, participants engaged in some unprovoked self-reflection on their belonging to a *global elite class*. Indeed, although our participants were diverse in country of origin and expertise, many of them attended the same elite schools and network in the same circles.[44] Participants acknowledged this homogeneity and spoke directly about how this might affect the selection of issues within global civil society networks:

> This global upper class to which we all belong, the class who does the talking and the meeting and who defines what's to be the agenda for the remaining 90 percent of the world: what is convenient to us and understandable to us, legible to us, has a far higher chance; what challenges us as individuals and our own values and our own sense of goodness will not move so far at all.

The concept of intranetwork relations as a set of explanations distinct from the external political opportunity structure suggests that relational factors within networks may be as or more important than factors intrinsic to organizations, issues, or their environment. But the concept also answers remaining puzzles about certain issue and actor attributes. Many factors that have been treated as attributes of issues or actors are socially constructed through perceptions about ties to other issues or actors.

For example, participants placed relatively little emphasis on the characteristics of issue entrepreneurs. Aside from the basic insight that "advocacy skills make a difference," entrepreneur attributes were mentioned least overall in the discussions, and even less in judging actual issues. However, respondents *did* place an emphasis on entrepreneurs' social ties to other actors as indicators of their (and therefore their ideas') merit.[45] They look to the density and composition of the entrepreneur's network ties as a clue to what sort of crowd they are joining if they acknowledge the campaign, and what sort of frame is embedded in the issue as a result.

The merit of the cause entrepreneurs champion is also judged by "issue attributes" such as "linkability" or "toxicity" that are really less about the issue itself and more about what else is already on the agenda or which intranetwork relationships may be compromised by a certain framing. These types of concerns form a crucial part of practitioners' estimate as to whether an issue "fits" their organizational culture. And as Oestreich has shown, how an organization's culture and mission is understood by its members can shift over time, so the question is how a particular constellation of preferences comes to accommodate new issues or norms in a particular context.[46] It is in large part relationships—to new issues, new coalitions, or new partnerships within the network—that help constitute gatekeepers' understanding of their own organizational interests. And these types of factors appear to be front and center in practitioners' judgments about the merit of new "human security" claims.

These dialogues with practitioners yielded a broad set of hypotheses about why some issues are more neglected than others: the nature of issues, the attributes of entrepreneurs and policy gatekeepers within networks, the relationships among advocates, and the broader political context. Practitioners were likelier to describe the broader context as a constraint on agenda setting in the abstract, but likelier to invoke factors related to the issue itself or their own organizational interests in expressing skepticism about candidate issues. Descriptions of intranetwork relations constitute an additional factor in practitioner narratives about agenda setting, one not adequately captured in scholarly approaches to TANs.

In the next few chapters, I illustrate how this works by chronicling three issue creation attempts that took place in the early twenty-first century. None of these has come fully to fruition at the time of this writing, but each is championed by tireless entrepreneurs engaging the power centers of transnational networks in an effort to build new global norms. Individually and together, these cases further illustrate both the causal and constitutive arguments in this book: that the issue adoption decisions of the most central nodes explain the rise and fall of issues within networks; and that the preferences of advocacy elites are constituted by perceptions of intranetwork relationships. *[handwritten: argument]*

The cases—campaigns for collateral damage compensation and against autonomous weapons and infant male circumcision—span humanitarian affairs, security, and human rights, showing that this same pattern holds true across issue areas. They involve different types of issue entrepreneurs: a small NGO in the collateral damage case, a network of scientists in the case of robotic weapons, a grassroots social movement in the case of circumcision. Yet the overall trajectory of the three cases is similar. In no case was norm entrepreneurship sufficient to spark a global campaign. In each case entrepreneurs gravitated toward a strategy of engaging advocacy hubs in wider humanitarian, disarmament, and human rights networks: the Office for the Coordination of Humanitarian Affairs, the International Committee of the Red Cross, and Amnesty International. In each case entrepreneurs' ideas initially received significant push back by advocacy elites, and during this period of push back their ability to market their new ideas stalled.

But the cases vary according to how much this changed over the course of the study. In the autonomous weapons case it changed decisively, with the indifference of disarmament gatekeepers shifting to open adoption of the issue and the launch of a campaign. Advocates for collateral damage victims made modest gains by the time I stopped gathering data, embedding their advocacy language in key international documents. Male circumcision, however, continues to be neglected by the human rights mainstream despite the efforts of grassroots activists. As the model predicts, the issues that were picked up by central organizations have risen in salience over the period of the study; those that were not remain of low prominence on the global agenda.

The following chapters shed light on these dynamics by documenting the interaction between issue entrepreneurs and the advocacy elites for the network whose agenda they aim to shape, drawing on iterated interviews, participant-observation, and process tracing of correspondence and documents. Each chapter shows how advocacy elites' perceptions of intranetwork relations explained the initial period of agenda vetting for all three cases. The chapters as a group also show how shifts in these perceptions of network ties made the difference between gradual engagement by advocacy elites (in the collateral damage case), full-blown issue adoption (in the case of autonomous weapons), and ongoing agenda denial (in the case of the circumcision campaign). Together with the data presented in chapters 2 and 3, the story of these campaigns demonstrates how intranetwork relations combine with configurations of other factors to shape the global advocacy agenda.

"You Harm, You Help"

Pitching Collateral Damage Control to Human Security Gatekeepers

In times of war, civilians are dismembered, burned to death, crushed, asphyxiated, eviscerated, buried alive, and shot. They witness the deaths or mutilation of close family members and friends. Their homes are destroyed; they become refugees, and in their displacement they become vulnerable to attack, robbery, rape, and death from exposure and malnutrition.[1]

And much of this is perfectly legal—so long as governments inflict such harms by accident, instead of deliberately; so long as they are incidental to some lawful objective, rather than directed at civilians.[2] Today, nothing in the voluminous international law of armed conflict holds warring parties accountable for such harms. Although governments are required under international humanitarian law (IHL) not to target civilians as such, accidental or incidental harm to civilians is considered an inevitable aspect of war.[3] Therefore, while states are sometimes required to pay reparations for war crimes, no international law requires governments to recognize or compensate the families of civilians killed or maimed in legitimate combat

Laws of war

Collateral damage

operations: those unfortunate enough to suffer such calamities are not victims of war crimes, merely "collateral damage."[4]

These "collateral damage" victims number in the hundreds of thousands worldwide, and available evidence suggests they are increasing both as a proportion of all civilians killed in interstate wars and also in absolute numbers. Proportionally, intentional civilian targeting is declining, according to datasets by Alexander Downes and Michael Hicks and his colleagues.[5] Case studies on specific wars by Ward Thomas and Colin Kahl also demonstrate that belligerents do comply with the civilian immunity norm to a greater extent than previously.[6] However, civilians remain at risk from lawful military operations. Even the most sophisticated weapons have significant humanitarian side effects.[7] Indeed, an index constructed by Marc Herrold suggests that the greater the share of precision weapons employed, the *higher* the rate of unintended civilian casualties as such weapons are likelier to be used in urban areas than earlier "dumb" bombs.[8]

In 2003, an NGO based in Washington, DC, the Campaign for Innocent Victims in Conflict (CIVIC), initiated a campaign to require states to recognize and compensate war's unintentional civilian victims. Now the leading force in a full-fledged movement, CIVIC presses all parties in conflict to "establish a new standard of behavior by providing recognition and help to civilians harmed by their bombs and bullets."[9] According to Campaign director Golzar Kheiltash, "Civilian harm has long been dismissed as collateral damage: to some extent it's legally permissible and viewed by warring parties as an acceptable cost of war. The concept we pursue is that civilian victims deserve amends, even when warring parties haven't violated their legal obligations."[10]

The novelty of the issue as originally defined by CIVIC may at first not be obvious, as civilian war victims, whether or not intentionally targeted, already draw a significant amount of policy attention from the UN system, humanitarian NGOs, and governments.[11] Hundreds of NGOs and international organizations, funded by donations from individuals, foundations, or government aid agencies, flock to the world's conflict zones delivering shelter, food, and medicine to displaced and traumatized war victims.[12] Others work in postconflict reconstruction, rebuilding houses, reintegrating refugees, and training former combatants for civilian jobs.[13] But since the system is based on voluntary donations, the resources for humanitarian aid and peace-building work tends to be transitory, flowing to the countries most in the media spotlight at any given time, and moving on when the attention of donors shifts. And since needs often vastly outweigh resources, aid agencies often engage in "humanitarian triage," and spend much of their time and resources begging governments for funding.[14]

The idea proposed by CIVIC represents a significant, if subtle, departure from this existing system.[15] First, by making "amends" for deaths and maimings an expectation of warring parties, rather than relying on the whims of donors and NGOs, they aim to turn what is currently a charity act into an entitlement owed to victims' families by belligerents.[16] Second, they sought a direct linkage between warring parties and the civilians affected by those belligerents' military operations—whereas previously the civilian humanitarian sector was a mechanism by which resources were transferred to besieged civilians.[17] Third, they openly challenged what many commentators had already identified as a serious gap in the laws of war—the indifference to unintentional harms inflicted on civilians.[18] By contrast, CIVIC emphasized the symbolic and moral significance of recognizing and responding to all civilian victims as an expression of human dignity and respect.

Many human security experts I interviewed as part of this project expressed an intuitive sense that this was a fantastic idea. And CIVIC was successful at lobbying both governments and military officials to make specific policy changes, including condolence payments. Yet the initial response to CIVIC's campaign for a new normative standard was far from uniformly positive within the human security network, slowing its efforts to build a coalition for a global norm campaign. Although CIVIC enjoyed some vital early support from matchmaker NGOs, and a relatively privileged position of access within the human rights and humanitarian networks due to the renown of its founder, many human security gatekeepers were initially skeptical about the idea that the existing rules of war were inadequate or that norm development in this direction would have a positive effect on civilian populations.

In this chapter I will trace the emergence of this idea and the process by which CIVIC has pitched it to other humanitarian NGOs and governments, and document the initial resistance to the idea from certain humanitarian heavyweights. The story of the Making Amends Campaign illustrates several aspects of the global agenda setting (and agenda-vetting) process.

First, it shows the various steps in the global agenda cycle laid out in chapter 2—entrepreneurship, agenda vetting, issue adoption, and proliferation. Second, it shows how even an idea with seemingly obvious normative value can initially produce skepticism among human security specialists. I show this is largely due to their perceptions about the networks of actors and issues in which they, the entrepreneur, and the new norm idea are embedded.

Third, this chapter highlights contests and negotiations between issue entrepreneurs and advocacy gatekeepers over how an issue can be framed so as to fit the existing issue pool without challenging existing ideational and structural relationships within a network, and how these framing choices can displace issue entrepreneurs' original ideas, causing "issue drift." Fourth, it suggests that with determination and strategic savvy, small NGOs with big ideas may succeed against the odds, even as they face hard choices about where and how to shop their ideas.

Political Entrepreneurship

The first step in social change is always politicization of a previously accepted social condition. Political entrepreneurship in this case took different forms over time depending on the agent and target of influence. First, it shifted from issue to norm entrepreneurship as the movement became more institutionalized. Second, it shifted from a focus on changing U.S. policy to an effort to inculcate new expectations at the global level. Third, the strategies used shifted from changing state practices one at a time to a focus on changing discourses within global civil society and multilateral institutions to affect state understandings, ultimately combining both approaches. In this section I outline the campaign's early history, emphasizing these conceptual shifts before turning to an assessment of how these ideas evolved through reactions from and interactions with global advocacy gatekeepers.

Problem Definition and Issue Entrepreneurship: "The Marla Ruzicka Story"

The movement to increase state accountability for assisting civilians affected by legitimate military operations began with Marla Ruzicka, a twenty-five-year-old grassroots activist from San Francisco who originally worked with Global Exchange. After the attacks of 9/11, the organization geared up for a mission to monitor and evaluate the civilian costs of the quickly looming war in Afghanistan.

Ruzicka found herself on the ground in Peshawar interviewing refugees and connecting with the expatriate journalist and aid worker community. Humanitarian and human rights organizations were in the field to assist, monitor, and protect. But "protection" by these organizations consisted primarily of reminding belligerents of their obligations under the rules of war; "assistance" was doled out to needy civilians as a kind of charity; and demand was always greater than supply. As Tom Malinowski of Human Rights Watch later told me, "Marla's approach was different—she went around hugging everyone."[19]

Inspired by first-person testimonials of lost homes, limbs, and family members, Ruzicka began collecting data on civilian losses one family at a time and approaching the guards at the U.S. Embassy, often with colorful demonstrations staged to be captured by foreign journalists, demanding restitution for civilian victims as a form of justice.[20] She also began building an informal network in Afghanistan with human rights and humanitarian organizations on the ground there, drawing the foreign aid community into her social circle through wild nightly parties in Kabul. Through these interactions, she developed the idea of an organization to lobby for war victims, an idea that came to fruition on a trip home in spring 2002.

Ruzicka landed in Washington, DC, in July on her way back to Afghanistan from San Francisco. Her goal was to secure a compensation fund from the U.S. government. Working through a Global Exchange contact, she was quickly introduced to Bobby Mueller of Vietnam Veterans of American Foundation, one of the cofounders of the International Campaign to Ban Landmines and an old hat at beltway diplomacy. Mueller in turn introduced her to Tim Rieser, aide to Senator Patrick Leahy of the Foreign Operations Subcommittee. Rieser, who had once unsuccessfully tried to get compensation for civilians harmed in the 1989 U.S. invasion of Panama, was skeptical of the idea but impressed by Ruzicka's passion. He began coaching Ruzicka on professionalism and advocacy work:

> Tim helped Marla metamorphose from a San Francisco leftist into a human rights advocate whom Washington would take seriously. "How do we get

the imp-
of using the
right language

compensation to the right victims who were bombed?" Marla asked one day. "Nobody will listen to you if you say 'compensation.' We need to find a way to get 'assistance' to the victims of the 'accidental' bombings," Tim corrected.[21]

Even this brief sketch suggests Ruzicka embodied many of the ingredients of a successful issue entrepreneur. Her charisma was beyond question: In a personal interview, Human Rights Watch advocacy director Tom Malinowski chalked up Ruzicka's success nearly entirely to her force of personality: "This was an inspired, charismatic, somewhat crazy, individual who had an idea that no one else had thought to pursue in the past and was very determined and relentless and charming and took it as far as she could."[22] Her credentials as a Global Exchange staffer bought her access and credibility with the rest of the NGO community, although she increasingly acted on her own initiative. She had the buy-in of the beneficiaries she sought to help: Afghan families she came in contact with were uniformly drawn to her and her message of empathy and condolences. She spoke the language of human rights and grassroots activism.

network
w/ NGOs
& the victims

But she also lacked a few qualities necessary for successful global advocacy: a sense of professionalism, procedural skills, and access to funding. She compensated with her intuitive ability to attract well-connected allies.[23] For the skills, she relied heavily on brokers who materialized through her intensely magnetic social schedule: Human Rights Watch legal research director Sam Zia-Zarifi, who encouraged her to assume the best of military personnel and learn to speak their language rather than scream at them; CNN terrorism expert Peter Bergen, who helped her network throughout the Beltway; and her friends in the U.S. Congress. By 2003, when she landed in Iraq, "everyone noticed the shift in her from radical activist to human rights professional."[24]

Ruzicka was also able to convert these connections into funding and soon decided to found her own NGO to promote her cause. Both the Open Society Institute and the Ford Foundation, as well as private donors, offered her new organization, CIVIC, financial support. By 2005, Ruzicka had helped Global Exchange complete the first testimonial account of civilian harm in Afghanistan.[25] Moreover, with Tim Rieser's help she had convinced the U.S. Congress to pass a law awarding condolence payments to civilians in Iraq harmed incidentally by U.S. weapons. Working family by family in Iraq, Ruzicka identified individuals in need of medical attention or solace, assisted them in completing the required forms to benefit from this new law and from existing condolence payment programs.

CIVIC's nonprofit status was still pending on April 16, 2005, when Marla Ruzicka was killed alongside her country director, Faiz Ali Salim, in a suicide attack. The tragedy galvanized her powerful network around her legacy. Members of the CIVIC board determined that her dream would live on through her organization, and the next chapter in CIVIC's history began.

From Issue Entrepreneur to Global Norm Entrepreneur

Although Ruzicka was an issue entrepreneur, she was not technically speaking a *global norm* entrepreneur. Her objective was to name a problem and directly help the suffering, not to create new international moral understandings. Her successors had farther-reaching goals, shaped by their personal convictions, their professional trajectories, and their evolving perception of the constraints and political opportunities in which they operated. They also had something Ruzicka never did: a solid organizational platform from which to work.

Ruzicka died leaving an organization on paper but one that scarcely existed in practice. The board had been pulled together as a means of pushing her 501(c)3 paperwork through, but was composed primarily of her friends and (after her death) her mother.[26] The organization had no executive director, no staff, and no institutional structure.[27] Its working budget was running out, and several funders were loath to provide more money, so guilty did they feel at having fueled the cause that led to Ruzicka's death.[28]

Those close to Ruzicka, however, were determined to protect and promote her legacy. Democracy in Action director April Pederson, who had been Ruzicka's best friend in Washington, DC, took over as acting executive director, and Tara Sutton became field director. Pederson sought new funding through Ruzicka's social network, making the case that her work should live on and promising to professionalize. Pederson also began pushing to hire staff grounded in security policy as well as human rights,[29] and with expertise in marketing and nonprofit management.

As incoming executive director the board chose Sarah Holewinski, a graduate of Columbia University in security policy with consulting experience at Human Rights Watch, connections to the progressive security establishment, and years of policy/advocacy work in the Clinton White House. Holewinski was joined by Associate Director Marla Keenan. Keenan had a master's in international policy from Carnegie Mellon University and experience in the private sector prior to graduate school, and had been working at Citizens for Global Solutions in global outreach.

This infusion of young, professional staff with marketing, management, and policy advocacy skills transformed the organization. Between 2005 and 2007 CIVIC shifted from a focus on identifying service recipients to lobbying governments and militaries, writing op-eds, and identifying funding streams with which to pursue its efforts to change policy. By late 2007, CIVIC had an office space in downtown Washington, DC, a new website, a small staff, and a thriving internship program. The organization now had senior leadership managing it day to day and looking to the future. It also had a reconstituted set of goals, targets of influence, and strategies—a set that continued to shift over time through interactions with government and advocacy gatekeepers.

New Goals, New Targets, New Tactics: CIVIC 2007–11

Three significant changes took place in CIVIC's organizational behavior between 2007 and 2011. First, CIVIC's *goals* shifted during its early years. For all her revolutionary intensity, Marla Ruzicka's aims had been modest: to secure resources from a single warring government and get them into the hands of certain needy civilians. Under Sarah Holewinski, CIVIC's agenda quickly broadened as it became clear that this problem was bigger than the United States and bigger than any specific conflict. Although CIVIC continued to catalogue victim testimonials and secure condolence payments for specific civilians through its connections with the military,[30] its work increasingly took on a third track as well. Between 2005 and 2007, the content on the website expanded from "service delivery" and "voice for victims" to include "change the rules."[31] By March 2008 the website highlighted the lack of responsibility for lawful civilian harms in the laws of war, using the evidence gathered in the field to call for new international standards:

In the past century, we've seen marked improvements in how we treat each other. . . . Through the Geneva Conventions and treaties banning weapons like landmines, nations have promised to protect civilians when they go to war. But no treaty, custom or norm requires nations to help those they fail to protect. No matter how many civilians are killed in a war, no matter how many are left homeless, no matter how much property is destroyed, those who do the damage have no legal duty to help. We hear time after time "war is war"—the standard explanation for overlooking harm to innocent people. It's time for a change.[32]

This goal of "changing the rules" was also expressed through CIVIC's staff recruitment and outreach. The organization hired Jessi Schimmel straight out of the University of Denver's Korbel School and put her to work researching global norm development and providing recommendations to the CIVIC leadership. When I was first contacted by Schimmel and Holewinski in 2007, it was as part of a set of feelers to academics with expertise in "global norm development," seeking ideas and strategies on how to change normative understandings at the global level.

The shift in goals entailed a series of shifts in CIVIC's *targets of influence* as well: from the U.S. government to the global community of states and the structure of international law broadly. Ruzicka's target had consistently been the United States, and she had worked through U.S. policy networks in both Washington, DC, and the expatriate aid communities in U.S. zones of occupation. But in learning how to "message" the notion of "help where you've harmed" to the U.S. government, Holewinski and Keenan began taking the message to other governments as well: "We began to question why, if the U.S. is making the effort to help civilians it has harmed, other countries shouldn't be doing so as well?"[33] Indeed, CIVIC was documenting civilian harm in many conflicts, and in each case the absence of formal accountability by belligerents left needy civilians without recognition or assistance.[34] It also undermined security policy, they argued, making it harder for well-intentioned governments to maintain the moral high ground against terrorists and war criminals.

Governments bought the pragmatic argument. But making the case that governments had a *moral obligation* to civilians was harder. Increasingly, CIVIC took the opposite tack, arguing that if there *was* no existing expectation that warring parties will make amends, then there *should* be:

> We believe this should be a global norm and value, but when you look at in
> ternational law nothing there states "collateral damage" victims should be
> recognized and helped. And that's when we started to say, this could be the
> next place for international law to go.[35]

What the content of that global norm should be precisely was a consensus that evolved over time within the organization. In conversations with
me over the course of 2008, Holewinski often ruminated aloud about
what precisely CIVIC's normative goals were and how to fit them into the
strategic context while remaining true to Ruzicka's vision of concretely
helping people.[36] Even the reference point of the norm was up for debate. Whereas Schimmel argued that CIVIC's niche was "people who are
harmed in the cross fire," as late as January 2009, for example, Keenan expressed doubt about whether the focus should be unintentional victims
only or *all* civilian victims: "As we go into more conflicts I don't think
we're going to be able to draw that line [between international and unintentional harm] so clearly."[37]

A key early question was what "changing the rules" actually meant in
practice. International law is structured by the distinction among codified treaty law (which binds parties to a treaty), customary law (based on
a historical pattern of practice), and nonbinding yet sometimes powerful
soft law (the moral consensus of the international community as reflected
in the language of international documents and resolutions). Should
CIVIC call for updates to the laws of war, work toward a customary law
standard, or adopt a soft law approach? Unlike landmine campaigners
and those who sought to end child soldiering, CIVIC decided early on
not to propose a new treaty or formal amendment to existing humanitarian law, nor did they at first attempt to spread this sensibility through
global civil society. Rather, they argued that a new expectation of conduct
would emerge organically as more and more states began to normalize
condolence payments through their defense ministries. In 2007, CIVIC's
key strategy was to change and improve state *practice* one warring party
at a time.

The belief that changed practice could lead to normative change was
grounded in the notion of customary international law: law that is based
on state behavior rather than codified in treaties.[38] It also stemmed from
the observation of CIVIC's staff that numerous "norms"—such as the
responsibility to protect—get codified in UN resolutions but are poorly

implemented. By contrast, "We wanted our norm to be built from the ground up. We were trying to knit together instances of amends into a larger momentum."[39]

For a tiny NGO, CIVIC was wildly successful at convincing warring governments to establish condolence payments and other mechanisms to recognize civilian suffering.[40] But over time it became clear that these programs alone did not necessarily change governments' perceptions about their moral responsibilities: changed practices did not necessarily change expectations unless the *meanings* of those practices were changed as well. The U.S. condolence payment program was often held up by CIVIC as an example of emerging practice when encouraging other governments to follow suit. But Holewinski told me in 2008, "I don't think any of these countries want to think of themselves as setting a precedent."

CIVIC staff continued to lobby governments for concrete policy shifts. But between 2008 and 2009 CIVIC expanded its repertoire of contention to include a concerted effort to change global *discourse* as well, or how transnational actors talk and think about the laws of war. While a treaty or other changes to codified law still seemed unrealistic, they wanted to embed the language of making amends widely in human rights and humanitarian discourse, changing the normative environment in which government diplomats would think about civilians and keeping unintended victims on the advocacy agenda.

This involved another shift in the targets of influence to include global civil society organizations and multilateral institutions: in short, CIVIC recognized the significance of obtaining symbolic support from global advocacy gatekeepers. Between 2008 and 2011, CIVIC actively targeted leading development, human rights, humanitarian law, and transitional justice NGOs, UN bodies, and government "champions" to join their coalition. A separate website was established to promote the concept of "making amends." CIVIC hired a new staff person in summer 2009 to garner support for the idea in UN circles.

In the rest of this chapter, I explore CIVIC's interactions with these "advocacy elites" between 2007 and 2011, even as the organization continued its pathbreaking work in the field. The next section describes and explains the varied support and push back CIVIC received from advocacy hubs in several adjacent issue networks; the final section traces the evolution of CIVIC's messaging in this context. My overall claim is that the factors that first stymied and ultimately fostered CIVIC's emerging success were related to network dynamics—perceived relationships between issues, between issue areas, between organizations, and between individuals in the broad transnational area of human security.

From Agenda Vetting to Issue Adoption by Network Hubs

Early on, CIVIC had enjoyed support from several powerful allies, providing the organization several natural advantages as a political entrepreneur. The Open Society Institute had provided an infusion of funding early on. And CIVIC had the ear and sympathetic support of the Washington, DC, branch of a key human rights organization, Human Rights Watch. Holewinski told me unequivocally in 2008, "We couldn't have done this without Human Rights Watch."

But this support by these particular organizations fell short of global issue adoption in certain important ways. First, because Ruzicka had been focused on U.S. foreign policy her network focused on Washington. ConnectUS, Democracy in Action, Citizens for Global Solutions, even the Washington, DC, chapter of Human Rights Watch were all focused on changing U.S. foreign policy, not on spreading thematic moral understandings at the global level. Second, the type of support given by these organizations is closer to what Bob describes as "matchmaking" rather than "issue adoption." Groups did not adopt the issue of "making amends" so much as they adopted CIVIC, providing office space, contacts, and introductions, brainstorming with its staff on advocacy strategy, and helping the organization stay afloat at key junctures.[41] None at that time provided regular, forceful, public legitimation of the "making amends" concept.

To spread a new normative expectation at the global level, CIVIC needed (and sought) to cultivate more formal alliances with organizations focused and networked thematically at the global level, in issue areas adjacent to the idea they were promoting. Such alliances were seen as valuable not simply in practical terms but for the boost in legitimacy that accompanies formal alliances with advocacy heavyweights in particular issue areas.[42] For example, Jessi Schimmel emphasized the legitimating effect of formal gatekeeper adoption when she described CIVIC's strategy in 2008, stressing the value added of simply associating the CIVIC cause with the organizational brands characteristic of several key issue areas. "I would aim for several organizations that really do build up our credibility, names that people who don't know CIVIC will still recognize," Schimmel said. "We want Human Rights Watch, International Crisis Group, also land-mines/cluster [munitions] organizations, victim's assistance groups. We aren't frankly asking for much: their name, their support if someone says, 'what is this norm, do you believe in it?'"[43]

But although some individuals inside specific organizations were supportive, CIVIC had difficulty getting human security NGOs to sign on. Instead, their early efforts to market the issue to broader thematic coalitions had resulted not in support from these organizations at large but instead significant push back. In 2008 Holewinski described her surprise when pitching the issue to progressive NGOs in Los Angeles: "It was my first month on the job and I was going to talk to this large group of pacifists, humanitarians, and I thought, 'This is going to be great! These are our people!' Not at all. I got blasted. It was really eye opening."

Agenda Vetting by Human Security Gatekeepers

Why were leading human security actors initially reticent about an idea that would seem to have such humanitarian merit? To some extent, certain *issue attributes* created concern for potential adopters. The making amends issue possessed many important attributes for an emerging issue—emotional appeal, "linkability" to various existing discourses, and reference to bodily harm to vulnerable populations—but in other respects it was not perceived as "ripe" for attention by the mainstream human security network. Concerns expressed by the staff of leading human security organizations I interviewed in 2008–09 referred to the issue's measurability, magnitude, or solvability.

Some human security specialists cast doubt about the scope or magnitude of the problem itself. When CIVIC approached the U.S. chapter of a leading international disability rights organization for support, senior officials there turned to the organization's counterparts in Europe before agreeing: "We wanted to know: *Is* this a thematic issue that's emerging? Or is the U.S. the only context where such a movement has emerged strongly?"[44] Others enthusiastic about the idea of amends were also initially skeptical of a rule that seemed unduly aimed at particular states or, as one Washington, DC–based humanitarian official put it, at "victims of Western wars."[45] "Is this a global norm or an anti-U.S. norm?" a Canadian human security expert asked skeptically when students in my class questioned him about the amends concept.

Even those who acknowledged that collateral damage was probably an issue in numerous contexts were uncertain how much importance to attach to this in the broader scheme of civilian harms. Some continued to argue that the bigger problem was the intentional targeting of civilians. CIVIC's website was full of testimonials, but in the absence of comprehensive global mechanisms for counting the civilian dead and injured in armed conflicts, it was difficult to say with certainty how serious incidental harms were as a proportion of the total.[46] Some practitioners were leery of a campaign where technical knowledge was unavailable to confirm the testimonials: in campaigning, *statistical measurability* is an important step in problem construction.[47]

Another concern related to *feasibility*: the ability to implement amends as a specific solution to the problem CIVIC had identified. In focus groups, human security practitioners generally demonstrated enthusiasm about the problem but skepticism about compensation as a solution. Some argued that "you'll never get governments to do that," pointing out the ways in which it would complicate counterterror operations. Some pointed out that many war-affected governments would be incapable of complying with such a norm: "Rwanda and Congo are in a conflict: Who's going to pay compensation?"[48]

Others raised concerns over the practical problems of implementing amends: "It's an interesting campaign, but as an actual kind of structure, a regulation, or norm, it would be extraordinarily difficult: how would you determine who the victims are, and what the compensation should be and all these other kinds of questions."[49] Some argued that the key problem was simply reducing collateral damage in the first place by enforcing the proportionality rule. A staff person from a refugee relief organization said, "Norm-building takes time and energy: Why not just devote that to enforcing existing norms?"[50]

Ultimately, however, these issue attributes are insufficient explanations for gatekeeper reticence since many other similar issues with the same attributes had been adopted by the same communities of practice. Few thought a ban on landmines was politically feasible when it was originally proposed.[51] Far from being opposed to campaigns singling out Western states, human rights organizations in fact routinely do so.[52] Many campaigns have been launched on inadequate evidence (such as the case of sexual violence in Bosnia) or on numbers that have been made up entirely, as in the extrapolation that there were three hundred thousand child soldiers.[53] And humanitarian law organizations have often sought to fill gaps in international law, promulgating new treaties and treaty language on weapons, children, and crimes such as sexual violence, as well as successfully building norms through nontreaty approaches. The guiding principles on internal displacement represent an example of a successful "soft law" process.[54]

Seemingly, no single issue attribute could have sunk the "making amends" idea—the question is why some human security elites constructed the issue in this way and came to believe that these concerns outweighed the other ways in which the issue *was* a plausible candidate for advocacy. Why did these issue attributes have such salience for this particular issue, pushing gatekeepers toward an initially reticent rather than receptive stance?

The answer is that many of these attributes were not merely intrinsic to the issue but rather relational. What mattered was not the issue itself but how the issue was perceived to be situated within networks of issues and relevant actors. In short, *intranetwork relations* helped constitute key actors' perceptions of the "making amends" issue and of CIVIC as a norm entrepreneur.

An obvious and somewhat circular relational effect was precisely the absence of formal adoption by a major advocacy hub. At the start, this affected CIVIC's credibility as an entrepreneur when pitching the issues to other advocacy hubs.[55] But other specific features of CIVIC's network position—and that of the issue it was championing—also affected the organization's initial ability to attract supporters.

One of these features was intersectionality: "making amends" constituted a "between the cracks" issue, falling at the interstices of different issue networks. Depending on which piece of the concept one focused on, it could be a humanitarian law issue, a human rights issue, a development issue, a justice issue, or a protection issue.

For emerging issues, this sort of liminality can contribute to effective coalition building, or it can incentivize "buck-passing" within civil society. For example, as I show in my earlier work on children born of wartime

rape, the fact that the issue could be viewed through either a child protection or a gender-based violence lens meant groups in either camp could
assume away their own responsibility to incorporate such children into
their programming.[56]

In the case of "making amends," individuals I spoke with at development and humanitarian organizations saw it as more of a postconflict
issue, whereas the postconflict justice community saw it as a humanitarian
law/human rights issue. In each case, the sense that the issue "belonged"
elsewhere was an obstacle to formal issue adoption:

> We understand that for a sustainable peace you need to address some of these
> issues; but our central thing is that when people are in conflict their basic needs
> are met. . . . We're mostly a water and sanitation organization. . . . Postconflict
> amends is something we could move into but we're not there right now.[57]

> We are interested in seeing that victims of conflict are addressed. I think the
> differentiating point for us is that our work is rights-based, and what I think
> [CIVIC] has done is carve out an area where they see a gap, where the law
> doesn't apply. . . . They're pulling on sort of a humanitarian motivation, an
> apology for what happened but not saying we did something wrong. . . . So
> we've kept in touch with them but we're just not part of their campaign.[58]

According to Holewinski, this sort of buck-passing often occurred in her
early efforts to pitch the issue to different sectors:

> We heard from a lot of organizations that there are already movements
> out there we should be joining. And whenever we looked into those move-
> ments, we realized that's not at all what we're saying. So "there are groups
> that are working on gender violence, why don't you do into that?" Well, a
> lot of war victims are men . . . so that leaves out a segment of war victims
> and we don't want to do that either. Or "you should link this to children and
> armed conflict." And, yes, our issue fits into that, but not all the way. So we
> have to find the channel that can give us a clear path to building this norm.[59]

Intersectionality of issues across issue domains doesn't necessarily doom
them: After all, some of the most high-profile issues in the campaigns
of the 1990s were those in which entrepreneurs could mobilize broad

coalitions around a master frame. The landmines campaign was framed as a disarmament, humanitarian, *and* development problem.[60] Conflict diamonds bridged human rights, trade, and security.[61] HIV-AIDS metamorphosed from a health to a human rights to a security issue.[62] But another intranetwork effect initially inhibited this easy concordance across issue areas: the fact that the frame originally proposed by CIVIC was perceived to conflict with master frames associated with the relevant issue areas.

Individuals thinking through a conflict prevention or peace frame were concerned, for example, that the idea of amends constituted a legitimation of violence. By drawing attention to the notion that some deaths and maimings were in fact not against humanitarian law, some organizations worried that this would provide a legitimating discourse for armed violence. This perception of disconnect between the peace movement and the CIVIC idea dated back to Marla Ruzicka's early days lobbying in Washington: members of Code Pink were among the idea's earliest critics.[63] A focus group respondent said: "The notion that 'that's OK, who we kill, we'll fix with a little money'; it's making me uncomfortable."[64] In 2009, a representative from one humanitarian organization similarly told me, "We're not comfortable being inside negotiations with the military—we don't want to be there saying that we think certain levels of collateral damage are OK."[65]

Within the humanitarian sector, a key concern was whether the "making amends" idea would compromise the well-defined distribution of labor between militaries and the civilian humanitarian sector. Humanitarian organizations operating in conflict zones rely on a discourse of political neutrality to gain access to needy civilians: open association with weapons bearers can compromise this image.[66] A norm that belligerents would themselves distribute payments as compensation was seen to both compromise the association of aid with political neutrality and jeopardize "humanitarian space": some humanitarians feared a further militarization of humanitarianism that could undermine the neutrality of the entire system.

According to CIVIC, there was also a sense among some humanitarian and development organizations that outsourcing victim assistance to the military would create redundancies, removing opportunities for NGO work. On a more normative level, some were concerned that such a norm would introduce inequalities among victims. Transitional justice groups were focused on reparations for war crimes: expanding the notion of compensation to those legally harmed through noncriminal military operations was viewed by some as an unhelpful dilution of their key focus. And finally humanitarian law organizations were quite skeptical of claims that the laws of war might need expanding—reflecting a general concern that if you open up the "Pandora's box" of the Geneva Conventions existing standards might be negotiated away.[67]

So shopping their preferred frame among these different communities of practice at first led to frustration and stalemate. At times, CIVIC staff were offered the opportunity to gain supporters by modifying their focus, but they resisted.

> We went to one organization working on Darfur, Congo, Chad, and they said, "We've been working on responsibility to protect, that's a natural fit, you should be coming into R2P." Well, that's about mass atrocities, not accidental deaths. By linking that with R2P, not only do we get off track of what we're trying to do, we water down R2P.[68]

By spring 2009, Amnesty International, Survivor Corps, and Oxfam had all declined to formally join the campaign.[69] Handicap International, which had previously been a member of the steering committee, withdrew later in the year. But CIVIC retained heavyweight Human Rights Watch, as well as advice from their wider network of contacts. And by early 2010 the campaign's prospects had shifted. International Crisis Group joined the steering committee. The UN Security Council began to take an interest in the issue, and several governments had begun talk of championing it. The campaign's list of members and signatories began to grow. By 2011, it included well-known human rights and humanitarian groups such as Physicians for Human Rights, Women for Women International, and the International Rescue Committee.

How did CIVIC shift the organization's and the issue's relationship to the broader human security network in such a way as to encourage gatekeeper adoption? CIVIC was able to successfully shift key gatekeepers' perception of the organization and the issue by reconstituting its network ties from Washington to New York; by developing conceptual and interpersonal strategies to span the discursive empty space between advocacy "silos"; and by zeroing in on a master narrative in which to embed the making amends issue: the "protection of civilians" discourse percolating in UN circles under the auspices of the Office for the Coordination of Humanitarian Affairs.

Advocacy Countermeasures: Shifting Network Ties

In the winter of 2008–09, CIVIC began taking stock of its strategy. It had already reached out to academic institutions for ideas and as advocacy targets, inviting strategy papers and briefings from the University of Massachusetts's Center for Public Policy and Administration and from Harvard University's International Law Clinic.[70] It was becoming clear that while they continued to be successful at affecting state practice here and there, a rethinking of advocacy frames and coalition strategies was needed in order to cultivate the broader norm change they desired for the "changing the rules" part of CIVIC's work.

In January 2009, CIVIC staff organized a brainstorming meeting with human security practitioners in the Washington, DC, area. Representatives from Human Rights Watch, Oxfam, Survivor Corps, Citizens for Global Solutions, and others in CIVIC's network attended to provide conceptual and tactical advice. Part of the purpose of the meeting was to nail down a frame for the campaign as part of the wider effort to convince groups in the room to officially join if they hadn't already. In planning how to elicit commentary and thoughts from participants, CIVIC staff prepared carefully to articulate "civilians caught in the cross fire" as a vulnerable group falling through the cracks, and to stress the key principle that they deserve aid without privileging any specific practical pathway to implementing this. They were also careful to emphasize that they wanted to build a customary norm, not push for a treaty.

The agenda also included a discussion of how to establish benchmarks for success "since we have no treaty to work toward"; where to pitch the concept ("having the U.S. on board, does that help or hurt?") and what to "hook it" to (the fiftieth anniversary of the Geneva Conventions? the release of the secretary general's report on the protection of civilians, although "not sure that's a perfect fit"?); and the timing of the formal campaign launch: "We could launch in spring, then sign people on; or we could sign people on and then launch."[71]

Those attending the meeting offered several kinds of feedback. First, they provided advice on *networking*: which individuals to try to attract in

UN circles and why, and how and when to catch them; or how to determine the right configuration of government allies ("get one country out of each of the five regional groups," and "find out which countries donate voluntarily to tribunals—it's a good barometer of who is good on humanitarian issues"). Second, they provided strategic advice on the *advocacy process* at the global level. For example, CIVIC was advised not to push for a General Assembly resolution as it would take too long to be helpful. Finally, they provided advice on *messaging*. CIVIC was encouraged to work on narrowing down the message into sound bites, but also to find the sweet spot between "something concrete" yet "universal enough." They were also told to avoid certain language: "If you use the word 'norm' you're dead. Package it differently."

Over the course of spring 2009, CIVIC began to implement these ideas through a significant expansion in its strategy. First, while it continued to work separately on promoting the amends concept through direct advocacy with specific warring parties, it refocused its energy on coalition building within global civil society. The campaign strategy document circulated internally in June 2009 called for a steering committee that included a faith-based organization, a women's organization, and an organization headquartered in the global South; it focused on governments as potential allies rather than targets of influence. Second, it formally repackaged the "changing the rules" section of the CIVIC website into a separate campaign, the Making Amends Campaign (MAC), with its own web portal. In this way, CIVIC sought to protect its service-oriented niche while beginning to formally combine efforts with a wider coalition on the norm-building side. In so doing, CIVIC reconstituted its relationships both with the issues and the actors in the wider human security network and yoked the "amends" concept successfully to the wider issue area of "protecting civilians."

New allies, new issue linkages.   A key decision taken in spring 2009 was to move the focus of the MAC campaign from Washington to New York. This marked a significant shift from CIVIC's earlier strategy of working through Marla Ruzicka's original DC-based networks. Those earlier connections (based on getting the United States to do something) had given CIVIC access to and leverage with congressional leaders and the U.S. Department of Defense. But it limited its reach in global civil society.

For example, many of CIVIC's DC-based NGO contacts worked for the U.S. chapter of their respective organizations and so were focused on influencing U.S. policy. Scott Stedjan at Oxfam USA, Joe Volk at the Friends Committee for National Legislation, contacts at the Washington offices of Human Rights Watch and the ICRC: even though these individuals were enthusiastic about CIVIC and generous with advice, they lacked the institutional authority to formally associate their international counterparts with what the CIVIC team wanted to characterize as a global, not a U.S.-based, norm-building process. They also lacked the connections to broker such relationships for CIVIC with their counterparts at the global level.

As CIVIC recognized at the January 2009 meeting, the appropriate gatekeepers for global agenda setting are not national chapters but international secretariats: the New York headquarters of Human Rights Watch, rather than the Washington, D.C. office; ICRC headquarters in Geneva; and UN bodies. Shifting their coalition targets from Washington to New York and Geneva wasn't simply about creating new connections. It was also about constituting the "amends" idea as a global thematic issue of concern to many stakeholders in many different contexts, rather than associating it primarily with U.S. foreign policy.

Pitching to new actors meant cultivating new connections. In March 2009, CIVIC hired a new campaign fellow to do just that. Scott Paul was a first-year law student at New York University with a stipend from New York University to do pro-bono work for the summer and a history of coordinating advocacy campaigns through the DC-based Citizens for Global Solutions. He was recruited for CIVIC by board member Heather Hamilton, who had worked with Paul at Citizens for Global Solutions. Heather described Paul as "the kind of person who can go out and just meet, meet, meet, and he understands that how these things happen is you form personal relationships and just push people to get involved."[72]

Indeed, Paul spent his summer arranging coffee chats, buying drinks, attending briefings, and pitching the MAC in formal meetings all over New York. He fastidiously followed up on referrals, bouncing from New York–based NGOs such as the International Center for Transitional Justice to the office of the "civilians" liaison for the Austrian delegate to the UN; to the Quaker UN Office and ICRC headquarters in Geneva and back to New York to see the civil society liaison at the UN Office of the High Commissioner for Human Rights. Paul reported back his impressions, intelligence, and trajectory to CIVIC headquarters in Washington through regular and detailed e-mails, and the DC-based team engaged in strategy and brainstorming sessions nearly every day by phone. By summer's end, CIVIC had already achieved one of its benchmarks—to expand the campaign membership to a thematically diverse range of NGOs.[73] But more than that, they were creating a buzz among government representatives and UN civil servants.

Paul did not simply possess the ability to rapidly generate social ties to a wide range of global civil servants bustling around UN headquarters in New York. He also embodied—and knew how to cultivate—conceptual and interpersonal connections across issue areas. Coming from a sustainable development background and then moving into foreign policy and international organizations, Paul was accustomed to working across congruent circles of theory and practice. For example, at Citizens for Global Solutions he was involved in several campaigns, including the Law of the Sea Campaign and the Stop Bolton Campaign,[74] that were not, in the words of Hamilton, "siloed in the human rights world . . . which is great because silos in advocacy kill your advocacy."[75]

Indeed, the necessity of finding a way to exploit their ideational position at the interstices of advocacy silos—rather than seeking to situate the amends concept in one or the other—had become increasingly apparent to CIVIC staff over the years. For example, in 2008 Holewinski had expressed concern about pegging the campaign to specific issue areas such as "women and children," but by late 2009 they were rethinking this approach. Maybe the best way to build a coalition was precisely to engage small pieces of the issue in multiple sectors simultaneously to see where it might gain traction. "We needed to find where our audience was," Holewinski said. "Who are the stakeholders in an issue that is so cross-cutting?"[76]

Paul did precisely this as he built social, professional, and conceptual connections in New York and Geneva one coffee meeting at a time. In each encounter, he tested the resonance of amends among a variety of different advocacy communities and frames, engaging important players around transitional justice, peacekeeping and peacebuilding, children and armed conflict, human rights, humanitarian law, and humanitarian affairs. One of the most resonant connections was the nexus between humanitarian affairs and hard security issues. Whereas victim assistance groups were increasingly skeptical of the campaign (Survivors Corps finally turned

CIVIC down for the steering committee in fall 2009 and Handicapped International bowed out later), groups specializing in conflict prevention— such as the International Crisis Group—were more interested. Through iterated discussions, Paul honed and narrowed CIVIC's message to find the "sweet spot" that would bind together intersecting advocacy communities, rather than cause amends to fall through the cracks.

Part of this process involved dampening down aspects of CIVIC's message that attracted push back from the wider human security network. As early as spring 2009 Holewinski and Keenan were moving away from the idea that there was a "missing law of war," looking instead for ways to "build on human rights law instead of humanitarian law" and in particular to think of amends in terms of the overlap between the two: the concept of human dignity.[77] At the suggestion of Golzar Kheiltash, a colleague from Citizens for Global Solutions who provided legal advice to the campaign (and later was hired as full-time campaign director), the MAC began deemphasizing terms like "norm," which carried more of a legal than moral connotation among advocacy targets, invoking images of the very treaty process that CIVIC had long since decided to avoid.[78] In reaction to push back on the merits of "compensation," the campaign also stressed that "amends" was about respect and dignity as much as about material assistance.

Though his New York University summer stipend ran out, CIVIC hired Paul part-time in fall 2009 to continue pushing the concept of "amends." By this time, not only had CIVIC's network ties to specific communities of practice changed radically, but their sense of how to frame and pitch amends had also transformed from an emphasis on humanitarian law and human rights law to an emphasis on "protecting civilians" as an issue area. It had also repositioned the "amends" concept conceptually in a way that created new ties to new actors and embedded the issue in a preexisting framework, bridging several distinct advocacy clusters.

Embedding "amends" in "protection of civilians" discourse. The emphasis on amends as a "protection" issue later seemed to the CIVIC team as a "natural fit," but at the time it constituted a subtle shift from CIVIC's earlier framework. In 2008, Keenan had mentioned protection as one of several advocacy discourses where the "amends" idea *didn't* resonate. In January 2009, the "protection of civilians" concept was raised as a possible way to "hook" the MAC campaign to preexisting advocacy rhetoric, but even at that time there was uncertainty whether it was the ideal frame. In part, this perception stemmed from CIVIC's sense, based on interactions with their Washington-based network, that "protection" meant too many different things to different people and wasn't firmly rooted in the concept of humanitarian law.[79] Another concern was the need to differentiate CIVIC's niche—redress by warring parties for unintentional harms—from a protection agenda that had heretofore focused almost exclusively on preventing intentional targeting, and whose response was structured through the relief sector rather than militaries. In early 2009, Holewinski and Keenan were leaning toward embedding the MAC in a combination of human rights rhetoric and humanitarian law rather than engaging "protection" as a normative concept.

Turning toward New York changed this conceptual incentive structure. The concept of "protection of civilians" had much greater resonance in UN circles than in Washington; and more resonance there as a way of describing the MAC niche than "human rights" or "humanitarian law" due to the concept's traction in specific forums at the UN. In fact, although CIVIC had learned through their DC-based contacts that open support from the ICRC on amends was off the table, Scott Paul discovered on a trip to Geneva that the ICRC was in fact more receptive to formal involvement than they expected—so long as the frame was "protecting civilians affected by armed conflict" rather than "filling gaps in humanitarian law."[80]

Similarly, one of the first pieces of advice Paul reported back to CIVIC headquarters when he hit New York in June 2009 came from a human rights organization: when contacting the UN missions, he *shouldn't* ask to speak with the human rights officers because for many countries, the human rights officers would primarily be dealing with General Assembly Third Committee issues. Instead, Paul was advised to ask for the officer responsible for the protection of civilians. These individuals were positioned differently, engaged not with the General Assembly committees but with the Security Council, which held thematic debates on civilian protection each summer and issued resolutions each November in response to a secretary general's report. Such individuals therefore constituted brokers to a different configuration of social and ideational networks within UN circles.

This demonstrates how global policy networks are simultaneously networks of issues and of actors. Indeed, these components of networks are mutually constitutive: marketing an issue to a specific actor can shift an issue's framing, and to some extent the frame chosen by a campaign determines who the best allies will be. Generally speaking, human rights officers are tasked with covering the Third Committee of the General Assembly, and protection of civilians (POC) experts focus on the Security Council's POC agenda (and often Women, Peace and Security or Children and Armed Conflict). According to Paul, "The choice wasn't really just about human rights vs. protection of civilians; the choice was really about General Assembly vs. Security Council."[81]

The Security Council made sense as a target strategically, tactically, and conceptually. First, as a high-profile global institution involved in the "high" politics of international security, success there would raise the profile of the amends issue in unique ways.[82] Second, there was a set of practical concerns relating to the relative institutional environment of the Security Council versus the General Assembly. As Paul put it, "A ton of NGOs compete for attention in the Third Committee, while the Security Council's protection of civilians mandate was actively seeking input and direction from NGOs." Indeed, as Cora True-Frost has shown, the Security Council has been an active "consumer" of human security norms since 1999.[83] Like any small NGO with limited staff and resources, CIVIC had to make strategic decisions about where to target its energy in order to garner timely and meaningful progress on the practice and principle of amends.

But third, according to Paul, linking amends to humanitarian affairs and armed conflict made more sense conceptually than framing it as a human rights problem per se: "We weren't prepared at the start of this campaign to articulate the MAC in a rights framework." Although in some respects protection of civilians *is* a human rights issue and stems from the concept of human dignity, and although ultimately CIVIC's allies came to involve human rights and humanitarian affairs organizations, in practice the distinction was conceptually helpful given the ideational and institutional distinctions between human rights law and architecture (which typically address states' obligations to their own citizens) and humanitarian law, which governs the treatment of foreigners in conflict zones, including the protection of foreign civilians.

By the time the website was launched the following year, the "protection of civilians" trope was featured front and center in the new online description of the MAC campaign: "Protection of civilians is built into the laws of war. But when these protections fail, warring parties have no formal responsibility to help."[84] The concept of "protection" was especially helpful because it could be invoked as policy shorthand for the existing laws of war, with incidental harms treated as a "protection failure," *or* as a policy project aimed at improving the welfare of civilians, in which CIVIC could argue that warring parties should be involved. This suited CIVIC's dual need to spread the concept among the discourse of the POC community while also pursuing amends-as-practice through policy channels.

The shifted advocacy frame meant new institutional targets. The most important hub for the "protection of civilians" in the UN system is the UN Office for the Coordination of Humanitarian Affairs, a department within the UN Secretariat. As a hub in the humanitarian sector, this international bureaucracy has three distinctive characteristics relative to other humanitarian organizations. First, it is more of an advocacy hub than an operational organization: its field offices are small and, unlike most humanitarian groups, it does little in the way of service delivery, focusing instead on promoting the humanitarian agenda at the international level. This profile gives it particular power to construct and market the overall advocacy agenda for the humanitarian sector. Second, in this capacity it therefore has close ties both to the NGO community and to government ministries, so OCHA occupies a structural position of relatively high "betweenness" at the interstices of the "high politics" of governments and UN delegates and "low politics" of the NGO world. It is thus a humanitarian hub in every sense, yet insulated from some of the pragmatic politics of service delivery that led field-based NGOs to be particularly wary of the amends idea.[85]

Third, through its work with the Security Council, OCHA constitutes an ideational broker between two somewhat weakly tied issue areas: hard security and humanitarian affairs. The UN secretary-general presents a periodic report on the protection of civilians to the UN Security Council, a report that the under-secretary general for humanitarian affairs plays a key role in drafting. The presentation of the report constitutes a focusing event that engages delegates to the Security Council in a diplomatic discussion about how to mitigate armed conflict, and is thus an important agenda-setting exercise for the humanitarian sector. It embeds human security concerns in Security Council discussions that otherwise tend to focus on nonproliferation, use of force, and other "hard" security issues, legitimates them as global issues by associating them with the realm of "high politics."[86]

Although the campaign focused significant attention in 2009 and 2010 in engaging state delegations directly, it was obvious to Paul that he needed the support of OCHA and the Secretary-General's office more broadly to really engage the Security Council on amends as a "civilian protection" issue. As Cora True-Frost has shown in her study of the Security Council's approach to thematic human security resolutions, innovations in language that end up in such resolutions are generally first filtered through communities of experts in other relevant UN bureaucracies.[87] Thus OCHA's gatekeeper role functions less in openly endorsing issues itself but in passing along concepts, language, and ideas throughout the UN system informally and in official UN documents that then receive the seal of the Secretariat.

Attracting formal support from OCHA was slow going at first. Although key individuals at OCHA were sympathetic to the CIVIC idea (one I spoke with had known Marla Ruzicka before she died), the organization was unprepared to easily endorse the concept. Paul had slightly more luck meeting with individuals from the UN Office for the High Commissioner for Human Rights. The OHCHR was an imperfect fit for the amends issue insofar as most of its work focuses on enforcing human rights law applicable to peacetime. Moreover, Paul's initial contact there in October 2009 was somewhat ambivalent about the amends principles as they stood. Paul was advised to delineate more clearly the gap that CIVIC sought to fill for victims of armed conflict, making it clear that victims of lawful conduct have no formal recourse from warring parties, and to articulate why amends would not simply duplicate other standards.

This issue of "duplicativeness" had also been raised by another key humanitarian heavyweight, the UN High Commissioner for Refugees. UNHCR is the UN's key hub for work on both refugees and the internally displaced. In a July meeting, Paul learned through his contact there that the "Guiding Principles on Internal Displacement" already included the concept of compensation but not the concept of *recognition* for suffering. On the one hand, this was useful to the MAC because it could hook the compensation concept to earlier precedent in small pockets of the humanitarian world.[88] On the other hand, Paul felt pressure to identify what was unique or new about the MAC idea specifically in the context of this wider ideational landscape, and so over the course of fall 2009 the campaign began to focus much more on the concept of recognition and less on compensation per se.[89] However, humanitarian gatekeepers in the UN remained reticent.

Instead, CIVIC had more initial success directly pushing amends with specific government delegations to the Security Council. Besides expanding the organization's social networks, this injected the MAC message into diplomatic circles, and CIVIC was able to garner support from specific sympathetic delegations such as Uganda, Austria, and Chile. In the lead-up to Security Council Resolution 1894 on the protection of civilians, CIVIC pushed hard with specific governments for the inclusion of language on amends. Ultimately, however, the language in the November 2009 resolution fell short of CIVIC's hopes.[90] The key concern here was not duplication but rather potential *competition* with a related issue: delegates were focused on the concept of reparations for war crimes, and were worried about watering down the message by addressing compensation for civilian victims more broadly.[91]

However, in the same session, the MAC received a boost from an unexpected ally: the Ugandan delegate to the Security Council. Paul had met with the Ugandan mission earlier in the summer, and had been intrigued by their receptiveness to the idea. Although no language on amends ended up in the resolution, the record of the discussion reflected the following statement by Uganda:

> This draft resolution calls for national reparation programs for victims as well as institutional reforms. However, my delegation would like to go a step farther and also recognize the need for all parties to armed conflict to emphasize the dignity of civilians by recognizing losses that result from lawful combat operations as well as providing meaningful amends to affected individuals and communities, such as financial assistance or funding for humanitarian aid programs. . . . My delegation encourages all member states to embrace the concept of making amends—not because there is any legal obligation to do so, but simply in the interests of mitigating suffering and promoting humanity. This has been the policy of the Uganda People's Defense Forces and it continues to be implemented by

the Uganda People's Defense Forces troops serving in the African Union Mission in Somalia.[92]

Aside from being incredibly validating to the MAC campaign, this statement caught the attention of officials at OCHA. Shortly after the November Security Council meeting, Paul finally met with a representative of OCHA's Civilian Protection Unit. According to Paul, the OCHA representative expressed interest in the amends concept for future reports, particularly in light of the Ugandan delegate's statements. The Ugandans had not only raised the issue in a high-profile forum but they had also signaled an emerging practice among states that went beyond the United States' condolence payment programs.

However, CIVIC's OCHA contact was relocating to Geneva; the best he could do was put CIVIC in touch with his successor and with other helpful contacts in the UN system.[93] It was several more months before Paul was able to liaise with his contact's counterpart to begin pitching and refining the amends concept, with a view to embedding language in subsequent civilian protection reports. From his initial contact, Paul understood that demonstrating the emerging practice among states would be key to providing OCHA with the ability to make the case at the Security Council.

The new OCHA POC representative reiterated this view when I spoke with him in June of the following year. However, at that time his key concern was that compensation should not replace proper legal accountability for war law violations, and raised concerns about the possible "moral hazard" if parties to a conflict were more likely to cause civilian harm knowing they need only pay compensation afterward. Like other gatekeepers, OCHA's concerns centered on the concept of compensation specifically rather than the broader principle of amends. He also pointed out that in general OCHA didn't have the capacity to research the topic fully.[94]

Despite his on-the-record reticence, however, Paul's contact actively supported the MAC informally, brokering meetings and providing advice. In February, he invited CIVIC to provide the information OCHA would need to make the case for putting amends language in the next POC report—"both on amends in practice and amends as an emerging norm as evidenced by public statements, reports, meetings and member state support."[95] He also encouraged CIVIC to organize a "side event" during the May/June Security Council debate on protection of civilians. In May, after meeting with a supportive Austrian delegate, he agreed to introduce CIVIC, through Paul, to the incoming section chief for the protection of civilians.

CIVIC's side event—a roundtable discussion on the amends concept—was held July 2012 in a UN conference room, organized to attract potential state supporters of the concept and convince them to integrate mention of amends into their prepared statements at the ongoing Security Council debate on protection of civilians. Tom Malinowski of Human Rights Watch presented, along with a former UN human rights officer. CIVIC learned through a state delegate that the side event help quell some OCHA officials' theoretical questions around amends, helping flesh out the concept and practical application of amends in a way that hadn't been done before. Several state delegations were also convinced to take note. Subsequently four Security Council member states—Brazil, Turkey, Austria, and Uganda—mentioned amends in their opening statements, each emphasizing the distinction between reparations for illegal acts and amends for damages that result from lawful combat operations. In mid-July, CIVIC was permitted to brief OCHA's incoming section chief about amends.

By the end of 2010, the "making amends" concept was gaining sway among global elites, buoyed by the support of important human rights and humanitarian gatekeepers constructing "civilian protection" as a set of ideas for the global community. The Office of the Special Representative to the Secretary-General for Children and Armed Conflict was receptive to the idea. In June 2010, Philip Alston, the UN special rapporteur on extrajudicial, summary, or arbitrary executions, devoted a section of his annual report to the Human Rights Council on amends for harm: as Paul wrote to me, "this is a game-changer." In November 2010, the concept of amends was addressed squarely in the Secretary General's Report to the Security Council.[96] A presidential statement followed the presentation of the report, stating that "all civilians affected by armed conflict, including those suffering losses as a result of lawful acts under international law, deserve assistance and recognition in respect of their inherent dignity as human beings."[97]

By summer 2012, OCHA itself had not yet formally adopted the amends issue. However, it had given the campaign a boost by incorporating amends language in the UN Secretariat's reports, and with government champions increasingly supporting the idea, support for CIVIC throughout global civil society continued to grow. In September 2009, the MAC campaign included two organizations on the steering committee and ten additional members, most of them smaller NGOs. But one year later, following OCHA's engagement with the issue, the membership nearly doubled and included a more significant proportion of NGO "heavyweights": the International Crisis Group, the International Rescue Committee, and Physicians for Human Rights. The MacArthur Foundation provided an infusion of funding. CIVIC hired Golzar Kheiltash to direct the campaign full-time as Scott Paul returned to law school. The concept of amends was no longer a nascent idea but an issue embedded in the global agenda for protecting civilians.

By this time, CIVIC's frame had coalesced around a focus on *all* victims, *including* those harmed by lawful military operations, with an emphasis on the provision of "assistance" and "recognition." But by then CIVIC had also stopped talking about "changing the rules" per se, focusing on "creating an expectation" through soft law that went *beyond* formal rules. And it had stopped talking about a missing law of war, instead aiming to build on the concept of "human dignity" underlying both human rights and humanitarian law, without changing the formal rules or insisting on a preexisting ethical standard.[98] The word "compensation" itself had been dropped in favor of "amends," a wider concept associated with recognition and dignity rather than primarily with material recompense.[99] CIVIC had decided against creating a new legal rule or binding norm, but it had subtly shifted the rhetoric of civilian protection, guaranteeing that the harm suffered by civilians through lawful combat operations was at least acknowledged at the highest levels of the global community. And this new language and the validation of humanitarian gatekeepers gave CIVIC added leverage and deepened credibility as it continued to work with governments and militaries on the ground to "heal the wounds."[100]

What does the CIVIC case tell us about issue creation in global politics? First, that norm entrepreneurship, while crucial, is insufficient to set the global agenda, and new normative understandings don't necessarily emerge even through successful direct advocacy with governments. Instead, much depends on the dialectic between entrepreneurs and powerful players in global civil society—leading NGOs, UN agencies, and government champions. But these organizations make their issue adoption

[handwritten marginal note: in goals & messaging to make the issue agenda]

decisions not based on their appraisal of the entrepreneur or the issue per se but how both are positioned within *networks*: networks of issues, of issue areas, and of organizations all structure the way in which an issue's fit and chances of success are interpreted by agenda leaders in advocacy networks. Moreover, successful direct advocacy with governments, while insufficient to build a norm itself, may be a catalyst to adoption of a new issue by powerful advocacy gatekeepers—an act that legitimizes new issues in transnational networks, providing space for new normative understandings.

Second, network gatekeepers may offer significant support short of formally adopting issues, so the "issue adoption/agenda-vetting" dichotomy should be unpacked by future research on advocacy campaigns. Indeed, given the single-issue orientation of small-NGO norm entrepreneurs, issue adoption in the sense of a large NGO launching a report or a study can sometimes be a double-edged sword: entrepreneurs need multi-issue gatekeepers to legitimize their specific cause in a wider issue area, but they also need to retain ownership of the specific issue as their entire organizational identity and funding streams are at stake. Entrepreneurs have a menu of options for negotiating legitimation by gatekeepers, and what they ask—that gatekeepers join a campaign, accept a place on a steering committee, adopt language in a document or on a website, or simply provide advice and contacts—will be a function of their particular strategy. Given the issue drift often required to gain support from adopters, and the ideational path dependency that results from embedding an emerging issue within the network of a powerful early adopter, norm entrepreneurs must be particularly selective in how they build their coalitions.

Finally, while this chapter has stressed structural relations between organizations, issues, and issue clusters, it also demonstrates how the personal social networks of individual entrepreneurs matter to the perceptions of gatekeepers—both in creating connections and in signaling how a campaign is positioned in the wider landscape of global advocacy. Marla Ruzicka exemplified the ability to connect simultaneously and with equal intensity to vulnerable populations and global elites. This gave her power, opened doors for advocacy, and drove her legacy; but it also meant she never rooted the CIVIC idea in a particular advocacy frame. Sarah Holewinski's hire both "professionalized" and "securitized" CIVIC by infusing the organization with professional contacts in the security sector. Her rolodex of NATO generals both ensured CIVIC would be taken seriously by the military and that it would be viewed with a skeptical eye by antiwar and humanitarian organizations.

Scott Paul's hire brought with it a wider network of professional contacts on the UN side, and the ability to manufacture the sort of "chance meetings" that lit a fire under influential officials. Paul's war stories of wooing bureaucrats and delegates over drinks illustrates how the work of global agenda setting happens away from the conference rooms and plenaries of international institutions and in the everyday spaces of cordial human social relations. It was his particular cachet with the diplomatic sector in New York that enabled the MAC campaign to "leapfrog" to some extent past humanitarian gatekeepers to representatives of key states at UN headquarters in New York. This buzz among state delegates helped construct OCHA's understanding of the issue's salience, and drove its eventual willingness to include amends language in UN reports—a milestone that helped sell the concept to the wider Security Council.

Indeed, the individual social networks of political entrepreneurs are not just vital as conduits of emerging ideas. They also constitute part of an issue's identity and location within an advocacy arena, and as such they signal to potential adopters what's at stake in endorsing a campaign. In the next chapter, I demonstrate how this dynamic played out in a very different issue area, as campaigners against the use of autonomous weapons struggled to find an advocacy frame that resonated with organizations involved in arms control.

5

From "Stop the Robot Wars!" to "Ban Killer Robots"

Pitching "Autonomous Weapons" to Humanitarian Disarmament Elites

Warfare is increasingly carried out by machines. Automated systems already routinely defuse explosives, conduct reconnaissance, serve as mechanical beasts of burden over inhospitable terrain, and assist medics, but militaries worldwide are increasingly developing and deploying robots with the capacity to deploy lethal force as well.[1] Although many members of the U.S. security establishment have argued for years that a human will always remain "in the loop" when making the decision to kill human beings, in fact both the U.S. Army and U.S. Navy have circulated research and solicitations for proposals on fully autonomous weapons systems (AWS) as early as 2005.[2] South Korea and Israel have both deployed armed robot border guards with the capacity to make autonomous targeting decisions. Other nations, including China, Russia, India, Singapore, and the United Kingdom, are developing similar technologies.[3] Indeed, systems such as the Phalanx gun on U.S. Navy vessels are already designed to operate autonomously under certain circumstances.

Since approximately 2007, an epistemic community of researchers has been arguing that this shift in military technology has significant and as yet largely ignored moral implications for implementing the laws of war. Some are concerned with whether machines can be designed to make ethical targeting decisions.[4] For others, the key question is how responsibility for mistakes is to be allocated and punished.[5] Some have considered whether, even if the weapons can meet humanitarian law standards, the ability to wage war without risking soldiers' lives might remove incentives for peaceful conflict resolution and alter the relationship between war and the warrior in such a way as to have spillover effects on the behavior of human weapons bearers.[6] High-profile accidents with unmanned or semi-manned weapons have fueled these concerns.[7]

International law generally proscribes the use of certain means of war. The Hague Conventions codify the principle that "the right of belligerents to kill or injure the enemy is not unlimited" and the Geneva Conventions reiterate that means and methods of warfare must conform to norms of "necessity, proportionality and discrimination." In addition to these general rules, specific weapons deemed to be incapable of distinguishing between civilians and combatants or whose effects cannot be controlled are inconsistent with international law. Moreover, Article 36 of the 1977 Additional Protocol to the Geneva Conventions requires governments to consider these factors both in deploying existing weapons and in developing new ones. Indeed, human security campaigns have emerged bent on regulating or banning certain weapons on precisely the grounds that they do not meet these criteria. Campaigns against landmines, blinding lasers, cluster munitions, and the illicit trade in small arms have each resulted in new norm development since 1990, including several outright bans.[8]

Yet, the cluster of organizations responsible for championing global codes of conduct regarding other types of ethically questionable weapons—cluster munitions, landmines, chemical and biological weapons, blinding lasers—was sanguine about developments in the area of autonomous weaponry until late 2012. Although a campaign formed to lobby governments for such a ban as early as 2009, it struggled for years to attract open support from humanitarian law hubs. In September 2012, I was told by an ICRC representative that the organization had no formal opinion on the matter. Correspondingly, during the period of this study, there was little policy attention to the matter by governments. As Peter Singer's wrote in his extensive 2009 study of developments in this area, "In the hundreds of interviews for this book, not one robotics researcher, developer, program manager or soldier using them in the field made a single reference to...the international law on weapons."[9]

Consistent with the "gatekeeper" model, all this began to change significantly in late 2012 with the publication of a Human Rights Watch report on the matter. This case thus illustrates the power and influence of Human Rights Watch as a "hub" in humanitarian disarmament: prior to its legitimation of the issue, entrepreneurs made little headway, but soon after HRW launched its report numerous other organizations began to take "killer robots" seriously. But why did HRW decide to adopt the killer robot issue in 2012, when it had for years treated the issue as a nonstarter?

In this chapter I examine the efforts of political entrepreneurs for a global precautionary principle against "lethal autonomous robots" between 2007 and 2012 and the initially lukewarm response of humanitarian law hubs such as Human Rights Watch and the International Committee of the Red Cross during this period. As I show, judgments about an issue and its entrepreneurs are shaped by their perceptions about the ideational and social ties between the issue entrepreneurs—who in this case are not NGO activists but members of the scientific community—and other issues and actors within the human security network. Perceptions of these "intranetwork" relations shaped advocacy elite preferences around autonomous weapons. Chances for norm development in this area shifted as those perceptions changed, and shifted decisively when network hubs acted on those changed preferences. This chapter shows how and why that happened.

Academic Networks and Political Entrepreneurship

Two decades ago, Peter Haas explored the political significance of "epistemic communities" of experts and scientists whose principled and causal understandings converge around a specific policy enterprise.[10] Whereas much work on epistemic communities has dealt with their role in policy formulation and enforcement, networks of academic experts and scientists also play important roles in issue formation and agenda setting.[11] Our focus group research found that endorsement by the academic community was one of the "broader context" factors that lent credibility to emerging issues, other things being equal. In fact, individuals affiliated with academic institutions were the original norm entrepreneur in 33 percent of all the advocacy campaigns in the Busby dataset.[12]

In the area of weapons advocacy in particular, networks of scientists, academics, and technicians have long been instrumental in agenda setting around new weapons bans.[13] The small arms issue was constructed by scholars such as Michael Klare and Edward Laurence and Keith Krause and only later expanded into an NGO network.[14] Groups such as the Federation of American Scientists, International Physicians for the Prevention of Nuclear War, and the Pugwash Conferences on Science and World Affairs have long constituted sites where science and global norm-building on emerging military technologies intersect.[15] This emphasis on "expert authority" as a legitimizing component in issue creation around weaponry explains why advocacy hubs have often convened "expert conferences" drawing together scientists, doctors, generals, and lawyers at early stages of the issue adoption process on issues such as blinding lasers and landmines.[16]

Academic experts do not merely influence policy through the formation of epistemic issue networks: they constitute an important part of the landscape of issue networks themselves. Universities and think tanks are important sources of new policy ideas, and academic experts who circulate from the academy through think tanks or policy positions play a significant role in carrying and framing new ideas through policy networks.[17] Several key nodes in the human security network itself are research entities, including the Liu Institute for Human Security at the University of British Columbia, the Stockholm International Peace Research Institute, and the Peace Research Institute of Oslo. Indeed, 64.5 percent of those responding to our survey of the human security network identified themselves as associated with universities.

That said, academic expertise often mitigates against the skills necessary for effective advocacy, and access to expert networks does not guarantee an audience with advocacy elites or that one's pet issue will resonate with those in a position to take political action. As the case study of autonomous weapons advocacy shows, this can particularly be the case when a prescriptive consensus among experts on an emerging issue does not yet exist.

Issue Construction, 2007–2010: The International
Committee on Robot Arms Control

Concern over the ethical implications of autonomous weaponry was already percolating within scientific circles in the early years of the twenty-first century. For example, a 2004 paper on emerging weapons technologies, written by physicists Jürgen Altmann and Mark Avrum Gubrud, included an early articulation of a proposal to ban such weapons.[18] In the same year, philosophers, lawyers, and engineers met in San Remo, Italy, for the First International Symposium on Roboethics, which included some attention to robotic soldiers.

But it was between 2006 and 2009 when Noel Sharkey, a roboticist based at the University of Sheffield in England, began to politicize various theoretical concerns about autonomous weapons by publicly constructing trends toward lethal robotics as a social problem and by establishing an organizational platform from which to campaign. Sharkey had begun his career as an experimental psychologist, after "being a chef and apprentice electrician, a railway worker, apple picker, everything," and later moved into computer science and artificial intelligence.[19] An extremely charismatic renaissance man with the ability to communicate as easily with princes or laypersons as with peers in his discipline, Sharkey combined applied research with public outreach. He was appointed professor of public engagement by the University of Sheffield and spent much of his career popularizing the science of robotics on television shows such as *Robot Wars* and events such as Techno Games, and through speaking tours and large-scale museum exhibitions.

As he followed developments in military robotics, Sharkey began to share a concern expressed by many of his colleagues with the ethics of autonomous weaponry. According to Sharkey, "One of the fundamental laws of war is being able to discriminate real combatants and non-combatants. I can see no way that autonomous robots can deliver this for us." Sharkey had heard of developments in military robotics through his media contacts. As a professor of robotics and public engagement he often interfaced with the media: "Journalists kept asking me about it. They'd say, 'What's going on? We keep reading little bits.' So I went and read little bits, and then I discovered the sites with all the U.S. plans and spent six or seven months reading, thinking: 'This can't be true.'"[20]

Sharkey decided to use his media and professional contacts to "make a fuss" because "I don't know how to access governments." He agitated through his professional societies, including the British Computer Science Society, the Institute of Electrical and Electronics Engineers (IEEE), and the Royal Academy of Engineering. The British Computer Science Society spoke to the Royal United Services Institute, an independent British think tank specializing in defense and security issues, and set up a small conference on his behalf to draw together other roboticists, ethicists, and military officials. This event provided Sharkey contacts within the British military and led to a variety of speaking engagements with European militaries. Meanwhile, he continued to publish popular articles on the dangers of automated weaponry in the mainstream press, scholarly journals, and trade magazines, and spent a significant amount of his time making presentations at scholarly conferences and media outlets[21] in opposition to autonomous military robotics.[22] By 2008 he was calling for governments to create a "global code of conduct" against the acquisition, deployment, and use of such weapons—in essence, a new norm against autonomous weapons systems.

Between 2007 and 2008 Sharkey gave a variety of talks in military and industry venues. He also put feelers out to the NGO community, including U.K. organizations working at that time on landmines and cluster munitions. Originally he had hoped they would take up the banner, with him contributing technical expertise and time, but when this did not happen he began to think about creating his own organization of concerned individuals.[23] An Australian acquaintance, Robert Sparrow, provided an opportunity when he passed through Europe in 2009 seeking a meeting of like-minded academics, including Sharkey and other critical voices in the emerging academic literature on military robotics. Sparrow had been corresponding with Sharkey since publishing his own call for "arms control of robotic weapons" in *Technology and Society*.[24] Sharkey hosted Sparrow and Jürgen Altmann, the German-based physicist, at his home in Sheffield that October; over the Internet the three also connected simultaneously with Peter Asaro, a New York-based philosopher/computer scientist specializing in military robotics and just war theory, whom Sharkey had interviewed a few times on his radio show.[25]

This four-way 2009 meeting resulted in the formation of the International Committee for Robot Arms Control (ICRAC), the establishment of a website, and the drafting of a mission statement that read: "Given the rapid pace of development of military robotics and the pressing dangers that these pose to peace and international security and to civilians in war, we call upon the international community to urgently commence a discussion about an arms control regime to reduce the threat posed by these systems." The group described itself as "an international committee of experts in robotics technology, arms control, international security, international humanitarian law, human rights law, and public campaigns, concerned about the pressing dangers that military robots pose to peace and international security and to civilians in war."[26]

At the suggestion of Altmann, the group decided to convene an "expert meeting" on the topic in Germany the following year to generate discussion and perhaps a consensus among experts about the importance of "arms control for robots," with a particular view toward reaching out to the German Foreign Office.[27] With funding from the German Foundation for Peace Research and the U.K.-based Joseph Rowntree Charitable Trust, the group also issued a broad invitation to individuals who had written on the ethics of autonomous weapons,[28] civil society organizations working on arms control issues,[29] and members of the U.S. military.[30]

The meeting took place over three days in late September 2010, and drew arms control experts from the German Foreign Office and Bundestag. It began with a series of presentations by experts, including engineers, philosophers, and law of war experts. Participants then broke into task groups to consider "proposals for international humanitarian law" and "proposals for arms control." It concluded with a presentation of recommendations, and a discussion of "political strategies for achieving robot arms control," after which participants were invited to sign a declaration of principles outlining the importance of global ethical norms guiding further development of such technologies.[31]

The meeting, particularly its breakout sessions, was characterized by considerable ferment over whether and how to move forward. A key point of disagreement was about whether the purpose of the meeting should be to discuss empirical and philosophical realities as researchers or to develop an advocacy agenda.[32] Another debate concerned whether to focus narrowly on fully autonomous weapons or on the full spectrum of semiautonomous or teleoperated systems, as "drones" with humans in the loop appeared to present different ethical conundrums than fully autonomous weapons.[33] Third, there was some acrimony about whether the goal of international governance in this area should be to ban the use of such systems rather than to simply remain seized of ethical considerations in this realm.[34]

Until the end of the meeting, it looked as if consensus might not be reached on these points, but according to those present a compromise position gradually developed. ICRAC's resulting "Berlin Statement" called for the international community to "commence discussion" toward an "international convention" addressing "the pressing dangers that these systems pose to peace and international security and to civilians." However, it distinguished between fully autonomous systems, for which it proposed a complete prohibition, and teleoperated systems, for which it suggested only restrictions, with the exception of nuclear-armed drones, which it wanted banned entirely.[35]

When put to a vote, a majority of the participants chose to endorse the statement, and of those a small number formally joined the ICRAC network at its conclusion: ICRAC membership grew from four to fourteen core members by the end of the meeting, which also culminated with a press conference. Forty percent of the attendees, however, did not sign the statement. According to individuals present, some participants demurred out of uncertainty over the substance of the statement; others objected to it as a strategy. Some individuals, in their capacity as representatives of organizations without an official stance on the issue, were sympathetic but not in a position to endorse its specific tenets.

Norm Entrepreneurship and Its Discontents, 2009–2011

Among those attendees at the original Berlin meeting who did not sign the outcome document was Ronald Arkin, a U.S. roboticist based at Georgia Tech. Like Sharkey, Arkin was something of a renaissance man, having stumbled into robotics after early training in chemistry, applied mathematics, and computer science. Moreover, he increasingly began to move in philosophical, theological, and policy circles after 2004, when engineers and ethicists began to jointly consider the ethical implications of human-robot interactions. As early as 2004, Arkin was invited to speak on the issue of military robotics at the First International Symposium on Roboethics, where he discussed the implications of human emotive ties to machines in military contexts.[36] This symposium brought him into contact with wider international networks, in particular the Pugwash Conferences, the Vatican, and "representatives from the Geneva Conventions."[37] Arkin recognized the importance of experts able to communicate intelligibly to the public on these issues: "The stakeholders of the technology we're creating are not only roboticists. We need to be able to inform, educate, and receive buy-ins from these other communities as well."[38]

Over the course of the next few years, Arkin began to ponder the ethical questions of robots designed to kill. Yet Arkin's approach to the issue of autonomous lethal robotics differed significantly from Sharkey's. The key problem as he saw it was that "human beings cannot comply effectively with the laws of war ... so how can technology help? ... Autonomous weapons systems can potentially outperform humans under limited conditions."[39] Arkin describes a tipping point in his thinking on the matter when he viewed a video entitled *Apache Rules the Night* at a Department of Defense workshop in mid-2005, detailing the unlawful execution of a noncombatant at a roadblock by U.S. soldiers. According to Arkin, this experience "moved me into an activist stance and spurred me to think of potential research solutions to violations of the laws of war."[40]

These ideas were published in a 2009 book, *Governing Lethal Behavior in Autonomous Robots*, in which Arkin began with evidence of "human failings on the battlefield," then argued in favor of autonomous weapons as a potential solution *if* such weapons could be designed to comply with the laws of war.[41] In talks at myriad institutions between 2007 and 2012 Arkin emphasized that while the latter was only a hypothesis, he was convinced on the basis of his experimental lab research that it could be done: "It is not my belief that an autonomous unmanned system will be able to perform perfectly in the battlefield, but I am convinced that they can perform more ethically than human soldiers are capable of performing.... There is clear room for improvement, and autonomous systems may help."[42]

Ronald Arkin first met Noel Sharkey in February 2008 on a panel discussion at the Royal United Services Institute, a British security studies think tank. The combination of their disparate views and lively personalities quickly attracted press attention and they were soon dubbed the

"Siskel and Ebert" of the killer robots issue.[43] Both Arkin and Sharkey exhibited deep respect for one another as intellectuals publicly and in private interviews with this author, though they differ prescriptively and tactically on the question of autonomous weapons.

When Sharkey invited Arkin to Berlin he was pleased to attend, but it was no surprise to Sharkey that Arkin stopped short of signing on to ICRAC's statement of purpose due to its clear insistence on a ban against AWS. By contrast, Arkin continued to argue at Berlin that AWS held some promise as a humanitarian tool. Although he supported the development of a global ethical discussion and "might have considered a temporary moratorium," he did not agree with ruling out the use of AWS altogether without strong evidence. "We absolutely need to be discussing this issue.... If the international community decides on a ban, I'd have no problem with that. But I think we can do better than an outright ban."[44] From Sharkey's perspective, while Arkin's system might work well in the lab, it would have limited ability to discriminate between civilians and combatants in field situations.[45] Subsequent to the Berlin meeting, Sharkey and Arkin often took these opposing perspectives in public and scholarly forums on the issue, attending the ICRC circuit together, speaking to the same journalists, and publishing in the same special issues of scholarly journals.[46]

Not only did Arkin and Sharkey differ prescriptively, they were networking differently during the period following Berlin. Arkin did not join ICRAC, but he did develop strong social and professional ties to a network of military ethicists and engineers connected through the Consortium on Emerging Technologies, Military Operations and National Security. CETMONS was established in 2009 as a network of six ethics centers from different American universities, including (after they invited him as their inaugural keynote speaker) Arkin's institution, Georgia Tech.

According to its website, CETMONS is a "multi-institutional organization dedicated to providing the basis for the ethical, rational, and responsible understanding and management of the complex set of issues raised by emerging technologies and their use in military operations, as well as their broader implications for national security." Autonomous weapons are one of several "thrust areas" of CETMONS, whose work also includes attention to cyberconflict, nonlethal weaponry, and bioaugmentation of warfighters. The smaller Autonomous Weapons Thrust Group (AWTG) works collaboratively to promote interdisciplinary discussions and collaborative work on ethics and military robotics among members, as well as outreach to the public, through "publications, research grants, workshops, conferences and other mechanisms."[47]

As a network, AWTG-CETMONS is structurally different from ICRAC in important respects. First, it is composed of American institutions and contains few transnational linkages.[48] Second, while a civilian network, its members have strong ties to the U.S. defense establishment: 20 percent of its members formerly served in the military; another 20 percent of members receive funding from the defense establishment.[49] Third, as a network of institutions AWTG-CETMONS members enjoy backing and funding from the donors of their respective ethics centers, and are therefore constrained by the institutional norms in which they are embedded, whereas ICRAC during this period was a network of individuals only, with no funding, organizational structure, or constraints.[50] Fourth, although the AWTG-CETMONS mission statement included "outreach, public service and participation in policy development in order to support creation of a secure, ethical, and rational future," they perceived and presented themselves as a community of experts rather than advocates, in contrast to ICRAC's open position in favor of a specific prohibitionary norm.[51]

At the same time, in calling for ethical attention to autonomous systems, AWTG may be thought of as an *issue* entrepreneur, if not a norm entrepreneur. Certainly members think of themselves as "thought leaders." One example of an issue advocacy effort put forward by AWTG is a jointly coauthored law paper on governance for autonomous systems published in May 2011 in the *Columbia Science and Technology Law Review*.[52] This article acknowledged the "broad agreement that now is the time" to discuss the ethical and legal issues of such systems and aimed to "start that legal and ethical dialogue."[53] However, unlike the Berlin Statement, this article did not call for a bright-line ban on autonomous systems, and in fact expressed skepticism about treaty bans as a means to govern emerging technologies, specifically contrasting its views to those of ICRAC.[54] Instead, the authors suggested that "soft law," industry codes of conduct or other nonbinding instruments, and transgovernmental dialogues might be sufficient.[55] Nonetheless, the purpose of the paper was clearly to encourage policy engagement with the ethical questions of autonomous lethal systems.[56]

Even though these two networks possess different network ties, adopt different outreach strategies, and are somewhat at odds prescriptively (both in their substantive claims and the extent to which they take open positions), they do enjoy considerable synergy and interaction. Both groups aim to spark a wider discussion about the ethics of autonomous weaponry in advance of their widespread deployment and use in contemporary battle spaces. And while these are correctly understood as distinct epistemic networks, individuals in each enjoy social ties with both. Events or collaborative efforts have brought members of both communities together, including Patrick Lin's edited volume *Robot Ethics* and the CETMONS-sponsored special issue of the *Journal of Military Ethics*, each of which featured contributions by individuals spanning these communities. And importantly, both were simultaneously courting advocacy elites to legitimate and disseminate the notion that the ethical dimension of advances in autonomous weaponry should be front and center on the international agenda.

From Agenda Vetting to Issue Adoption by Network Hubs

From the start, both CETMONS and ICRAC's founders recognized that to really promote ethical standards they needed the assistance and legitimation of professional advocacy organizations. Indeed, most were extremely humble about their own abilities as advocates, preferring instead to incite a discussion that would be promoted by others. In 2011 Robert Sparrow told me, "ICRAC suffers from being an organization comprised of academics.... Academic research and political activism aren't the same thing. People have full-time research or teaching commitments, and at the moment we don't have the activist base to really motivate arms control around these particular weapons." Similarly, Ron Arkin never pictured himself as an advocate, often describing himself as "just a roboticist" who recognized that if norm development would take place in this area it would be organizations with credentials and connections in the area of war law that would need to carry the banner. According to Sharkey:

> I'm not trying to be an advocate. I would like other people to take it up who are better able to. All I am is an academic with some access to the media and some technical expertise, but I don't see myself talking to the UN or

something. I'm talking to Landmine Action, and I'd be happy to take a backseat and leave it with them. They know what they're doing. They understand access to political things that I don't. I'll help them write the reports and things, but I'm quite happy for them to do the negotiations.

The most important human security institutions involved in the development of weapons norms are specialized departments within human rights and humanitarian law organizations such as the Arms Unit of the International Committee of the Red Cross and the Arms Division of Human Rights Watch. The ICRC is one of the oldest international nongovernmental organizations—founded independently by a network of Swiss elites in the 1860s—though as guardian of the Geneva Conventions it also has a formalized role with states that gives it a status similar to that of an international organization.[57] Human Rights Watch is by contrast a relative newcomer to the NGO scene, better known for its work in human rights: protecting individuals from their own governments.[58] Since the early 1990s, however, it has branded itself as a heavyweight in humanitarian law and weapons issues as well through its Washington-based Arms Division, which has been formally involved in high-profile humanitarian disarmament campaigns around landmines, cluster munitions, blinding lasers, and, more recently, incendiary weapons.[59] HRW also has close ties to the ICRC, cultivated during the blinding laser campaign and maintained through subsequent social interactions and personnel transfers.

Together, these two organizations have the highest centrality score for all "humanitarian disarmament" organizations in the human security network.[60] Both have been prominent actors in every successful arms control campaign that has occurred since 1991. Both have also been notably absent from those campaigns that have emerged but failed to gain political salience, such as depleted uranium, psychotropic weapons, fuel-air explosives, and napalm.[61] Indeed, if there is one thing that distinguishes weapons that have been banned from those that have not in the postwar era it is the endorsement of one or both of these humanitarian heavyweights.[62]

Agenda Vetting by Network Hubs, 2007–2011

When I first spoke with him in 2008, Sharkey reported considerable success in disseminating his ideas to militaries, epistemic communities, and the public.[63] But during the same period, he had trouble getting his ideas to resonate with human security organizations, and autonomous weapons remained absent from the formal agendas of important organizations entirely until late 2011.[64] Mark Steinbeck of the ICRC Arms Unit and Joanne Mariner from HRW's Terrorism and Counterterrorism Program did attend the initial ICRAC conference, "to show up, listen, see what's going on." But while Sharkey had aimed for the meeting to culminate in a declaration of purpose with the ICRC and HRW as signatories to a new campaign, neither Steinbeck nor Mariner was in a position to take such a formal stand on behalf of their organizations.[65] Neither was either convinced at an individual level that an immediate ban was necessary. For example, Mariner wrote an online post for FindLaw describing her impression of the arguments at Berlin:

> The workshop is timely: there is a perceptible trend toward combat robots that are "fully autonomous."... A recent USAF strategy paper lauded the trend.... Noel Sharkey warns, "We are sleepwalking into a brave new world...." I don't think I quite see the situation either way.[66]

Network hub reticence throughout this period had a powerful contagion effect as well: other, more sympathetic organizations within the human security network were hesitant to formally pursue the issue given this perception of disinterest by central hubs such as the ICRC. Richard Moyes, then the policy director of Landmine Action, a "middle power" NGO in the network around technologies of violence, developed an interest in robotic weapons after connecting with Sharkey and reading military reports in 2008. Subsequently, he publicly expressed an interest in pursuing autonomous weapons at the close of the cluster munitions campaign.[67] Yet this agenda was not pursued openly by his organization—in particular because he sensed that to colleagues at the ICRC and HRW, the issue still seemed "like science fiction." By 2009 Landmine Action had gone in a different direction under new leadership, and Moyes explained in a follow-up interview: "I have expressed a personal interest in this issue, but it's not my expectation that the wider landmine advocacy community is interested.... So many of them have never heard of it."

Actually, some key insiders at ICRC and Human Rights Watch were in fact aware of the autonomous weapons issue. Indeed, the ICRC Arms Division had raised the question of sensor-fused weapons (bomblets that make targeting decisions independently after deployment) at the Wellington

Conference on Cluster Munitions in February 2008—a set of remarks that influenced Moyes's original interest in the issue and prompted him to reach out to Noel Sharkey. Nonetheless, this percolating interest did not develop into a policy priority within the Arms Division, as Moyes discovered when he put out feelers to various hubs about a potential "anti-killer-robot" campaign in 2008. The same year, ICRC officials told Peter Singer, who was then conducting interviews for his book *Wired for War*: "We have no particular viewpoint or analysis to provide."[68] In 2009, I was told by an ICRC official: "We have questions, but we aren't really conducting any focused work on this." This lukewarm approach had a dampening effect on the issue within the humanitarian disarmament community until 2011.

Given their percolating interest, why did arms control elites formally shy away from the issue of autonomous weapons during this period? Focus group research suggests that this reticence among advocacy elites was particularly puzzling. Of all the candidate issues we tested on human security professionals in 2009, fully autonomous weapons was the one that fewest human security practitioners objected to on its merits. Respondents easily drew the connection between fully autonomous systems and landmines, and raised questions over the ability of such systems to discriminate.[69] Moreover, many of them saw a campaign around AWS as not only desirable but *feasible*, in ways that other meritorious issues might not be: participants acknowledged "killer robots" as a "fundamentally terrifying issue" that "plays easily to people's fears," and that could unite various groups under a "big tent," suggesting that "this one's got legs."

> I think it's absolutely an issue, because it throws open the whole idea of the laws of war and how they would apply and what it would mean for them. If we don't have human beings that make these decisions but machines, then obviously you have a big question on your hands. I have to admit I've never heard of this.... Why *hasn't* it attracted more attention?[70]

One thing that focus group participants agreed on was that the issue wouldn't become an issue until key organizations known for humanitarian disarmament spoke out:

> This would have to come from the NGO community ... some big NGO that is against it or in support of an arms control regime for it. A group like that would have to be pushing this agenda.

When asked why no such advocacy had occurred to date, focus group respondents suggested one feature of the issue that might mitigate against advocacy was the absence of documentable humanitarian costs from autonomous weapons. Whereas landmines and cluster munitions had been harming civilians in large numbers prior to campaigns against them, autonomous weapons would need to be banned preemptively. Focus group participants put it this way:

> My reaction is it's a very interesting set of issues, but it's not ripe: it's almost ahead of its time. You would really need to see these weapons in use, and the actual collateral damage, in order for this issue to begin to get leverage and momentum.

> You can't create a norm around something that you don't fully understand. People will say it's science fiction: we don't need a norm for science fiction.

Although some autonomous systems were already in use at this time, I corroborated the "science fiction" perception with practitioners embedded in the arms units of both Human Rights Watch and the ICRC.[71] For example, one HRW staffer told me: "I don't think there's much of a taste for being too forward leaning on science fiction, if I may be blunt. The emphasis is definitely on existing state practice, not on laboratory weapons that are unproven....It's a little too speculative. Just stuff on the Internet is not a sufficient basis for us to pick something up and go with."[72] As late as 2009 I was told by an ICRC staff person in the Legal Division that "as far as I know right now, this is still science fiction."[73] In short, while autonomous weapons might be similar to landmines in legal terms, they were very different politically, particularly given the absence of statistically documentable humanitarian costs and stories of noncombatant victims with which to create public attention.[74] Aside from the "giggle factor" (a term used by interviewees to describe the tendency to dismiss the threat of killer robots as science fiction) mentioned in some interviews the issue attribute of "measurability" might be hard to demonstrate.[75] Previous weapons-ban campaigns had relied on statistical evidence of widespread harms and photographs of victims and survivors to document the problem. One respondent said cynically: "You will see a campaign for a killer robot ban when a humanitarian worker is shot dead by a robot."

But the "ripeness" and "measurability" factors cannot solely explain the lack of attention to autonomous weapons because other emerging military technologies have been banned preemptively, before being widely deployed or understood and before causing significant humanitarian harms. The very first multilateral antiweapon ban, against exploding bullets in the late nineteenth century, took place before the weapons were widely deployed.[76] Similarly, the deployment and use of blinding lasers[77] was banned on the basis of "superfluous injury" prior to widespread adoption of the technology.[78] This occurred after an NGO campaign outlawing the weapons *before* their use became widespread during a period where "laser weapons" still sounded like science fiction.[79] As with other successful campaigns in the weapons area, the blinding laser campaign took off not because there was evidence of harms but because the ICRC and HRW threw their weight behind the ban.[80]

Why were advocacy elites more reticent on autonomous systems? Moreover, why did their stance on robotic weapons shift in 2012, while these attributes of the issue in terms of measurability and ripeness remained objectively constant? In truth, many considered autonomous weapons an important issue, just as did focus group respondents. But as with the Making Amends Campaign, an important determinant of elite preferences regarding formal adoption was less about the intrinsic attributes of the issue and more about network effects: perceptions of the issue and the various entrepreneurs in relation to existing advocacy agendas and their extant sociopolitical networks. These perceptions shifted between 2009 and 2012, overriding concerns about measurability and reconstituting perceptions of "ripeness."

As with the making amends idea, one feature of this issue itself was its *intersectionality:* arguments against autonomous weapons could be and initially were connected to a range of other advocacy domains: peace, human rights, counterterrorism, humanitarian law. Moreover, ICRAC's concerns ranged from fully autonomous weapons to remotely piloted systems—such as drones that kept a "man in the loop" but raised concerns about conflict prevention and extrajudicial killings—to nuclear arms control, conflict prevention, and limitations on space weapons.[81]

In short, ICRAC faced a "frame soup" as did CIVIC in its early days—only in reverse. Whereas the MAC had forum-shopped its issue narrowly to a variety of places in search of the right frame, resisting efforts to co-opt its core message into ideationally acceptable domains, ICRAC cast the problem as widely as possible in hopes of appealing to many communities.

However, this approach made it hard for even sympathetic campaigners to latch onto the piece of the issue that "fit" their agenda without implicitly endorsing the parts that didn't—or being associated with advocates promoting goals inimical to their own work.[82] As late as mid-2011, a campaigner told me, "There really does seem to be a growing momentum and concern, but NGOs and donors are still at the stage of not being able to pin it down to anything.... ICRAC is not yet at the stage of being able to articulate what the main debate is."[83]

For the ICRC particularly, this "all-over-the-map-ness" made certain key players hesitant at first to formally liaise with the AWS issue as articulated by ICRAC. The ICRC prefers to be seen as initiating campaigns where they are formally involved, to avoid being seen as bandwagoning, and to exercise some control over the frame.[84] Moreover, their mandate limits their work to issues that clearly engage humanitarian law, and their credibility with governments on military issues is contingent in part on avoiding connections to peace activism, a rule of thumb expressed to me by more than one practitioner as the "no tree huggers" rule. Part of how they cultivate and maintain this image is by careful selectivity regarding social ties to other activists: while the ICRC specializes in staying abreast discreetly of what is going on in many sectors of civil society, "we are very careful who we formally are seen as associating with."[85]

Practitioners at Human Rights Watch expressed similar reservations in this early period: despite what was already in 2009 an ongoing interest in the issue of autonomous weapons, I was told there were "no serious internal discussions on this issue." Some concerns had to do with the conflation of anti-AWS sentiment with a broader pacifist critique of U.S. imperialism. But the wider question of whether HRW would be "needed" on a campaign that was already attracting a coalition came up as well:

> It's a question of *how big is the crowd* already doing this work. How is it being looked at? What can our organization itself contribute in terms of the whole operation? How is that going to make a unique contribution and not just be seen as another one in the crowd?[86]

This posture of formal aloofness from the AWS issue certainly did not mean practitioners in these organizations were apathetic. Insiders at both ICRC and HRW followed developments and engaged with entrepreneur networks around autonomous weapons in the years between 2009 and late 2012, when Human Rights Watch finally adopted the issue. But for both organizations decisions about whether, how, and when to formally adopt the issue or call for a new norm were constituted in part by perceived network effects—including perceptions of the relative social networks of the different entrepreneurs, perceptions of how the AWS issue was tied to other existing and emergent issues, and perceptions about how other great and middle-power organizations in humanitarian disarmament were going to position themselves.

Network Effects and Issue Engagement by Network Hubs, 2010–2012

Despite concerns over relational factors, there was in fact considerable percolating interest in the issue of autonomous weapons on its intrinsic merits. Faced with dueling norm entrepreneurs, arms experts within the ICRC engaged openly with both.[87] But between 2009 and 2011 they gravitated toward the entrepreneur with the sociopolitical network most closely aligned with ICRC's organizational culture. Although Noel Sharkey did not see Mark Steinbeck again after the Berlin meeting, and spoke at an ICRC event again only two years later, Arkin and other members of the CETMONS network enjoyed increasingly dense social ties to the ICRC during the same period. After connecting informally with Steinbeck at the Royal United Services Institute and then at the Berlin conference, Arkin was invited to present his arguments in 2010 at the Bruegge Conference on Emerging Technology. There ICRC vice president Christine Beerli heard him speak and he was subsequently invited to brief both the ICRC Assembly and staffers in Geneva. In 2011 he made a presentation to ICRC lawyers at San Remo, Italy, as well as meeting personally with ICRC president Jakob Kellenberger. When he invited Steinbeck to join him for a CETMONS meeting on emerging technologies at Chautauqua, New York, Steinbeck accepted and brought with him a colleague from the ICRC's Armed Forces delegation in Washington.

    In part this synergy between Arkin and ICRC officials came from a sense of "fit" between their understandings of the issue. The ICRC is a heavily conservative organization whose cachet with states comes from its strict neutrality and commitment to working within the framework of international humanitarian law. This means taking care not to criticize war per se or take sides in particular conflicts, limiting itself to promoting constraints on war. They are especially careful to avoid issues where they might be seen as criticizing *particular* states as opposed to the international community as a whole; and they are careful to cultivate good relations with national militaries so as to retain influence. Arkin's strict and single-minded focus on the laws of war and civilian protection were much more consistent with ICRC's central message than ICRAC's wider antimilitarist frame.[88] Moreover, Arkin's social network affected ICRC's perceptions of his credibility as a messenger on the subject. His techno-optimistic views and connections to the defense industry provided a useful match to ICRC organizational culture, and ensured he could communicate easily and professionally with generals and military lawyers whose thinking the ICRC sought to influence. And his *lack* of social ties to what ICRC officials believe states would see as the left-wing fringes of global civil society gave him an extra modicum of professional credibility.

But the ICRC engaged with Sharkey too over this period, if less frequently. Access for and receptiveness to one entrepreneur or another in a given context was somewhat idiosyncratic and depended on how each entrepreneur was networked socially with specific individuals within the organization. Ron Arkin developed a particular rapport with Mark Steinbeck, who had attended the Berlin meeting and had joined him in refusing to sign the document given what they both perceived as its prematurity. Even after leaving the Arms Unit, Steinbeck served as an important point of contact for Arkin in his interactions with other in-house entities. But Lou Maresca, still embedded in the Arms Unit, spent an evening in early 2012 in Sarajevo drinking with Noel Sharkey, who had been invited to speak at a regional meeting on weapons issues. Subsequently, when asked by the Norwegian Red Cross later in 2012 to suggest interesting speakers on emerging weapons issues for a side event at the upcoming Cluster Munitions Convention, Maresca suggested Sharkey rather than Arkin, providing an important opportunity to network with the wider cluster munitions NGO community. Peter Herby, the head of the Arms Unit, connected at different moments with both Arkin and Sharkey, and continued to take an agnostic, balanced stance on the subject up through 2012. Like other insiders, Herby knew the ICRC was not yet in a position to weigh in definitively on the question of a ban. However, as a skilled diplomat and bridge-builder, Herby focused less on the differences in Sharkey's and Arkin's approaches and more on how their agendas converged around the seriousness of the issue and the primacy of international discussion on how best to protect civilians given these trends.

This measured stance by Herby both reflected and helped constitute the position of the organization on AWS as it evolved through this period. In periodic and sometimes simultaneous interaction with both Sharkey and Arkin, ICRC insiders gradually accepted that AWS was an issue they should keep an eye on, yet the organization carefully refused to endorse either a preemptive ban or a fully techno-optimistic approach: theirs was a middle ground between these two positions that acknowledged the potential humanitarian value of AWS while highlighting potential risks. At the conclusion of the 2011 San Remo Roundtable on emerging technologies co-organized by the ICRC, at which both Sharkey and Arkin spoke, ICRC president Kellenberger issued a public statement mentioning AWS for the first time.[89] He began by noting the difference between teleoperated, automated, and autonomous systems, and regarding fully autonomous systems he stated:

> The deployment of [fully autonomous] systems would reflect a paradigm shift and a major qualitative change in the conduct of hostilities. It would also raise a range of fundamental legal, ethical and societal issues which need to be considered before such systems are developed or deployed. A robot could be programmed to behave more ethically and far more cautiously on the battlefield than a human being. But what if it is technically impossible to reliably program an autonomous weapon system so as to ensure that it functions in accordance with IHL under battlefield conditions?

Though this statement fell far short of adopting ICRAC's call for a ban, the implicit acknowledgement of the issue by ICRC sent ripples through the human security network. And it gave a boost to a far more robust set of understandings closer to the position of ICRAC, percolating quietly behind the scenes within the Arms Division of another powerful arms control hub, Human Rights Watch.

Early on, Human Rights Watch officials were in much the same boat as the ICRC with respect to this issue: they were concerned about "having a man in the loop" after following these developments. But they worried about being "too far ahead of the crowd," and thought ICRAC's call for an outright ban could be premature. For HRW, the key concern with autonomous weapons was not so much that the issue came with the "wrong" social network—HRW has a long history of diverse civil society coalitions—but that the issue was being linked to other issues that they didn't want to be on the record as opposing.[90] Whereas ICRAC's frame included concern over drones, nuclear weapons, and conflict prevention, Human Rights Watch took a very specific, legalistic perspective. And they did not share a gut-level concern over the rapid pace of technological advances per se:

> [Drones] to us are not problematic...in fact they're very positive. Long loiter time allows you to then determine whether or not your target is military in nature or a civilian object. If you're going to shoot at somebody, we'd rather you use something like that than blindly lobbing a bomb at somebody.

> The question we would ask is: Is there something inherently problematic about this weapon based on the way it's supposed to function and the way it's actually functioned in conflicts? Generally we are protechnology. We think advances in technology in the past ten to twenty years are generally very positive.

In some respects, this position dovetailed more with Arkin's view than with Sharkey's. Nonetheless, by 2011, at the time of Kellenberger's San Remo statement, currents were under way within Human Rights Watch to launch a formal campaign against autonomous weapons systems that went far beyond the ICRC's simple call to "remain seized" of the matter.[91] And in late 2012 these currents coalesced into formal adoption of the AWS-ban idea at the NGO Summit on Humanitarian Diplomacy in New York. This event culminated in the first press releases by Human Rights Watch to acknowledge the need for a campaign against fully autonomous weapons and the formation of a steering committee.[92] HRW staff and consultants began tweeting about the issue, and a report on the subject was released in November of that year.[93] On April 22, 2013, the Campaign to Stop Killer Robots was formally launched in London and hailed as a successor to the landmines and cluster munitions campaigns. By the end of that year, NGO campaigners had succeeded in convincing governments to take up the issue under the auspices of the Convention on Conventional Weapons process.

What factors shifted in HRW's thinking from 2009 to 2012? And why did the organization decide to throw its weight behind a ban on fully autonomous weapons while the ICRC stalled on the issue? A few weeks before the campaign steering committee was formed, I attended the Third Meeting of States Parties for the Cluster Munitions Convention conference in Oslo and asked humanitarian disarmament veterans gathered there what had generated the buzz on killer robots that seemed to be percolating by that time. Many of them mentioned that starting around mid-2011 the issue had just seemed "ripe," and they cited the growing media attention to drones and autonomous weapons and the wider sense that there was a momentum on the issue. However, a closer look reveals changes in the network structure of the issues and organizations during this period that contributed to this sense of ripeness. Human Rights Watch—and a specific individual within the Arms Unit—was uniquely receptive to these factors due to a particular structural position and social ties within the human security network.

Shifting ideational networks reconstituting issue and entrepreneur attributes.   Issues are understood and legitimated not merely on their own merits but on their perceived relationships to sociopolitically adjacent issues. As noted above, in 2008 one of the key impediments to addressing the issues of autonomous weapons was their close relationship to a related but distinct (and less problematic) issue: the presence of unmanned aerial vehicles, or drones, in armed conflict zones. ICRAC had intentionally collapsed both concerns into a single call for action.[94] Outside the arms circles within both HRW and ICRC, practitioners tended to conflate these two issues during that period, arguing that AWS was not a problem because drones were not a problem. Within arms control circles, practitioners understood the distinction and did worry about AWS, but were hesitant to go on record as opposing AWS because they did not want, by extension, to be seen as criticizing drones per se. However, as the nature of the political networks and political discourses around the drone issue shifted, so did the political implications of addressing AWS as a distinct problem. This shift occurred in three ways between 2009 and 2011.

First, mass concern for drones shifted what one informant called the "giggle factor" on autonomous weapons due to the public's perception that drones were synonymous with "killer robots" and that such killer robots were therefore already a reality.[95] Although significant changes did not occur during this period in the deployment of fully autonomous weapons, what had previously seemed like a "science fiction" issue "ahead of its time" had begun to acquire an element of ripeness and urgency through erroneous ideational association with teleoperated systems. By summer 2012, practitioners I spoke to about what tipped the scales toward attention to AWS repeatedly invoked the sense that somehow "people just started to get it." The ICRC's acknowledgment of the issue in September 2011 helped.[96] And media attention to drones had risen significantly between 2008 and 2012, with media and practitioner attention to fully autonomous weapons rising correspondingly.

Second, the ideational adjacency to the drone debate thus became more of a benefit than a liability by producing two previously missing issue attributes: humanitarian cost and ripeness. Although there were no examples of fully autonomous weapons killing people, evidence of civilian harm from drones mounted yearly, attracting a cottage industry of specialists aiming to document humanitarian harms.[97] As for "ripeness," public awareness of drones (combined with the sense that these were "killer robots from the sky") transformed the concept of autonomous weapons from a "Terminator-like fantasy scenario" to an only half-incorrect public perception that "these weapons are here now."[98] HRW Arms Division director Steve Goose later described how his organization was able to draw on this perception to create a sense of urgency to compensate for the absence of documented humanitarian harms: "In addition to drones becoming a very hot topic issue there is the growing evidence that increasing autonomy is the future of warfare…and that the more entrenched this becomes the less likelihood there will be of success with governments. So that's what we're relying on to create this sense of urgency, which every successful campaign needs."[99]

Third, and importantly, the drone debate itself shifted in this period from being centered on antimilitarist arguments associated with the

Code Pink crowd to being more fully rooted in a mainstream human rights/international humanitarian law framework. In May 2010, Philip Alston, the UN special rapporteur on extrajudicial executions, took on the drone debate from a human rights/IHL/UN Charter perspective, examining questions about the appropriate use of armed force.[100] Regarding drones per se, the report underlined that the use of any weapons should include appropriate intelligence-gathering and legal safeguards. In particular, whereas earlier questions had been raised about whether the use of drones would make war itself easier or more frequent (*jus ad bellum* concerns), the Alston report emphasized whether their use would make targeting decisions in war more permissive (*jus in bello* concerns). Rhetorically, Alston situated the issue of drones more firmly in the realm of humanitarian law and distanced it from the wider pacifist critique, rendering it more palatable to the human rights/humanitarian law mainstream. In the following year, numerous scholarly articles, white papers, and commentators began addressing these concerns much more squarely; by June 2012, Navi Pillay, the UN high commissioner for human rights, was echoing the same rhetoric.[101] By fall 2012, foreign policy elites were calling for an international treaty governing the use of drones.[102] Alston's successor, Christof Heyns, began work on a new report explicitly drawing the connection between drones and AWS as part of a continuum of lethal military robotics that might threaten international law and human life.

For Human Rights Watch, these developments helped create an opportunity to "add value" conceptually by clearly distinguishing the legal concerns in the drone debate from the question of fully autonomous weapons. Insiders saw these as distinct concerns from a legal perspective, a point being lost in the wider media debate (see figure 5). With respect to drones, a man was in the loop, so the key question from HRW's perspective was whether the weapons were being used lawfully—in several other reports or press releases they echoed the UN's discourse on targeted killings and military accountability.[103] Drones were also implicated during this period in an emerging discourse about the use of explosive weapons in populated areas—a campaign in which HRW played an early role as a steering committee member. At the same time, the assumption was that drones *could* be used lawfully if they were subject to appropriate governance mechanisms, and used solely in unpopulated areas. However,

"While violent extremists may be unpopular, for a frightened population they seem less ominous than a faceless enemy that wages war from afar and often kills more civilians than militants."[1]

"The intense discussions about water-boarding are distracting us, perhaps intentionally so, from the much more serious moral transgression of the continuing robotic killing of innocents."[2]

"These are targeted international killings, no less real, and indeed more insidious, for their video-game aspect... The very phrase 'go to war' becomes hard to distinguish from going to work. That's a conflation fraught with ethical danger. The barriers to war get lowered."[3]

"The use of the drones therefore is violating the war-fighting principles of distinction, necessity, proportionality, humnity."[4]

Figure 5. Qualitative analysis of the drone debate. (1) David Kilcullen and Andrew Exum, "Death from Above," *New York Times*, May 16, 2009; (2) Gary Kopf, "When Drones Kill Civilians," *New York Times*, May 24, 2009; (3) Roger Cohen, "OfFruit Flies and Drones," *International Herald Tribune*, November 12, 2009; (4) Cesar Chelala, "Drone Dependency Trivializing Afghan War," *Japan Times*, March 30, 2010. Tag cloud represents frequently used words among a dataset of twenty-nine hits from DailyOpEd.com using the search terms "drone warfare." Search was conducted in February 2011; only op-eds on drones specifically were retained and coded for several analytical themes. Graphic created by Charli Carpenter, Dan Glaun and Lisa Shaikhouni. Tag cloud results rendered by DiscoverText and visualized with Wordle.

autonomous weapons would have no human in the loop, so HRW's focus here was on whether this would mean the weapons were *inherently* indiscriminate:

> The drone issue is quite newsworthy, but we see that as a weapon that is just being remotely piloted. There's still a human involved; it's not truly autonomous. So, being able to break that off kind of liberates you from a lot of the controversy around targeted killing, or CIA use of drones. It lets you focus on: What's a truly autonomous weapon and what are the principles we should be looking at there? What we're essentially trying to address is, is there a principle in IHL dictating that a human should be in the loop on making the decision whether to engage a target or not. Some within our organization will say that's an instant distinction violation: that if an autonomous weapon can't distinguish between a combatant and a noncombatant, it's inherently indiscriminate. I don't think we have the answer on that yet. But the thinking has been made easier by the fact that we're taking the consideration of drones out of it.[104]

Ironically, it was perhaps the argument articulated first and most forcefully by Arkin that most clearly honed in on the central question from a humanitarian law perspective: whether these weapons could be trusted to discriminate between civilians and combatants as well or better than human beings.[105] Whereas Arkin believed the burden of proof was on advocates to prove the contrary, HRW and the landmine community had a long history of "reversing the burden of proof," of requiring governments to demonstrate in advance of deploying weapons that their use would not violate humanitarian standards.[106] This strategic thinking, coupled with the need to delink the question of AWS from the drone debate, set the stage for the development of a precautionary principle on fully autonomous weapons.[107]

Organizational ties reconstituting ideational networks. What else was driving these shifts in the ideational landscape? A second important change in 2011 was the establishment of a new NGO, Article36, whose focus is the humanitarian control of weapons technology. This small organization quickly came to occupy a brokerage position among disparate weapons campaigns, and became the first NGO adopter of a ban against autonomous weapons in April 2012. Launched in 2011 by experienced humanitarian advocates Richard Moyes and Thomas Nash, the organization took its name from the provision in the 1977 Additional Protocol to the Geneva Conventions that requires governments to consider the legality of new weapons and methods of warfare.[108]

Richard Moyes, former policy director of Landmine Action, and Thomas Nash, former Cluster Munitions Coalition coordinator, built on the social connections and skill sets cultivated on the landmines and cluster munitions campaigns and very quickly begin pushing a developing agenda on explosive weapons through civil society networks.[109] However, rather than conceiving itself primarily as the coordinator of the explosive weapons campaign, the organization instead sought to occupy a broader, vacant structural gap in the human security network by constructing itself as a multi-issue NGO operating at the nexus between weapons and humanitarian affairs (see plate 6).

First, from a network theory perspective, this structural location was extremely advantageous politically, imbuing Article36 with a level of influence due to its "betweenness centrality" that could not be explained by reference to either the organization's longevity, resources, or name recognition. Previously, humanitarian disarmament networks had tended to form around specific weapons in isolation: the International Network Against Small Arms, the International Campaign to Ban Landmines, and the International Coalition to Ban Uranium Weapons are examples. As demonstrated by plate 6, these campaigns have tended to be disconnected from one another. They also vary greatly in their connectedness to wider civil society networks.[110] By establishing itself as an organization focused specifically on humanitarian disarmament as a broad, multiweapon issue area, Article36 constituted itself as a new kind of actor within the network.[111]

Second, Moyes and Nash worked to yoke together smaller weapons networks conceptually and socially to strengthen the cohesion of "humanitarian disarmament" as a subcluster within the human security network. Conceptually, they did this by establishing connections, formal and informal, to multiple substantive weapons issues, such as nonlethals, incendiaries, and uranium weapons, and through cross-cutting work on procedural issues not limited to specific weapons, such as casualty recording and regulating the arms trade.[112] Socially, they worked to cultivate connections between colleagues in disconnected issue networks, to help socialize marginalized actors into successful civil society networks, generate ideational synergies, and encourage the wider marketing of new ideas to colleagues in hub organizations.[113] Formally, they joined multiple existing coalitions; informally, they maintained ties with many others. Thus Article36 actively cultivated a position of betweenness in humanitarian disarmament, connecting distinct subnetworks in the arms area.[114] By 2012, on the basis of formal coalition memberships alone, Article36 had the second highest betweenness centrality of any organization in the humanitarian disarmament area (see plate 7).[115]

Third, Article36 staff were positioned to link the more isolated subnetworks not only to one another but to the wider human security movement through Moyes's and Nash's interpersonal cachet with major human security hubs such as Human Rights Watch's Arms Division, the International Committee of the Red Cross, the UN Office for the Coordination of Humanitarian Affairs, and the UN Institute for Disarmament Research (UNIDIR). Although their new organization was hardly a human security hub like HRW or ICRC, the staff of Article36 possessed close professional and social ties to arms control specialists in those organizations. As former advocates for landmine and cluster munitions' bans, its staff had procedural and social expertise with the NGO grouping around humanitarian disarmament, the ability to broker connections between ICRAC and humanitarian hubs, and to legitimize ICRAC and its members through association.[116] It was Moyes who had initially "tested the waters" on AWS with the ICRC and Human Rights Watch after reaching out to Sharkey in 2008, and the fact that he and Thomas had joined ICRAC did not escape the attention of HRW insiders. Moyes continued to discuss the issue with both Sharkey and Mary Wareham, a key Human Rights Watch campaigner, who eventually met with Sharkey as the organization began considering how to frame their emerging position on autonomous weapons. This April 2012 meeting established a working relationship between Wareham and Sharkey, who later reviewed HRW's working memorandums on the topic, provided technical advice, and briefed the organization.

Fourth, Moyes and Nash worked to socialize ICRAC members behind the scenes on how to work productively in a coalition.[117] Part of this advice (not all of it followed) was about branding.[118] But some of it centered around how to adjust the internal network structure of ICRAC to enhance the organization's credibility and functionality vis-à-vis the wider human security community. One challenge for the group was that its consensus-based, theoretically driven nature made it impossible to make decisions on the group's behalf.[119] Thomas Nash explained to Sharkey how vital it was that the committee have an internal decision-making structure and become an NGO for campaigning purposes. Indeed, as Wendy Wong's research has demonstrated, the more centralized such an internal structure is, the more effective transnational groups can be.[120] In January 2013, Article36 paid for the incorporation of ICRAC as a registered organization in the United Kingdom.

Finally, by pioneering a "humanitarian disarmament" niche with its own early call for an AWS ban, alongside its work on landmines, cluster munitions, and other more mainstream issues, Article36 connected AWS conceptually to the humanitarian disarmament agenda, making robots—and nuclear weapons, and pain weapons, and even depleted uranium, now reframed as "toxic remnants of war"—seem less like fringe issues associated with the radical Left and more part of the human security mainstream.[121] In fact, the very concept of "humanitarian disarmament" was developed in part to reclaim disarmament issues from the antimilitarist movement: to make disarmament about civilian protection, a cause that militaries and humanitarian organizations could get behind, rather than about ending war altogether.[122]

In all these ways, the emergence of Article36 on the scene and its decision to adopt an autonomous weapons ban helped reconstitute the networks adjacent to ICRAC, thereby reconstituting mainstream perceptions of the AWS issue. Yet the fact that Article36 endorsed the autonomous weapons issue without itself attempting to take the lead on a campaign also left HRW room to "add value" by being the first NGO to publish a report and initiate a coalition. According to HRW Arms Division director Steve Goose:

> Richard and Thomas were paying some attention to it, their organization had become a part of ICRAC, but it seemed they did not have the resources to put toward working on it because they were so focused on explosive weapons.... We observed that there was no NGO doing serious research or advocacy on the issue of fully autonomous weapons, and no NGO ready to push for or lead a new, coordinated campaign. And the more we looked at the issue, the more we became convinced of the need for urgent and extensive research, advocacy, and campaigning.[123]

Interpersonal ties reconstituting organizational interests.   Finally, the autonomous weapons issue got an important push in 2011 based on the interpersonal social networks of key elites within Human Rights Watch. Steve Goose told me about how the issue adoption process in the Arms Unit often depended on the personal interests of staff, and how these could be constituted in part through their interpersonal relationships:

> Personalities and individuals come into play.... We picked up on incendiary weapons partly because Mark Hiznay [senior researcher in HRW's Arms Division] wanted to do it. We've been working on explosive weapons for a few years because UNIDIR was interested in it: John Borrie [senior researcher, UNIDIR], Richard, and Thomas were talking about it, talking about it. So that makes a difference in the way these things happen."

As for killer robots:

> My wife beat me over the head for a couple of years on this. We'd have never gotten to this point without her bugging me.[124]

And Steve Goose is not married to just anyone: his wife is Nobel Peace Prize winner Jody Williams, who ran the International Campaign to Ban Landmines in the 1990s and possesses perhaps the widest social network and greatest name recognition of any individual in the humanitarian disarmament network. As a member of the Nobel Women's Peace Initiative, which she established in 2007, she also occupies a conceptual brokerage position between the more conservative, military law–focused humanitarian disarmament community and the peace and women's sectors of global civil society. Though even she needed the institutional authority of the humanitarian disarmament hub to push the issue forward, her close interpersonal ties to a particular gatekeeper in that network constituted an important advantage.

In 2011, Williams stumbled across Sharkey's writings in the course of some research on the dangers of drones, and immediately recognized that this issue was distinct from drones and more "fundamentally terrifying."[125] Her resulting paper on drone warfare began by referencing the film *Terminator* and ended by discussing the slippery slope from drones to fully autonomous weapons, including an entire section titled "When There's No Man in the Loop!"[126] Though the published paper itself was not widely circulated, Williams's research taught her enough about the issue to begin championing the "killer robot" cause in her personal, social, and professional circles.

Williams was positioned structurally to give credence to the issue in the media and among campaigners in the wider human security network.[127] Perhaps most crucially, she was well positioned socially to influence elites in key humanitarian disarmament hubs. Williams's influence can be seen not only in Human Rights Watch's willingness to push hard on the issue but also in the way the issue was framed in the HRW report *Losing Humanity* and subsequent advocacy documents. Although one might have expected an organization like Human Rights Watch to take a conservative, law-focused, protection-of-civilians framework to speak both to the ICRC and the military establishment, *Losing Humanity* frames the issue as simultaneously a humanitarian, human rights, and peace problem, as simultaneously a problem of law and of ethics. Thus, through her cachet with insiders and far-flung ties to the wider human security community, Williams's personal investment in the "killer robots" idea encouraged issue adoption at HRW, which sparked off a cascade of interest in global civil society. But her concern, as someone with credibility in the issue area forged by earlier network ties, also signaled to advocacy elites a wider sense of the issue's linkability to various domains and "fit" in the humanitarian disarmament network, opening up diverse possibilities for issue creation.

The issue of autonomous weapons was pushed onto the global agenda by academic entrepreneurs who captured the attention of key human security elites in and around organizational hubs. They did this by engaging the media, through published scholarship, and by networking through academic/practitioner communities. The issue was vetted for a time based on ideational and interpersonal associations about how it was anchored in advocacy space, but was later mainstreamed into humanitarian disarmament as perceptions of these associations shifted. Once a highly connected organization took the issue up, it quickly proliferated within the human security network, with numerous organizations joining the campaign and other international documents calling for either a ban or a moratorium on AWS appearing in the weeks and months after HRW's initial report.[128] The case study confirms that the structural position of actors confers access, authority, and legitimacy on the issues they champion.

This case study also provides a few other insights about the emergence of issues within global advocacy networks. First is the significance of academic experts and institutions as generators of ideas within global networks. In weapons advocacy, as in other issue areas, academic networks not only have the potential to spawn epistemic communities, in Haas's formulation, but to play key roles as brokers and players in wider networks of meaning, even where common causal and principled ideas are missing. It was a series of academic panels through British think tanks that brought Ron Arkin into contact with Noel Sharkey and later Mark Steinbeck from the ICRC. It was scholarly articles that initially influenced Jody Williams's orientation to the issue and her sense that fully autonomous weapons were distinct from other military robots in ethically problematic ways. To some extent, having a norm and counternorm entrepreneur, both of whom agreed on the importance of an ethical discussion, helped strengthen the push for attention to the issue, which laid the groundwork for a prohibitionary norm campaign.

Indeed, a second insight from this case is the importance of exploring the division of labor among key organizations—in this case, between the ICRC Arms Unit and HRW Arms Division on weapons issues. Powerful organizations function differently and pay close attention to one another's activities. The ICRC's carefully cultivated aloofness means that simply acknowledging a normative debate (even without taking a position) can be of enormous political import. This then legitimized efforts by HRW to carve out a stronger campaign position over time. This worked both for HRW staff, allowing the organization to gauge the ripeness of issues through the ICRC's tacit support and to be seen as an initiator of campaigns, and for the ICRC, which was happy to pass the buck to its counterparts in the HRW Arms Division in order to protect its reputation for neutrality. In some respects, ICRC's continuous and ideologically neutral engagement with counterentrepreneurs in CETMONS bought HRW the time it needed to formulate a strong but credible position, in alliance with ICRAC and Article36, against the piece of the robotic weapons issue most clearly at odds with humanitarian law. Future analyses of campaigns should focus as much on relationships *between* gatekeepers as on relationships between NGOs and states or between marginalized and elite nodes in advocacy networks.

Finally, the role of the media in agenda setting bears closer study. Several studies posit a direct relationship between media attention and global advocacy.[129] But this case suggests that rather than driving advocacy, the relative media politicization of a particular issue can pose an initial constraint on issue adoption by human security hubs. Media coverage and the "sexiness" of an issue are not always a good thing for global agenda setting: it depends on the nature of the media frame, and its "fit" with a particular node's organizational culture. For example, established organizations' willingness to put their reputations on the line with respect to autonomous weapons was at first constrained by the sensationalization of "killer robots" in the media and popular culture. Similarly, depleted uranium (DU) activists damaged their likelihood of attracting mainstream support when the movement's frames became perceived as diffuse and unprofessional.

However, at some point sufficient media attention, even of the sensationalized sort, creates a tipping point that incentivizes advocacy. This is less bandwagoning on the popularity of an issue as it is stepping in to helpfully reframe a debate. Sometimes, the media can push the advocacy agenda less through information dissemination and more through getting it just wrong enough in enough volume to incite a reaction from mainstream advocacy "experts."[130] The media plays another role in agenda setting, however: it can broker connections between actors in an issue's emergent stage. Noel Sharkey told me that a significant number of his socioprofessional connections around AWS were formed through joint media interviews that led to correspondence with a widening circle of stakeholders.

These structural factors can make all the difference in determining whether and how issues are accepted within issue networks. In the next chapter, I turn to a cause that has been less lucky than the killer robot idea: a ban on routine infant male circumcision. Lacking endorsement by advocacy elites and the access and legitimation that confers, this cause has remained of low salience to the global community; and as with autonomous weapons, human rights gatekeepers often think in network terms when vetting the agenda.

"His Body, His Choice"

Pitching Infant Male Circumcision to Health and Human Rights Gatekeepers

The World Health Organization estimates that 30 percent of infant boys are circumcised annually worldwide, often without anesthetic and primarily for cultural reasons.[1] Previously justified on social or medical grounds, routine circumcision of children is not now recommended by medical practitioners.[2] However, neither have medical associations gone so far as to recommend *prohibiting* the practice, which continues in the United States, Canada, Israel, Australia and New Zealand, much of the Muslim Middle East and Central Asia, and among some immigrant populations in Europe.[3] Circumcision is also on the rise in Africa, where it has become the subject of attention since 2005 by global health and development organizations due to its purported effects in reducing HIV-AIDS.[4]

A growing coalition of advocacy groups argue that nontherapeutic circumcision of nonconsenting minors is a violation of children's bodily integrity rights and an unwarranted infliction of pain on a vulnerable infant even when conducted with analgesic.[5] These critics cast doubt on the veracity of studies linking the practice with medical benefits, pointing out that earlier medical justifications have always been debunked, and citing a wide range of side effects.[6] Hypothetical health benefits aside, they argue, even with anesthesia the practice involves irreversibly altering a person's bodily integrity without his consent.[7] For several decades this "intactivist" movement has argued the practice should be treated as a human rights violation, prohibited by governments, and eradicated as a routine medical practice.

Yet while other bodily integrity rights against children, including other forms of genital cutting, have been recognized as human rights abuses within the UN system for over two decades, issue entrepreneurs have had little success in pitching a ban on infant male circumcision to human rights gatekeepers.[8] In 2009, Debra DeLaet observed: "UN agencies and human rights NGOs have not made statements or taken positions that explicitly condemn male circumcision."[9]

This chapter describes the intactivist movement's origins, claims, and tactics, documents the process by which powerful human rights organizations have exercised "agenda denial," and provides some insight into why intactivist claims have not resonated with organizations at the center of the human rights network. As with the earlier cases, network effects made the difference: even though this particular issue has certain characteristics that make it harder for human rights elites to focus on than some others, a key element of the explanation revolves around dynamics among organizations in the health and human rights networks, and perceptions of ties among human rights issues themselves.

Political Entrepreneurship from the Practitioner/ Claimant Grassroots

As Len Glick documents, anticircumcision sentiment, including from within the Jewish community, had roots at least as far back as the nineteenth century.[10] But the U.S.-based movement against routine infant male circumcision coalesced in the 1980s around the grassroots efforts of mother and registered nurse Marilyn Milos. Milos was a former educator and midwife who began training as an obstetrics nurse in the late '70s. In an interview, she described how her life was changed in 1980 after witnessing a baby boy strapped to what she described as a "rack" and circumcised without anesthetic:

> We were told that we were going to be allowed to watch a circumcision, and I thought, well, this is interesting, because my sons had been circumcised. Of course, it was done behind closed doors and nobody ever saw a circumcision. All the students walked into the room and the baby was strapped to a plastic board with four-point restraints. The baby started struggling against restraints, he was getting more and more frantic. I said to my instructor, 'Can I comfort him?' and she said, "No, wait 'til the doctor gets here." I thought, we're supposed to be *nurses*, this is a healing and helping *profession*—and we're just going to stand here and watch this baby struggling and suffer? When the doctor came in a couple of minutes later, I said, 'Can I go comfort the baby,' and he said 'Sure, go stick your finger in the baby's mouth.' That was interesting to me because he didn't know where my fingers had been. But I put my finger in the baby's mouth and I started to rub his little head and he started to *suck* so hard and I said to him, this is only going to take a minute and it's not going to hurt—just the same things that I had been told when my own sons were circumcised. So there I was in front of all my classmates and my instructor, and the doctor put this little drape over the baby—they make these drapes with holes in the middle so the baby's penis can be stuck through it, you know, just so it could be mutilated, it's just so amazing. They don't want to cut the head of the penis off, so they have to separate the foreskin from the glans... this means literally tearing the foreskin from the glans. Imagine, it would be like sticking something between your finger nail and the finger nail bed... meanwhile, the baby let out a scream I have never heard come out of the mouth of a human being before, and started shaking his head back and forth, of course my finger was out of his mouth at this point because he wasn't sucking... but screaming, screaming, screaming....I started to cry—my bottom lip started to quiver, tears started welling up in my eyes, and I knew, I'm losing it here. And I did. And, it wasn't even happening to me, but I was watching this baby being tortured and mutilated before my eyes, and I started to cry. The doctor looked at me and said: 'There is no medical reason for doing this.' That was the day and the very moment that changed the course of my life.[11]

Milos began researching the issue and was shocked to discover little scientific evidence of medical benefits from neonatal circumcision. Haunted by the realization of what her own sons had endured without her knowledge, she became an advocate for a parental right to informed consent:

> I had a doctor who lied to me and said it doesn't hurt, it only takes a second, and it will protect my sons from a myriad of ills. And of course it was behind closed doors and nobody ever saw a circumcision. I didn't even know enough to recognize that my babies had a wound on their penis, that I had brought a wounded baby home from the hospital."[12]

Seized by the idea of protecting other children and their parents, Milos began mobilizing nurses to inform parents about the procedure so that they would know what they were consenting to. However, this campaign at the hospital quickly drew condemnation from her superiors and she was asked to stop talking. Milos refused and was fired from her position. By then, she had already begun filing 501(c)3 papers to found an organization to work on raising awareness about the nature of routine infant circumcision and particularly its absence of verifiable health benefits.

Early in her research, Milos had come across a book entitled *Circumcision: An American Health Fallacy* and befriended the author, Edward Wallerstein. His landmark study had been the first detailed historical genealogy of the medicalization of circumcision, a process that had occurred during the nineteenth century in large part to prevent masturbation.[13] Appalled at the lack of information that now perpetuated what they saw as an outmoded and barbaric practice, together Wallerstein and Milos conceived of an organization that would provide factual information to parents and challenge the notion that routine circumcision was medically necessary. The National Organization of Circumcision Information Resource Centers (NOCIRC) was established in 1985.

Network Formation and Issue Construction

During this period Milos began networking at the grassroots level with other early intactivists. Drawing together local parents, nurses, and activists from the antiwar, women's rights, LGBT, and men's movements, Milos began picketing local medical ethics boards, the offices of doctors who performed circumcisions, and companies that produced the Circumstraint, a restraining device to which babies were strapped before unanesthetized surgery. At these protests the groups engaged in various forms of direct action such as audio-recording the screams of babies undergoing circumcision to play on loudspeakers, distributing flyers, or producing street art including shoes with their toes cut off for dramatic effect. Milos also courted the media, and was launched to national renown in 1987 when she appeared on the *Phil Donahue Show*. Referrals to her organization began to appear in anticircumcision literature of the period, including *The Joy of Uncircumcising*, a popular book that led numerous survivors to the movement.[14]

Beginning in 1989, Milos also began organizing biannual NOCIRC symposiums, which became the key focusing events for the growing movement. Primarily an opportunity to present and publish scientific findings to which mainstream medical journals were unreceptive, the symposiums also enabled activists to network in solidarity with one another, to exchange ideas and information. Milos established a relationship with Springer Publishing, which printed the proceedings of each symposium. Thus NOCIRC helped cultivate a counterepistemic community that developed an internal normative and causal consensus about the harms of circumcision to counteract what they perceived as rampant misinformation and bias in the mainstream medical journals.[15]

But these symposia, the latest of which took place in Boulder, Colorado, in 2014, are not simply academic conferences. Presentations at the symposia alternate between presentation of scientific studies regarding the health risks of circumcision, presentation of historical, social, and religious aspects of the issue, activist pronouncements, testimonials from affected persons, photographic slideshows or documentary work, and performance art.[16] The events are part scientific exchange, part political brainstorming session, part solidarity site, in which participants' narratives are validated and a common identity forged through the sharing of war stories from efforts on the front lines of the movement.[17]

And the symposia are decidedly political rather than purely scientific: at the first symposium in Anaheim, California, in 1989, the movement adopted a Declaration, stating: "We recognize the inherent right of all human beings to an intact body. Without religious or racial prejudice, we affirm this basic human right.... We recognize that the foreskin, clitoris and labia are normal, functional body parts.... Parents and/or guardians do not have the right to consent to the surgical removal or modification of their children's normal genitalia.... Physicians and other health-care providers have a responsibility to refuse to remove or mutilate normal body parts."[18]

Other activists in Marilyn's orbit developed their own brands of intactivism throughout the 1990s. Tim Hammond and Wayne Griffiths, San Francisco Bay Area peace and women's rights activists who met through NOCIRC, established the National Organization for Restoring Men (NORM) in 1989 to support men in efforts at foreskin restoration. Inspired by his experience with ACT UP, Hammond founded a separate group in 1992, the National Organization to Halt the Abuse and Routine Mutilation of Males (NOHARMM), to function as a direct-action wing of the movement. He also encouraged J. Steven Svoboda, a patent attorney who had found his way to the movement through acquaintances, to start a separate organization to deal with the legal side of things. In 1995 Svoboda founded Attorneys for the Rights of the Child. Between 1995 and 2002, intactivist branches sprang up within other specific social and professional sectors as well: Doctors Opposing Circumcision, Mothers Against Circumcision, Students for Genital Integrity, and Nurses for the Rights of the Child. Many of these groups focus on supporting one another in resisting circumcision professionally or personally, disseminating information, and conducting outreach. A few focus on protest events. One, MGMBill.org (the acronym stands for male genital mutilation), attempts to use state legislatures to promote circumcision bans, and has also produced counterculture artifacts such as the controversial *Foreskin Man!* comic book series.[19]

In the early days of the movement, intactivists were careful to argue only against routine circumcision in hospitals, while acknowledging the legitimacy of circumcision performed for religious reasons. For example, a 1989 letter to the editor in the *Los Angeles Times* read, "*Unless religious scruples protected by the First Amendment require circumcision*, every human being is constitutionally entitled to his whole, natural, intact body until he or she decides otherwise."[20]

However, intactivists gradually broadened their views under pressure from Jewish activists in the movement. Tim Hammond, who founded NOHARMM, told me: "Because of my silence on the religious aspects of this issue I began hearing from Jewish men. 'How can you abandon us?' they said. 'Don't Jewish boys have the same right to their bodies that you claim you have?' I had to develop the moral courage to say yes, they do."[21] Jewish groups opposing circumcision proliferated throughout this period, and books appeared arguing that circumcision was not required by the Old Testament and proposing alternative ceremonies such as the *brit*

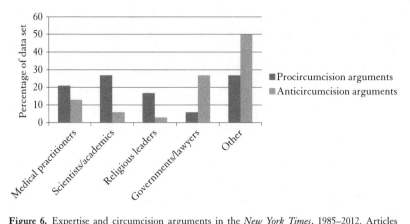

Figure 6. Expertise and circumcision arguments in the *New York Times*, 1985–2012. Articles were selected using the *New York Times* search engine for the term "circumcision." Opinion pieces were excluded. The orientation (pro or anti) and professional expertise of any individuals quoted in the article was coded. Those with no specific expertise (citizens, activist leaders, business representatives) are coded "Other."

shalom (naming ceremony).[22] Over the course of the 1990s, the movement began to argue more explicitly against all genital surgeries performed on nonconsenting minors—girls, boys, and intersex children.

Although the movement was U.S.-based in its early years, during the late 1990s it began transnationalizing. In 1995 a NORM-UK chapter was founded by four British doctors whose seniority and professional credentials lent a measure of gravity to the issue, given the dominant media framing of the movement as composed of non-experts.[23] NOCIRC chapters proliferated throughout the former British Commonwealth countries where routine circumcision remained prevalent. The International Coalition for Genital Integrity was founded in 1999 as an umbrella group to tie the fragmented organizations together and connect them to wider global networks around children's and women's rights. By 2012, the coalition included twenty-six organizations representing seven countries, including some organizations, such as Doctors Opposing Circumcision, with members from all over the world.

In the mid-2000s, the movement also evolved from a grassroots network to a more professionalized coalition at the urging of an angel investor, Texas billionaire Dean Pisani. According to my informants, Pisani had developed an interest in the issue after chafing under unwanted pressure from medical practitioners to circumcise his own son. Researching the subject, he and his wife decided against the procedure and instead developed a relationship with the movement. Pisani urged Milos to develop the sort of organizational infrastructure to which he could channel large sums of money for U.S.-based advocacy work. A series of meetings with movement leaders in 2008 resulted in a new advocacy organization: Intact America. Under the directorship of Georgeanne Chapin, it quickly emerged as a hub for movement activity. Chapin developed a savvy professional website and embarked on a series of campaigns to saturate the mainstream media with timely press releases and to mobilize the organization's grassroots to more effectively lobby medical associations and members of Congress. For the first time the movement had a figurehead, a budget, a business plan, and a uniform advocacy strategy.

International Issue Entrepreneurship and Agenda Vetting, 1993–2012

Besides lobbying domestically, U.S.-based intactivists also reached out to the global human rights network for legitimation and support throughout this period. Of critical importance, many mentioned to me, was getting "leading" NGOs in the movement to accept circumcision as an issue. Indeed, members of Congress, who were initially lobbied to support anti-circumcision legislation, reportedly told movement leaders that until "well-recognized human rights or health organizations" endorsed a plan of action, support for their efforts was unlikely.[24]

According to Clifford Bob, in the global human rights movement the most powerful organizations include "major NGOs such as Amnesty International and Human Rights Watch; international organizations such as the UN's Office of the High Commissioner for Human Rights and other prominent international bodies; and human rights intellectuals." Amanda Murdie's analysis of network ties within the human rights network confirms this view of the hubs, as does my research team's analyses.[25]

During the 1990s and 2000s, attention to infant male circumcision among these organizations was virtually nonexistent and remained so for the duration of this study. At the time of this writing, the UN Office of the High Commissioner for Human Rights does not include male circumcision on its list of harmful traditional practices; neither UNICEF nor the UN's Special Rapporteur on Violence Against Children addresses this issue.[26] Circumcision has been noted in one UN document as an example of sexual torture when carried out against adult prisoners in armed conflicts.[27] However, the routine circumcision of nonconsenting infant boys has escaped critical attention by UN human rights bodies and major human rights NGOs. For example, the 2006 UN Study on Violence Against Children makes no reference to the circumcision of boys.[28]

This is not due to a lack of effort by issue entrepreneurs. Over the last decade intactivists have pitched this issue to specialist networks and NGO hubs in the health and human rights networks, and directly to UN bodies. Yet, like many small NGOs, NOCIRC faced structural impediments to accessing this community. Gaining UN Economic and Social Council (ECOSOC) roster status was a convoluted process, achieved only in 1999. Even then, movement finances did not easily allow for interfacing with global human rights events: activists had to come up with their own funding to visit New York, Geneva, or London.[29] Instead, most efforts to "pitch" to human rights gatekeepers occurred at the local or regional level.

For example, in 1996 Tim Hammond traveled to Harvard University to present on the human rights implications of routine circumcision at a "Health and Human Rights" conference spearheaded by then World Health Organization head Jonathan Mann. His paper was accepted by the conference, and according to Hammond the Europeans in the audience were receptive, but women's advocates and human rights advocates seemed skeptical: "They told me there was no way Amnesty International would ever pick this up."[30]

Apparently they were right. In the United States, activists spent considerable time over the 1990s pitching the issue to Amnesty chapters in the United States. As early as 1992, resolutions were fielded at both the Boston and San Francisco Amnesty chapters, asking the organization to affirm circumcision as a human rights violation, but they failed repeatedly.[31] Tina Kimmel, who had joined NOCIRC in 1991, described an Amnesty meeting where California intactivists worked hard to get their item on the agenda, only to have the vote delayed until most members had left, after which Amnesty staff voted it down in what from her perspective was an "obviously orchestrated maneuver."[32] Ron Goldman fielded no fewer than five resolutions at Amnesty International USA Northeast meetings, each defeated after what he (and several observers) viewed as violations of Amnesty procedures.[33]

The Amnesty International Bermuda chapter did develop an interest through its director, Liyoni Junos.[34] Junos subsequently attended the 2000 Symposium in Sydney, Australia. But when Junos raised the concern at the AI International Council in South Africa in 1997, she was advised that to do promotional work on the issue they would first need to demonstrate that circumcision is an internationally recognized human rights violation.[35] Yet paradoxically it was precisely acknowledgment by Amnesty and other human rights gatekeepers that was politically required to certify such "recognition." Unsurprisingly, subsequent documents prepared by Junos and submitted to the International Secretariat did not elicit action.[36]

Meanwhile, Leonard Glick, a Jewish cultural anthropologist who wrote a detailed history of circumcision and Judaism and later served on the board of Intact America, wrote Amnesty International in 2000 to encourage action on the issue. His letter drew a detailed response from then director William Schultz, who allegedly told Glick that because the medical harms had not been proven it was impossible for Amnesty International to take a stand.[37] Another activist described corresponding with a staff person in the AI Secretariat and finally convincing him to broach the issue with the AI Board of Directors. After doing so his contact reportedly told him that he had been warned never to bring this up again.[38]

Human Rights Watch was equally standoffish. Steven Svoboda, a lawyer who had previously conducted fieldwork for Americas Watch in Latin America, tested the waters on the issue in 1997 with a former colleague who had also worked with the organization. According to Svoboda, she was so offended at the idea that she cut off contact with him subsequent to the conversation. Afterwards, he made no serious attempts to pitch the issue to Human Rights Watch due to what he perceived as a generally hostile institutional environment: "I felt I would be investing an enormous amount of time and emotional energy with an organization where I wouldn't get very far."[39]

Others in the movement did reach out to Human Rights Watch. Matthew Hess of MGMBill.org produced an elaborate online pitch packet and contacted HRW officials by e-mail: first Keramet Reiter, an associate in the U.S. Program, and then (at Reiter's suggestion) Kenneth Roth, HRW's longtime executive director.[40] Reiter explained that the organization was unlikely to work on issues where they had not conducted their own research, and in response to Hess's query about whether research might be forthcoming on the issue, Roth replied in a one-line e-mail that it was highly unlikely.[41] Other Human Rights Watch officials I spoke to beginning in 2008 confirmed the organization had been contacted by concerned citizens over the years. One told me, "Yeah, we were approached on that.... I can't say it was taken that seriously. We just didn't see it as a priority issue, as rising to a level that we need to take up."[42]

Absent the assistance of a powerful NGO ally from the human rights movement, some intactivists took their cause directly to the United Nations. While writing his treatise on male and female circumcision in 1997, Sami Aldeeb Abu-Sahlieh repeatedly contacted the United Nations special rapporteur for traditional practices affecting the health of women and children, Halima Embarek Warzazi, first soliciting her views on the matter for his research and later arguing in correspondence that it would be discriminatory to exclude consideration of the male child while advocating on behalf of girls. However, Warzazi responded that a girls-only approach was warranted because while female circumcision was a health concern, male circumcision did not have comparable health effects.[43] Only months after this correspondence, the title of the Special Rapporteur's office was switched from "Women and Children" to "Women and the Girl Child."[44] The Special Rapporteur went on record in later reports invoking this new title for her office and insisting that her mandate simply didn't cover male circumcision.[45]

In 2001, NOCIRC sent a delegation to pitch the issue to the UN Sub-commission on the Protection and Promotion of Human Rights, a subsidiary body of the former UN Human Rights Commission in Geneva, Switzerland.[46] There Steven Svoboda and his team presented a statement sharply criticizing the UN for failing to prioritize male circumcision, as well as for limiting its work on "harmful traditional practices" to those affecting the girl child, a practice he criticized as a form of gender discrimination.[47] Having cobbled together the funds out of pocket to travel to Switzerland, Svoboda and team members Tina Kimmel and Kenneth Dribak also spent three weeks networking and pitching ideas over lunches and in hallways. But with the exception of the Swedish delegation, they found UN officials unmoved by their arguments. Tina Kimmel told me that "it was hard to figure out who to talk to." Steven Svoboda recalled, "Some of the experts were pretty open minded, sympathetic, approachable, but nobody made any commitment to any specific actions, which we were hoping for."[48] Indeed, over the course of the week Svoboda began to feel more and more marginalized by the commissioners. According to

Swoboda and his team, experts at the World Health Organization were "even less receptive."[49] My qualitative interviews and focus groups with human rights advocates in elite organizations found a similar response.

Indeed, far from warming to the idea of a ban on circumcision, in 2007 health and development hubs with close connections to the human rights movement began instead to *promote* circumcision as a mechanism to prevent HIV-AIDS. Earlier studies had suggested a link between circumcision and HIV-AIDS rates, and three randomized controlled trials in Africa between 2005 and 2007 appeared to document a 60 percent transmission reduction rate from women to men after the operation.[50] Thereafter the World Health Organization, UNICEF, and the Joint United Nations Programme on HIV/AIDS (UNAIDS) enthusiastically undertook an advocacy program to promote male circumcision of adults in African countries, a call to action to which several important donors as well as the U.S. Agency for International Development quickly responded. By 2012, international agencies were not simply promoting circumcision for adult males but also nationwide mandated routine circumcision of male infants.

In response to this increasingly unreceptive environment, U.S.-based intactivists began to shift both their organizational strategy and their messaging. First, rather than continuing to link male circumcision to the female genital mutilation (FGM) agenda under the rubric of "gender equity," they engaged in "scale shift"—broadening their focus to include both. Particularly at the international level, the language moved from a focus on "circumcision" to "genital integrity," with attention to boys, girls, and intersex individuals. According to International Coalition for Genital Integrity director Dan Bollinger, "We try to look at the child regardless of who the child is."[51] Similarly, Genital Autonomy was founded in the United Kingdom in 2008 in part to distinguish the men's service-oriented approach of NORM-UK from the wider advocacy campaign to eradicate genital modifications for boys, girls, and intersex children.[52]

The movement's discourse also shifted laterally in this period from a focus on gender, parental consent, and health to a purely children's rights frame. In the early 1990s papers presented and published in conjunction with the NOCIRC symposia focused on cultural and epidemiological factors and framed circumcision as an "epidemic," emphasizing the parallels between male and female circumcision. Symposium titles referred to "circumcision" and "sexual mutilations" and "pediatric ethics" until 1998, after which they shifted to the terms "genital integrity" and "genital autonomy" with a combination of subtitles referring to human rights, bodily integrity rights, and human dignity.[53] By the time Intact America was founded, the movement had coalesced around a bodily integrity rights frame. According to Executive Director Georgeanne Chapin:

> We refuse to get sucked into arguments on the science of circumcision. I can never argue with an MD from Harvard who is making his living off money that's paying to circumcise the subcontinent of Africa.... We're going on ethics: the baby's healthy, the foreskin is a normal body part, adults don't have the right to cut body parts off children, period.

Nonetheless, as late as 2009, human rights gatekeepers remained unsympathetic, even dismissive of such arguments. When I queried that year about infant male circumcision as one of many potential "neglected" human rights issues, a Human Rights Watch staff person told me, "We're not working on it. I'm not saying we've never been contacted about it, but those kinds of letters would probably go in the nutty file."[54]

Explaining Human Rights Agenda Vetting

Why did human rights gatekeepers shy away from this issue? On an objective basis, this is hard to explain based purely on issue attributes, actor attributes, or the overall political context. However, as I will show, the social construction of international issues is always a subjective process, one very dependent on the imagined relationships among issues and among organizations networked together through the advocacy landscape.

That the issue itself failed to resonate seems puzzling on the basis of existing theory. The idea of protecting baby boys from mutilation at the hands of adults would seem to fit Keck and Sikkink's famous hypothesis that bodily harm to groups perceived as vulnerable or innocent should be easy cases for transnational advocacy.[55] The problem was clear and the solution was feasible and solvable through government action: because the procedure took place in hospitals rather than homes, governments could easily enact rules against it or simply refuse to include coverage of the procedure on the national health plan.[56] The issue could be and was linked to a variety of existing, universal international norms regarding bodily integrity rights. The magnitude of the problem was enormous and easily measurable. Although as discussed below this issue ranked closer to the "inconducive" end of the spectrum on the "toxicity" and "perpetrator attributes" criteria, it is little different from female genital mutilation in that regard—an issue that has attracted wide attention in the human rights community.

What of the attributes of the entrepreneurs themselves? Were these such as to affect gatekeepers' perceptions of the credibility of the issue? If anything, relative to other issues on the international agenda, intactivists' characteristics should have made it likely that the issue would gain credibility on the international stage. Many of them were credentialed professionals with field experience in the medical or legal community. Most were members of the claimant population themselves—adult circumcision survivors or mothers of circumcised sons who felt misled by medical professionals. Unlike the FGM movement, which was led by Westerners on behalf of southern populations and thus subject to claims of imperialism, the intactivist movement grew out of the U.S., U.K., Canadian, and Australian grassroots in opposition to practices in northern hospitals. In later years the movement attracted donor funding, and intactivists' advocacy skills began to mature over time. They were fluent in the primary language of the northern human rights movement. And the network included some "unlikely leaders" including numerous members of the Jewish community.

Were the attributes of the adopting organizations the key constraining factors? Certainly the agenda-vetting power displayed by Amnesty International's International Secretariat is consistent with Wong's analysis of the organization's culture.[57] Though country chapters may propose new items for international attention, discretion on whether to legitimize new human rights problems is controlled through the Secretariat. Although Wong does not explore how the Secretariat chooses to adopt or vet candidate issues, Stephen Hopgood's examination of AI's internal culture provides clues: the Secretariat's willingness to consider proposals from one country chapter depends somewhat on how much resistance they expect from other country chapters, as well as whether the issue will be seen to compromise their credibility on other issues, and how amenable an issue is to fact-finding.[58] Similarly, Thompson's analysis of AI's internal decision-making process on the death penalty suggests how careful AI has been historically in adopting new issues, particularly those that would threaten cohesion within the movement.[59] In short, country chapters themselves possess a greater agenda-vetting power through resistance to other chapters' proposals than they do the power to unilaterally influence the Secretariat.

Still, this doesn't explain why AI managed to develop a consensus around sexual orientation rights and the death penalty but seemed unwilling to seriously debate the issue of circumcision. Nor does it explain the equivalent reticence of Human Rights Watch, an organization unbeholden to national chapters, or of various UN bodies in which "rights talk" gets constructed and reproduced at the global level.

Did the broader political context work against the intactivist movement? A factor often bemoaned by intactivists is that neonatal circumcision is a $450 million year industry in the United States.[60] Key donors to human rights agencies include countries where the practice is widespread: Australia and the United States together donated over $130 million to UNICEF in 2011, and the United States is the single biggest donor to the UN Human Rights Council. Yet while there is a correlation between the position of donor countries and some human rights gatekeepers, I have found little evidence that these concerns directly influenced gatekeepers' preferences on the issue.

Indeed, most other "broader context" factors cited by practitioners as relevant were in fact conducive to advocacy in the case of male circumcision. Numerous academics and experts, including many members of the medical establishment, joined the movement. Claimant demand was high as evidenced in the widespread global network of intactivist organizations, led primarily by victims of the procedure or family members concerned for the well-being of their sons and including many representatives of the very religious communities that human rights elites may have feared offending. A legal framework existed in which to situate a global norm against routine circumcision. Media attention increased over the first decade of the twenty-first century. Trigger events such as the September 2011 death of an infant in New York, or the banning of circumcision by a German court after a toddler suffered from uncontrollable bleeding, brought notoriety and public attention to the issue.[61] Although the practice remained widespread within two powerful states (the United States and Israel) and through much of the Muslim Middle East, numerous other governments worldwide had already eradicated routine circumcision by this time. Indeed, on balance the political environment seemed at least as favorable to advocacy as the autonomous weapons issue, which gradually gained salience on the global agenda during the period of this study.

Why were the restraining factors—the "toxicity" of the issue, the perpetrator attributes, and the perceived opposition of powerful actors—sufficient to render the circumcision issue taboo within mainstream human rights circles for decades? One interpretation is that these factors are peculiarly salient in the minds of human rights elites, even when weighed against other enabling factors. However, I argue that what made this configuration of factors so salient were gatekeepers' judgments about the issue in relation to other issues on their agenda; and their judgments about the procircumcision lobby in relation to stakeholders with dense social ties to their own communities of practice.

Issue Conflicts: Child Rights vs. Religious Rights

First, resistance to the issue was framed in terms of *conflicts* with an issue already salient on the human rights issue agenda: religious freedom. The idea that circumcision is really a *religious rights* or *cultural rights* issue rather than a child rights' issue made it particularly difficult for gatekeepers to acknowledge the human rights implications, either because they themselves belonged to these faith traditions or because they feared being judged intolerant by those who did. Respondents in my focus groups were divided over whether they felt strongly in favor of such a right, but even those who didn't acknowledged feeling constrained by a norm to avoid denigrating religions, for both normative and practical reasons.[62]

> The minute you hit this issue, it's going to touch a nerve. It's the same as the cartoons about the prophet Muhammad and things like that. It's intruding into a religious issue from the Western perspective.[63]

> If it's not scientifically proven one way or another, then if you make this a human rights issue then you make it an imposition of Western values under the cloak of human rights declarations. And if you try to go impose a Western value onto another culture it actually becomes more problematic than the practice, it actually weakens human rights as a doctrine.

There is evidence to support these fears. Where circumcision has been openly raised it has often invoked accusations of anti-Semitism, cultural imperialism, or religious disrespect from religious communities themselves. Ballot measures to ban circumcision in the United States have been swiftly denounced by organized Jewish opposition. A June 2012 provincial ban on ritual circumcision by a German court after a four-year-old Muslim boy suffered uncontrollable bleeding drew an immediate backlash from Jews and Muslims in Germany and abroad, along with claims of a "second Holocaust" against non-Christian religious rights. When incoming Norwegian ombudsman Anne Lindboe included circumcision eradication on her platform for children's rights advocacy in Norway, she received a visit from representatives of the Simon Wiesenthal Center. According to Lindboe, she was told she was being disrespectful of Jews and that the only way to correct this was to change her mind.[64] In addition, one runs across accusations of anti-Semitism in letters to the editor[65] and even in the scholarly literature.[66]

Perhaps this explains the perception among intactivists that the mere worry about being perceived as anti-Semitic retards a greater policy response on this issue even among those sympathetic to the cause.[67] In fact, intactivists report hearing this expressed as a rationale for agenda denial by policy gatekeepers in various contexts.[68] However, my research suggests that "fears of anti-Semitism accusations," while present, are not the only or even the primary concern expressed by human rights professionals.

Rather, human rights elites express valid normative concerns with weighing different rights claims including the importance of religious freedom. But more important, the practice is prevalent in their own social networks, and both accepted and promoted in their adjacent professional networks. The need to tread lightly on it is therefore very much constructed by their sense of how it relates to their own political agendas and to that of their partners in the human security network, rather than to the transnational Jewish community per se.

Social Proximity to Alleged Perpetrators

Aside from concerns about religious controversy, in interviews and focus groups conflicts with "parental rights" were also often raised. But this was not because the concept of "parental rights" was a salient, competing agenda item in the human rights network. Rather it was because many human rights professionals themselves were circumcising parents who took the issue somewhat personally.

Unlike many other practices that human rights professionals condemn but do not participate in, the practice of circumcision was widespread in the human rights elite community itself. Confronting it evoked defensiveness from those who had circumcised their own children and were loath to think of themselves as human rights abusers. Indeed, in focus groups, personal narratives figured much more prominently in practitioners' evaluations of the merits of this issue than in discussions of other potential human security campaigns:

> I make decisions on behalf of my daughter every day. This goes against the rights of parents. Religious-cultural issues aside, this is about the state telling me what I can and cannot do.

> Is staying in the playpen a human rights violation? When you're a baby, your mother gets to tell you what to do.... I had to make lots of decisions about my child, to vaccinate, to breastfeed, to send to daycare—all kinds of parental decisions are human rights violations. So this doesn't seem as important to me as a lot of the other stuff out there.

Earlier research suggests that whether or not a human rights problem is caused by a "socially acceptable perpetrator" is an important causal factor in its likelihood to be condemned by human rights organizations.[69] Arguably, this is a more important factor than the attributes of the victim population in constructing advocates' sense of whether a campaign has merit.[70] If it is politically acceptable to treat a specific group as a perpetrator— dictators, greedy corporations, or other groups traditionally in power over vulnerable others—advocates are likelier to think a campaign can be marketed. When an alleged perpetrating group is viewed as a victim group itself, campaigns targeting its conduct are more difficult. The association of circumcision with Judaism, the sociopolitical status of the Jewish community as "ideal political victims" within the human rights movement, and concerns over religious rights may have exerted some effect.[71]

But the density of social ties between the potential targets of such a campaign and human rights elites themselves was also a constraint. Indeed, in many cases the two populations are synonymous, creating a cognitive dissonance in settings where circumcision was framed as a human rights problem. For example, an Amnesty USA official who had spoken out against one of Ron Goldman's several attempts to field a resolution on the matter described his reaction to the proposal this way:

> They wanted to argue it was a form of torture. I spoke out against this idea as both a presumed "torturer" and presumed "victim." Why should Amnesty make a decision so that [I] am now considered a perpetrator of torture on my eight-day-old son, and my grandfather and my parents should be considered a perpetrator for arranging for me to be circumcised in a religious ceremony when I was eight days old?[72]

Coalitional Politics: Health and Human Rights in Global Civil Society, 2005–2012

Yet it was not only human rights elites' (and by extension their membership's) implicit inclusion in the target population that constrained their ability to take male circumcision seriously as a human rights problem. Indeed, this resistance could conceivably have been overcome through persuasive action, since similarly close-to-home issues such as spanking had already been taken up by human rights gatekeepers by this point in time. A bigger problem was that to address circumcision, fingers would need to be pointed at global health professionals who had long accepted and perpetuated the practice.

This was problematic because mainstream human rights organizations have close social, professional, and in some cases personal ties to those working in global health organizations—relationships cultivated through years of civil society work in development or humanitarian contexts, and strengthened by Jonathan Mann's efforts in the mid-1990s to weld the "health" and "human rights" sectors in global civil society.[73]

These interpersonal connections were not only vital conduits for existing human rights work on adjacent issues at the health and human rights nexus, including HIV-AIDS, reproductive health, and disability rights. They also shaped the perceptions of nonmedical human rights specialists on circumcision in not inconsequential ways, making them particularly receptive to the frames and conventional wisdom being promulgated within the mainstream global health establishment. For example, one respondent, in explaining his indifference to this issue, invoked his marital ties to a medical health professional:

> I've never thought of it as a human rights problem. It's funny, because my wife is a HIV/AIDS worker for fifteen years now, and she is passionately convinced that male circumcision is one of the single most important ways we have of slowing down the spread of HIV-AIDS.[74]

Indeed, health groups were in the same time period both promoting the purported medical benefits of circumcision and linking the idea of circumcision as a "form of vaccination" to their existing discourses on health and human rights. In this framework, the human rights implications of circumcision were not about bodily harm or stigma but rather about ensuring equal access of men to a potentially beneficial procedure. A 2006 WHO document argues "it is an international human rights violation to deny circumcision on non-medical grounds," and also stressed the importance of safety and informed consent.[75] However, the "informed consent" and "voluntary" criteria for the program of action apparently did not extend to children, only to parents: the same document stated that no surgical intervention "should be performed on anyone without informed consent, *or* the consent of the parent or guardian." In the same year, a document produced jointly by UNICEF, WHO and UNAIDS stated:

> All decisions about undergoing the procedure need to be fully informed and completely voluntary. Parents must be responsible for weighing the pros and cons before deciding whether infants and young boys should be circumcised.... Governments need to consider whether the circumcision of male infants should be routinely offered and encouraged.[76]

Even though intactivists were normatively less concerned with genital surgery voluntarily chosen by adult males, the idea that this policy might be used to further justify the routine circumcision of infants caused significant concern. Some ink was spilled aiming to discredit the emerging consensus on the correlation between circumcision and HIV transmission; many activists pointed out that of industrialized countries the United States has both the highest circumcision rate *and* the highest HIV-AIDS rate. However, others simply argued that other prevention methods were equally effective, that babies don't need to be protected from sexually transmitted diseases, and that no one would recommend routine mastectomies of girls in order to prevent breast cancer.

Nonetheless, the mainstreaming of this idea by global health gatekeepers posed additional social constraints to human rights groups against taking a strong stand on the issue from a child rights perspective. Doing so would have risked disrupting civil-society alliances and would pit them against powerful players such as the World Health Organization—at the very time that they were cultivating such alliances on other emerging human rights issues, such as the right to pain relief or the human rights dimensions of HIV-AIDS. It also exacerbated the sense that promoting a ban would mean countering the position of donor organizations including the U.S. Agency for International Development and the Bill and Melinda Gates Foundation—organizations that found WHO's policy prescriptions compelling and were now funneling significant sums to circumcision campaigns in Africa. As one otherwise sympathetic human rights professional told me, "It's a much harder argument to make now that it's perceived that it can be important in preventing HIV [infection]."[77]

Even human rights professionals who personally doubted the veracity of the medical establishment's view saw the presence of a scientific debate on the matter as a reason for *inaction*, rather than action. One focus group respondent said:

> It's an issue that's got to be resolved within the medical community just like debates about vaccines or nutrition. I personally think that we've been lied to by nutritionists for the last twenty years about a lot of things that are making Americans sick right now. But that's not a human rights issue. We've got to engage in that debate in the medical health community and get a different consensus if we feel like that's needed. I mean, how can a human rights organization play a role in that without establishing that one side or the other in the medical debate is right or wrong? We don't have clearly the expertise or credibility to weigh in [on] one side or another in a debate like that.

Of course on other campaigns human rights groups had taken precisely the opposite position: that the burden of proof was on the scientific community, industry, or governments to demonstrate benefit/absence of harm, rather than on activists to demonstrate harm/absence of benefit. Under what conditions does the "burden of proof" argument in cases where no scientific consensus exists cause agenda-setting rather than agenda vetting? This case suggests that the crucial factor is the density of ties between the advocacy network and the expert communities in question. On balance, human rights groups will privilege the judgment of those organizations/ experts with whom they enjoy the closest social and professional ties. In this case, that meant that the bar was high for questioning the received wisdom of colleagues in the global health sector.

Issue Competition: The Male Circumcision/Female Genital Mutilation Debate

This sea change in the health agenda may help explain post-2007 reticence on the circumcision issue, but it does not explain why rights groups avoided the issue prior to the HIV-AIDS studies and WHO's policy position. Indeed, had a strong advocacy campaign against male genital mutilation emerged prior to 2006, it is much more doubtful that WHO, much less UNICEF, would have proposed painful, irreversible surgery on nonconsenting babies as an antidote to disease transmitted sexually by adults. The absence of a strong norm in this period enabled this policy agenda. What explains human rights agenda vetting around male circumcision between 1996 and 2005, at the same time that other "private wrongs" were experiencing a renaissance in the human rights sector?[78]

Aside from the inhibiting effect exerted by social ties to organizations in adjacent networks with a different view of the problem, another "network effect" we coded for that seemed particularly salient in this case is perceived *competition between issues*. Sometimes, transnational advocates avoid work on an issue not because it conflicts with other issues or with coalitional relationships, but because, however complementary it may be at a conceptual level, it is perceived to potentially divert resources and attention from an adjacent, presumably more pressing concern.[79] In this case, attention to male circumcision was seen to threaten the campaign around female genital circumcision. Focus group respondents explained:

> A campaign on this should automatically be compared to the campaign to eradicate female mutilation. I think this could actually backfire on that other campaign, which is *really* a priority.

It's so much worse for girls. If I were going to focus on this issue, boys would really have to be secondary. I would really focus my attention on girls.

The notion of a zero-sum relationship between the two issues is similar to concerns I heard raised in my earlier research on the protection of civilian men and on children born of war rape among UN agencies. Global civil servants worry about the co-optation of gender concerns by groups other than women, because so few resources already go to women's concerns in the UN system relative to global need. As an interview respondent stated, "You know what happens when you gender-mainstream: gender gets completely watered down."[80]

But this perception was also fostered by the cognitive association of male circumcision with female circumcision. In focus groups I found it very difficult to get participants to evaluate male circumcision on its *own* merits: instead they would pivot to FGM. Yet far from helping "make the connection," as intactivists hoped, the very conceptual adjacency of the two issues worked against the intactivist cause, since to talk of one was interpreted as displacing the other to which the human rights community was already committed. One focus group respondent criticized my selection of infant male circumcision as a focus: "Why didn't you ask about female circumcision? It's a much more burning issue."

To intactivists I interviewed, this reaction was baffling: they viewed the causes as inherently complementary and expected gender experts to be the last crowd to endorse what they viewed as gender discrimination. Tim Hammond described his surprise at being booed out of an Alice Walker award ceremony by hostile feminists and chided by gender-mainstreaming experts in the health and human rights community:

. People don't make the logical connection between the slogan 'my body my rights' that women use and the rights of males....I don't understand that disconnect....What I often hear is, "oh, now you're just playing the victim card...you're trying to copy women.' As if men don't have a legitimate right to complain about a violation of their bodies and their rights. I think feminists should be pleased and flattered that men have adopted a similar strategy.

Why did this argument fail to resonate? After all, while there are vast differences between the least severe form of male circumcision and the most severe form of female circumcision, it is true that the most commonly inflicted forms of each are roughly comparable in their scope and effects, as are the discourses that perpetuate the practices.[81] Anthropologists have noted these "rather contradictory policies" that seek to "medicalize male circumcision on the one hand, oppose the medicalization of female circumcision on the other, while simultaneously basing their opposition to female operations on grounds that could legitimately be used to condemn male operations."[82]

In fact, however, this argument undermined human rights elites' ability to see infant circumcision as a children's bodily integrity rights violation. As comparable as the practices may be conceptually, they are not at all comparable *politically* precisely because of the way in which ideas were networked socially within transnational spaces.[83] Ironically, the gender equity argument through reference to FGM linked circumcision not to children's human rights but to *health* and to *gender*—two issue clusters where the strong ethical argument about children's rights held far less sway.

Originally, female genital mutilation had been championed not as a human rights issue but as a health issue.[84] Moreover, precisely because it was so toxic, many practitioners continued to emphasize the health aspects of FGM to avoid being seen to peddle imperialist Western human rights arguments.[85] Even though FGM is undoubtedly also a human rights issue, its political association with the health sector meant that it had been rationalized in a very different way than was seen as appropriate for male cutting. It also meant that comparisons to FGM had to be made on the basis of health impacts, whereas intactivists' strongest arguments (and their intellectual expertise) lay on the human rights side.

Moreover, the gender equity frame undermined a strong child-rights argument against circumcision by encouraging human rights elites to think of this as a *men's* issue—just as the FGM movement had been framed as a *women's* issue—rather than an issue affecting boy and girl children. With adults as the frame of reference, the gender equity argument worked against male claimants. Whereas for advocacy purposes women could be framed as a vulnerable group oppressed by the practice, this argument was less compelling when males were the victims. Adult men had not traditionally been seen as vulnerable to gender-based violence or powerless in the face of oppressive social structures:[86] Focus group participants argued:

> There's no shortage of power within the affected community. If the men, particularly here in the United States, wanted to see this happen, it could

easily happen.... The people that are making the decisions around these issues are the ones that are impacted by this issue.

Of course, this statement would appear to miss the point that the babies
being subjected to circumcision are not "making decisions around these
issues." Nor are practitioners necessarily correct that men do not suffer from gender hierarchies: indeed, many scholars have demonstrated
that this too is a gendered discourse. However, that gendered discourse
is a social fact: "harmful practices," of which FGM is the classic example, are defined at the UN in terms of gendered power relations
with adult men and women (rather than children per se) as the frame
of reference.[87]

The fact that men are not *perceived* as a traditionally vulnerable group
makes this rationale for issue neglect dovetail nicely with Keck and
Sikkink's original formulation: it matters less that vulnerable infants were
actually the victims than that gatekeepers *perceive* the claimants as adult
men, a perception certainly exacerbated by intactivists' emphasis on "gender equity for males."[88] Particularly when compared to the still emergent
attention to women's rights in UN circles, this appeared to UN insiders
as an effort by adult men to steal thunder from the gender-violence
movement, rather than a campaign on behalf of children.

Intactivists missed several opportunities in the last decade to pursue
advocacy targets that may have shifted this perception. They did not, for
example, engage with the 2006 Violence Against Children Report process,
which might have been a logical framework for the movement to hang its
hat on as a child rights campaign focused on violence rather than health.
Nor did they pitch the issue to specialized agencies dealing with children,
such as UNICEF. But this is changing. The movement's shift toward a
child rights orientation has held promise for reframing this issue in human
rights circles.

In a presentation at the biennial Genital Autonomy Symposium in
September 2012, former Tasmanian children's commissioner Paul Mason
drew parallels not to FGM but rather to the problem of corporal punishment as it developed in UN circles, encouraging intactivists to "connect the
dots." Genital Autonomy-UK reported positive social interactions with
the Child Rights Information Network, which seemed more amenable to
intactivist claims than did FGM groups. The June 2012 Cologne ruling
was expressed in terms of children's bodily integrity rights, and the outcry

generated unprecedented publicity for genital integrity organizations, many of whom suddenly received media attention.

As the movement moves further away from a gender equity, health, or informed consent framework, it may both reconstitute the issue itself and the social networks globally where these frames may find resonance. Indeed, intactivists argue this is already happening.[89] Ultimately, however, the support of leading human rights organizations is a crucial missing ingredient in the quest to consolidate this emerging understanding into an internationally recognized norm against the cutting of infant boys with resonance in the wider human rights network.[90] Indeed, a member of Amnesty International USA suggested to me in 2012 that the organization should take the opposite position and champion the cultural rights of religious groups. How this story plays out will remain to be seen.

This chapter has shown how decisively central organizations in an issue network can keep new issues off the agenda when they threaten preexisting frames, alliances within the wider advocacy network, relationships among issues, or conventional wisdom within a global community of practice. Intactivists are waging an uphill battle against an entrenched cultural practice embraced by the states in which human rights gatekeepers are headquartered and by whom their organizational partners are funded, as well as many practitioners within health and development organizations to which human rights elites are closely connected.

Some of the factors inhibiting entrepreneurs' successful engagement with gatekeepers include money and resources; identity factors within the movement, and the strategies of the movement itself. But to a great extent intactivists simply face a tremendously unreceptive environment in the mainstream human rights movement due to the relative density of human rights professionals' social and professional ties to (a) the groups they perceive as perpetrators and (b) mainstream global health organizations. Moreover, the perception that the victim group is a network of men speaking as *claimants* rather than a diverse network of *champions* speaking on behalf of vulnerable children has made it difficult to incorporate their claims into the gender discourse popular in the human rights movement.

In short, the network structure of the issue and the actors relative to gatekeepers' own social and ideational perceptions of the existing network and issue agenda made all the difference in determining whether the cutting of infant boys resonated as a genuine human rights concern.

CONCLUSION

Big ideas always look impossible. So, you have to put them out there.

FOCUS GROUP PARTICIPANT #34, DECEMBER 2009

I have made two arguments about the importance of intranetwork relations in explaining variation in the global advocacy agenda. One is a causal argument about the significance of issue adoption by particular actors positioned to ignite a contagion effect within global civil society. I have shown that the causal impact of their issue adoption decisions is a function of their structurally central location within networks. The second is a constitutive argument about how those actors understand their preferences. I have shown that all things being equal, advocacy "gatekeepers" also judge the merit and timing of issue adoption based on intranetwork relations: how the issue connects to other issues, other organizations, and other networks of issues and organizations to which they enjoy more or less robust ties.

The three cases you have just read each illustrated different aspects of this process, but as a group they reinforce those key claims derived from the extant case literature and focus groups. They demonstrate that norm entrepreneurship in global politics is not enough to ensure that a cause will attract the attention of major human security organizations. All three cases included a dedicated entrepreneur, but the cases exhibited very different levels of success over the course of the research period. Nor is network formation sufficient, even when that network includes numerous organizations. The infant male circumcision movement had perhaps the widest, densest, and most diverse transnational network of all three cases, but the least success on the global stage.

Indeed, these cases were selected to control for factors inherent to issues, entrepreneurs, and to the broader political context that might be expected to sink new campaigns. All dealt with issues in which the bodily integrity rights of vulnerable individuals are at stake; in which the solution is reasonably feasible; in which there is a clear set of international laws to which the issue might be linked. All involved efforts by English-language-fluent Western-based entrepreneurs with either activist or expert credentials, with either claimant status or buy-in from the beneficiary population, with access to funding and to relevant gatekeepers, and with a similar learning curve in advocacy skills. And the cases face a similar political opportunity structure: they benefit equally from existing legal frameworks, from media attention, from forums in which to press their case; and they are similarly threatening to powerful interests. In short, these should have been easy cases—or at least similar cases—for issue creation in global politics.

How do these largely unknown cases vary from high-profile campaigns such as landmines, conflict diamonds, child soldiers, and honor killings? The key difference is that during the course of the study, none of these campaigns had yet attracted support from advocacy elites in central hubs for their causes. The entrepreneurs varied over time in the extent to which they were successful at engaging gatekeepers, both relative to one another and relative to similar issues in the advocacy pool. And they varied in how they and the issues themselves were *networked* vis-à-vis relevant advocacy and policy gatekeepers, relevant issue areas, and relevant stakeholders. These factors, I argue, explain the differences between these cases and otherwise similar yet salient issues, as well as differences among the cases themselves and within cases over the course of the study.

These three cases demonstrate that gatekeeper adoption matters, usually occurs after a period of agenda vetting, and often doesn't happen at all. Both the Making Amends Campaign and the anti-killer-robot lobby forum-shopped repeatedly throughout the human security sector before finding a framework and organizational forum on which to hook their ideas. The "making amends" concept, already well known in policy circles, diffused to transnational activist networks when humanitarian gatekeepers began to give it rhetorical support.

Similarly, the autonomous weapons issue percolated quietly around human security circles for years but only gained a foothold in the humanitarian disarmament community when mainstream NGOs began to acknowledge "killer robots" as a serious looming threat rather than a science fiction scenario. Conversely, the intactivist campaign tried to engage global gatekeepers, but their cause was vetted and remains a non-issue in the wider human rights network. When centrally networked gatekeepers adopt issues, wider networks listen; when they avoid or actively vet, their behavior exerts a dampening effect on the possibility of global norm development.

Additionally, while agenda vetting is a function of a cluster of factors, intranetwork relations play an important role in gatekeepers' judgments about when to adopt new issues or to exercise agenda denial. Not only do hierarchies among transnational actors confer power on central organizations to "vet" the advocacy agenda, but network effects also help constitute those organizations' preferences. Across my case studies, I observed this effect in three ways.

First, preexisting networks of ideas within an issue network can exert dampening effects on emergent issues under certain circumstances. Just as a gendered frame associating the protection of civilians with "women and children" prevented concerted advocacy to protect adult male civilians in armed conflict, the association of "women and children" as a single vulnerable group stymied agenda-setting efforts around populations whose life experiences complicate that frame, such as children born of rape or men advocating for bodily integrity rights for boys.

Second, perceptions of ties among organizations in existing networks and around a new issue can shape advocacy elites' willingness to join new campaigns. The anti-killer-robot lobby's social ties to antiwar activists initially limited its cachet with more conservative humanitarian organizations. CIVIC's embeddedness in the U.S. foreign policy community influenced global organizations' initial perceptions that theirs was a one-country campaign. The compartmentalization of issue turf can create opportunities for cross-cutting synergies, or pose pitfalls, as when actors pass the buck from one network to the next.

Third, perceptions of ties between issue areas matter. Relational dynamics among organizations in a network can shape gatekeeper preferences. Coalitional turf demarcated within civil society between women-focused groups and child rights groups influenced the invisibility of children born of rape; partnerships between the human rights and health sectors affected reticence around the issue of male circumcision as a human rights abuse. Greater attention needs to be paid in studies of global agenda setting to the relationship between emergent issues and coalitional politics within and between issue networks and subnetworks.

Finally, it is clear that a factor driving the success or failure of global agenda setting is simply the social networks of key stakeholders and drivers. Both Marla Ruzicka and Noel Sharkey exemplified this factor: their ability to connect simultaneously and with equal intensity with experts and with everyday people provided them power. But the individual social networks of political entrepreneurs and matchmakers are not just vital as conduits of emerging ideas. They also constitute part of an issue's identity and location within an advocacy arena, and as such they signal to potential adopters what's at stake in joining a campaign. Sarah Holewinski's rolodex of NATO generals both ensured CIVIC would be taken seriously by the military and that it would be viewed with a skeptical eye by antiwar organizations. Richard Moyes's connections to disarmament elites enabled him to "mainstream" the killer robot issue simply by acknowledging it in ways that ICRAC members could not.

This study has important implications for issue entrepreneurs, for global policy elites, and for students of international relations. The take-home message for issue entrepreneurs is that careful thought must be given to where and how one pitches one's issues if one is to build successful coalitions within global policy networks. Practitioners in such networks care deeply about social change but are selective and strategic in attending to different issues. And issues are judged less on their intrinsic merits than on the ideational and social networks surrounding them. Although issue entrepreneurs may have little control over the attributes of the issue they are promoting, they may be able to affect the perception of those attributes through their messaging. Additionally, issue entrepreneurs should carefully consider the organizational interests of those with whom they seek coalitions, and be aware that these interests are constituted as much by relationships with the rest of the advocacy network as by the organizational culture, donor economy, and broader political environment. They should also focus on developing the skills, alliances, and a professional profile that will give them credibility among the wider global advocacy community.

This study suggests insights for organizations in a position to accept or "vet" advocacy claims as well. My research team identified a perception among practitioners, particularly in the abstract, that their hands are largely tied by states, donors, and the media, yet this perception flies in the face of many successful advocacy campaigns, documented in an extensive social scientific literature. Global civil society is influenced by these broader factors, but it plays a role in setting the government, media, and donor agendas as well. Within these networks certain civil society organizations play a larger role than others. Organizations at the center of issue networks have a powerful legitimating effect on new issues. Organizations operating at the intersection of networks or ideas have the ability to bridge the distance between "silos" in new and synergistic ways.

Students of international relations will, I hope, close this book convinced that studies of advocacy networks should take networks as structures (rather than agents) far more seriously. International relations scholars have long appropriated the metaphor of the "network" as a way to describe the nonstate political sector, yet have rarely examined how relationships within networks shape the behavior of agents and therefore political outcomes. I have proposed some new ways to think about and to measure the impact of network structures on activism across borders.

However, I am not suggesting that scholars of norm development should abandon constructivist methods and turn to network math. Rather, I have shown that it is perceptions of network ties, rather than the ties themselves, that constrain actors. Qualitative, constructivist methods for understanding how actors embedded in transnational networks view these relationships, and their own preferences, are required to make sense of the ever-shifting issue agenda.

In general, a research agenda on issue construction and gatekeeping in transnational networks would take theorists of global civil society in some interesting directions. Is "no" ever final? Do the advocates give up and walk away? Do issues fizzle? Die? Do they get rebranded? Under what conditions do people give up? Many of these questions require a larger dataset of issues and nonissues. They require systematic and imaginative research methodologies capable of mapping out transnational space, capturing a range of nascent issues, and comparing them to cases of successful agenda setting. They require studying not only gatekeepers but also issue entrepreneurs. It is the dialectic between these groups that drives global civil society. And as I have shown, this dialectic produces significant outcomes and nonoutcomes in global governance.

Appendix

Studying Transnational Spaces

A Multimethod Approach

Transnational spaces and processes are notoriously difficult to study. This is because they are diffuse: constituted both in the fractured geographic localities of the physical world and the world of language and ideas, transnational ideas are both everywhere (that someone subscribes to or invokes them) and nowhere in particular. For that reason, such communities are challenging to access, and an accurate picture of their discourse and impact is difficult to capture properly through conventional "measures."

Sometimes, researchers do this by navigating somewhat at random between various "sites" of transnational activity, aiming at an overall picture. Those who adopt a more "replicable" approach must do so in comprehensively manageable yet incomplete slices. Thus, my colleague James Ron surveyed global South advocates where they gathered at human rights training events in the North, for example, letting the structure of the human rights network gather his sample for him. My earlier work on protection of civilians discourse used as a dataset all the documents on the OCHA's Protection of Civilians web portal as a replicable though not necessarily representative sample of "protection of civilians" discourse.

Such strategies for accessing transnationalism through specific sites are slightly more systematic but still incomplete and unsatisfactory: researchers can never properly "sample" transnational communities because we simply cannot know who is in our population. Migrating toward thinking about "global" rather than transnational ideas doesn't help much in resolving this problem. We are limited by our corporeality in accessing our population of concern, and ideas that circulate globally in real time are often tricky to capture and trace. One never really knows how nonrepresentative one's data are, and so it is difficult to make satisfactory claims about the world.

The questions I asked in my study were also difficult to leverage. Campaigns are easy enough to study, being concrete forms of social activism, but "issue creation" is fuzzier. What is an "issue"? Few scholars of issue emergence even define the term. But I struggled with another conceptual and ethical dilemma: If the object of study is people's awareness or lack thereof of certain "issues," rather than any particular approach for developing policy around them, how might I examine that variation while remaining reasonably aloof of the politics of issue creation itself? That is, how could I examine issue emergence "scientifically" without accidentally becoming an issue entrepreneur myself, without inadvertently influencing the very perceptions I wished to study?[1]

Given these dilemmas, I followed Patrick Jackson's advice in *The Conduct of Inquiry in International Relations* to think carefully about "methodology" around this project before selecting "methods."[2] I have no idea where Jackson or his students would place this work in his spare 2 × 2 grid of scientific approaches (more on this below). But it is enough to say for now that I do accept his notion of science as the "systematic production of factual knowledge about political and social arrangements," and I did think particularly hard about how to safeguard the role of social scientists tinkering on the edges of politics and policy, while engaging practitioners in such a way as to be able to access the data I needed for my analysis. In doing so, I made the following "philosophical wagers" as I set off and proceeded.

First, I am provisionally committed to the notion that there are "facts" out there in the social world unrelated to any specific actor's interpretation of those facts, but that accessing certain of these facts and formatting them as scientific findings nonetheless may require an interpretive process.

In such cases, I assume that intersubjective agreement on the validity of interpretations increases the external validity of one's findings. Therefore, to the extent possible I conducted my research collaboratively as a check on researcher bias. And I relied on teams of graduate and undergraduate students to assist in creating interpretations that will hopefully be convincing to others. Although the intersubjective validity of my finding remains woefully limited by many things (not least of which is the English language format of both my data collection and coding processes), it is nonetheless more valid, I think, than it would be had I done all my own coding.

Second, I see analytical utility in combining methods at different points along the continuum among neopositivism/critical-realism/analyticism/reflectivism in a single project. This is particularly true since different methodological cuts at the same problem often lead to divergent findings.[3] I think the choice of approaches is most helpfully driven by their purpose: a more positivist, explanatory approach is useful if the goal is to identify general patterns across many cases; a more interpretive, descriptive approach is helpful to understand single cases that can best be used to illustrate patterns but not, in my view, to explain broad generalities.[4] And some element of reflectivism is called for any time a researcher is "hooking up" directly to the social relations he or she is studying, which I think researchers can do in different degrees but which I definitely do as a public intellectual and a qualitative methodologist.[5] So I combined a reasonably transparent, quasi-replicable approach on the portion of the project from which I derived my "general" argument with a more interpretive ethnographic approach on those portions of the project designed to illustrate the general argument through references to the situationally specific configuration of factors that led to an outcome in distinct cases. Throughout, I kept in mind how my presence and structural position as a researcher influenced my interpretations, the data I was able to access, and the processes I was studying in ways that I hope have kept me humble about my conclusions.

Third, I wagered that it was possible to move among and engage practitioners in communicative action in ways that neither harmed entrepreneurs' efforts to promulgate their ideas nor exercised undue influence on the circulation of those ideas among advocacy elites, while accepting the inevitability of my embeddedness in the processes I was studying and leveraging this for insights about and access to the politics of agenda-setting. I see this as consistent with and constitutive of a variant of what Jackson and Kaufman call "Weberian activism," in which the purpose of social scientists is to engage policy processes not by articulating value judgments but by communicating relevant factual knowledge about political and social arrangements to stakeholders acting on their own value judgments.[6] Of course, this is trickier while research is ongoing than it is once research is done. It is also trickier in studying agenda setting than in studying policy development, because agenda setting is a moment in the policy process when the key question is not what to do about a problem but whether or not the problem exists. So simply providing factual information about that social condition itself involves efforts to reshape policyholders' value judgments about what "matters" and is therefore is political. I discuss more about how I resolved this dilemma in the last part of this appendix.

Three phases of the project served three different purposes. The first goal was to operationalize the human security network and the varying salience of its issue agenda, as well as gather an inventory of ideas from practitioners about what might be on the agenda but is not. The second goal was to see what practitioners in this network make of these patterns, document their narratives about agenda-setting dynamics in a conversational setting, and from that draw inferences about how advocacy elites think and evaluate new issues. The third goal was to see how the resulting inferences did or did not play out in the dialectic between entrepreneurs and advocacy elites on several emerging issues. I discuss the methods for each in turn below, and then return to broader questions of methodology in conclusion.

Capturing the Network and the Issue Agenda

We began this project by collecting data on the state of the human security network and the state of the issue agenda in human security through surveys and web analysis. We wanted to know which organizations and which issues were most closely associated with the network. Our solution to the dilemma of transnational sampling was to identify the core of a single multi-issue network. To do this, we treated in-coming hyperlinks as well as mentions of organizations in survey responses to be indicators of in-degree centrality in the network and we averaged organizations' rankings from these two measures to arrive at their overall centrality score.[7] We also used survey answers and web content as an indicator of the issue agenda at that time, and as evidence of how issues are clustered in advocacy space.

Data Collection

The survey was disseminated through an online snowball in spring 2008, beginning with the mailing list of what at that time was a key information portal in the human security network: the Liu Institute at University of British Columbia.[8] One of the questions asked respondents to name "three or more organizations that come to mind when you think of human security." The responses to this question were not themselves amenable to network analysis,[9] but they gave us a population of organizations cited and a frequency count that enabled us to identify the organizations most closely associated with the network by the most practitioners. The twenty most mentioned organizations are listed in the table in this appendix.

We complemented survey results with data gathered from the World Wide Web. Hyperlink analysis gave us a second centrality measure for human security organizations on the web, on the assumption that

Most mentioned organizations in human security

Organization	Frequency count
Amnesty International	36
Canadian Consortium on Human Security	34
Human Security Report Project	31
United Nations Commission on Human Rights	31
Human Security Network	28
International Committee of the Red Cross	24
Liu Institute for Global Issues	23
Human Rights Watch	16
United Nations Educational, Scientific, and Cultural Organization	14
International Crisis Group	14
Doctors Without Borders	12
North Atlantic Treaty Organization	12
Center for Strategic and International Studies	11
Foreign Affairs and International Trade Canada	10
Oxfam International	10
United States Central Intelligence Agency	10
Organization for Security and Co-operation in Europe	9
Canadian Foreign Ministry	8
United Nations Development Programme	7
United Nations	7
World Bank	7
United Nations Children's Fund	7
World Health Organization	7
United Nations High Commissioner for Refugees	7

Note: Names of organizations given when responding to the survey question, "Name three or more organizations that come to your mind when you think of human security."

hyperlinks between advocacy sites constitute recognition of organizational membership in a community of understanding.[10] Within advocacy communities, linking practices between organizational websites function as do academic citations, providing indicators of who is considered a member or a player within a specific community of shared knowledge and practice. And importantly for this project, hyperlink analysis tells us who the leaders or authorities are within the network, as represented by the relative number of incoming and outgoing links.[11]

We used Issuecrawler to identify the most prominent organizations in the human security network. Issuecrawler is a web network location and visualization tool developed by Richard Rogers and hosted at govcom.org at the University of Amsterdam. Although Issuecrawler has several modalities for searching the web, we used co-link analysis for this project. This is a form of hyperlink analysis that "crawls the seed URLs and retains only the pages that receive at least two links from the seeds."[12] In this way, we were able to isolate the websites most closely related to the original search term "human security."

Figure 7. Example of primary document for human security issue coding. http://www.hrw.org/advocacy/index.html.

Because Issuecrawler's results are somewhat dependent on the starting points used, we gave careful attention to how we picked starting points. Our goal was to identify the most frequently cited "human security" hubs online, so in October 2007 we leveraged Google's "Page-Rank" algorithm by using the top ten Google search results as starting points. We allowed the crawler to return results in three iterations, and yielded a core network of 106 organizations. Organizations in this core network were coded for centrality, for organizational type, and for thematic orientation through consensus coding by two senior personnel to produce the graph in plate 1. Notably, this graph illustrates the core, not the entire network; and it illustrates the network relationships as they existed at the start of the study, not necessarily as they exist today. The graph was generated by Alex Montgomery using R.[13]

Around the same time, a team of graduate students at the University of Pittsburgh collected text data from each website in the network manually by capturing the content for each organization's "mission statement" and page describing "what we do" or "issues we work on," reflecting the industry standard for the organization of NGO, think tank, and international organization websites at that time. These were saved as text files and we considered them in the aggregate an indicator of the overall human security network agenda at that time. Figure 7 is an example of the type of web page captured.

We assumed that both the survey data (disseminated online from a North American hub) and the web data (skewed toward organizations with more resources for websites) would be biased toward the industrialized West. And while we didn't identify a way to properly adjust for that, we did attempt to measure the level and nature of that bias through conducting a parallel study of the human rights network that could be triangulated through another source, by embedding identical questions in James Ron's survey of global South activists being conducted at Equitas's International Human Rights Training Program in Montreal.[14] We found significant overlap between southern activists' perceptions of the global human rights network and those of our broader survey respondents and the web analysis, with two exceptions: funding agencies were more prominent among organizations listed by southern activists, and global South activists were more likely to list economic and social rights among their descriptions of "neglected issues." The results from this side study appeared in a *Human Rights Quarterly* article: for this project, which focuses on the human security network, the analysis simply served to remind us of the necessary partiality of our view from the North and the limits of our methods.[15] At the same time, in the human rights network the view of the core is not so different from the South than from the North, not so different online than in surveys. Overall, this test strengthened our confidence that we were able to capture a reasonable approximation of the human security network as it existed in 2008 using these tools.

Data Coding and Analysis

However, the issue language used often varied across organizations, and varied somewhat between the online representations and the language used by survey respondents. This meant that only a few concepts like "human rights" could be auto-coded simply using search terms. So the research team developed and refined a set of codes and code definitions representing the issues described in the surveys and listed online. For example, we used a single "child soldiers" code for "child soldiers" references, and also for references to "child recruitment," as well as long passages describing the "use of children in armed groups" or anything else that a coder decided might qualify as a "reference to child soldiers or child recruitment as a practice."

Teams of undergraduate coders associated with QDAP-Pitt and later QDAP-UMass then categorized the survey answers using these codes to produce an overall frequency count using Atlas.ti. Because there were so many different issues and coders can only work with a few codes at a time, we disaggregated them conceptually, beginning with large buckets such as "development" and "governance" and "repression/persecution" and later creating subsequent waves of more specific codes such as "summary executions" or "corporate social responsibility." Code definitions were refined using a series of pretests based on the inter-rater reliability among coders as measured by Fleiss' kappa.[16] Coders achieved an average inter-rater reliability score of 0.67 for this set of coding. The same codes were applied to both survey data and web data.

We analyzed the coded results in two ways: salience and co-occurrences. The salience of issues varied slightly between the web sphere and the survey data, though the most salient issues were more or less constant across each.[17] To arrive at an overall salience score we averaged them: figure 2 reflects the average salience scores for an issue across both datasets. On the web data, we did an additional analysis, identifying co-occurrences of each code with each other code, which can be represented by Atlas.ti as a network grid and then subjected to network visualizations. With the help of R, Alex Montgomery converted this data to the graph in plate 2 to show the thematic clustering of issues online into a network structure.

Finally, I was especially interested in *low*-salience issues, because we wanted to know what sort of factors might prevent an issue from getting traction in order to better understand what factors enabled other issues to get attention from transnational networks. So I also asked survey respondents to name human security "problems" they knew of in the world that were not very prominent as "issues" within the human security movement. As described below, focus group participants were given a similar survey prior to participation, and a portion of the time in the focus groups themselves was spent brainstorming additional "missing issues." Participants were free to name any problem they could think of. The text box in chapter 2 contains problems that were reported missing from the human security agenda at the time the data were collected.

Understanding Advocacy Elite Preference Formation: Focus Group Research

To explore this question we drew on the experience and insights of forty-three senior officials drawn from organizations central to the human security network.[18] Our goal was to spearhead a discussion about why some issues gain attention within this network of networks, and why others do not; and compare the narratives presented by practitioners to scholarly understandings of these dynamics. Six focus groups were completed by University of Massachusetts–Amherst researchers at Tufts University's Fletcher School of Law and Diplomacy in fall 2009.

Focus groups, as conversational settings, provide an environment in which to examine what ideas, assumptions, or discourses advocates across issue networks hold in common: they are "particularly suited to the study of attitudes and experiences around specific topics" and to ways in which those topics are articulated in social settings.[19] Thus, in addition to substantive information on how advocates explain their issue selection decisions, the transcripts of such sessions provide data on the way in which particular issues are currently conceptualized, constructed, or discussed among practitioners themselves; which issues are conceptually linked to which other issues; and the extent to which advocates can agree that particular "nonissues" lack some factor required for advocacy.[20]

Data Collection, Coding, and Analysis

Two graduate students, Anna Tomaskovic-Devey (now Anna Rapp) and Sirin Duygulu, were hired to assist me with the focus group portion of the project—recruiting, coordinating travel for, and hosting almost fifty human security practitioners from multiple continents at the Fletcher School of International Affairs at Tufts University, and gathering nearly twenty hours of focus group transcripts. Peter Uvin was kind enough to provide facilities space and catering, as well as help from Tufts graduate students for the focus groups themselves.

Participants were recruited based on their positions within organizations identified in both the surveys and the hyperlink analysis. Although all 110 organizations in the network received a letter of invitation and a follow-up phone call, we recruited most aggressively from organizations with the highest centrality scores in the network.[21] This follows from the assumption that organizations at the center of a network have the greatest influence over the network agenda.[22]

We made efforts to recruit from the most senior ranks in each organization, in order to hear from individuals with some influence over each organization's internal agenda. This resulted in the participation of forty-three individuals from thirty-nine organizations, including practitioners from eighteen nations, based in five world regions, with representation from most of the major thematic clusters, organizational types, and geographical region.[23] We also aimed to create a diverse cohort of practitioners in each focus group, combining individuals operating in different thematic fields (human rights, humanitarian affairs, arms control, sustainable development, and conflict prevention) and hailing from different types of organizations (NGOs, international organizations, think tanks, academic institutions, and government agencies).

Each focus group began with a brainstorming session on issues missing from the network agenda. Participants were asked to list as many issues as they could think of that are not getting enough attention from human security specialists. The brainstorming session led into a larger discussion of why certain issues make it onto the advocacy agenda, and others do not. After a coffee break, the final segment of the focus group centered on thought experiments where I presented issues that had not yet (at the time) garnered international attention, drawn from a pool of candidate issues in our database, and the participants were asked to analyze why these issues lack saliency. Specific issues we described included three on which I was conducting case studies (infant male circumcision, collateral damage compensation, autonomous weapons) and also several others (foreign military basing, universal Internet access, forced conscription). At the end of the focus group sessions there was time for a more general discussion and for comments on the research methods.

Although this general format was held constant across all focus groups, minor adjustments to the focus group protocol were made as we went along. We found early on, for example, that the discussion was limited if we encouraged participants to organize their brainstorming sessions around specific thematic areas such as "human rights" or "environmental security" because so many issues are cross-cutting in nature. We also varied the specific "thought experiments" provided to the participants, retaining the ones that led to the liveliest substantive discussions and eliminating those that some participants considered to be "straw men." For example, "universal access to the Internet" was dropped.

Anonymity in the focus groups was protected by assigning each participant a number (some quotations in this book by these individuals are identified by the participant's number, others simply as a "focus group participant"). A student kept track of speaker order while another took notes. A third managed the audio-recording. We ended up with six hundred pages of transcripts from the various sessions. These, like the earlier survey and web data, were coded and analyzed using Atlas.ti 6.0, a qualitative data analysis software package with which multiple individuals can code large amounts of text for certain substantive themes or discursive properties.

With four research assistants, I developed the thematic categories for qualitative analysis. We began by using independent grounded theory review of the set of transcripts to derive a set of general patterns from a reading of the data themselves.[24] We also identified testable propositions from the agenda-setting literature and considered what we would expect to observe in the conversations if those propositions were true. Together, we developed codes both for substantive arguments made by focus group participants about the determinants of the issue agenda (drawn from both grounded theory and deductively based on what the agenda-setting literature would lead us to expect to see), and also for discursive patterns we observed during the conversations (such as "hat-wearing").[25] These analytical categories were applied to each passage of codeable text by at least two and up to four undergraduate student coders through a succession of coding waves in which we aimed to determine which codes could be applied most reliably and which were most subject to interpretation. We considered a codeable passage to be one speaker-statement (that is, each time a speaker took the floor, we would apply as many codes to that passage of transcript text as were applicable). So the total code frequency in plate 5 refers to the total number of times a factor was mentioned in the conversations—that is, it's *salience*—not the total number of speakers mentioning it. Inter-rater reliability for each code was measured using Fleiss' kappa, as before, and each code list was refined at least three times to derive the maximum degree of reliability among the coding team.[26]

This coding scheme, as well as the data being coded, was significantly more complicated than the simple tagging of survey answers or web content for the presence or absence of "issues." In this phase, students were asked to follow very precise rules regarding which portions of text to apply specific codes to.[27] They dealt with a lengthy and sophisticated code list designed to translate hypotheses from the agenda-setting literature into specific observable patterns in the text. The project was broken into pieces to make it easier, with one set of coders working on a cluster of codes regarding "issue attributes," and others looking at "broader context," "network effects," and "actor attributes" (later broken into adopter and entrepreneur attributes).

For example, subcodes under the "Issue Attributes" category included, among others, "emotional appeal," "feasibility/solvability," "linkability," "perpetrator attributes," and "measurability/data/evidence," each designed to identify observable implications of propositions from the agenda-setting literature about attributes of issues said to impact agenda setting. Here's an example of how we translated these propositions into a coding scheme: "Measurability/Data/Evidence" was meant to explore the hypothesis that practitioners react differently to issues amenable to data gathering.[28] This code definition read "use this code if speakers argue that an issue or

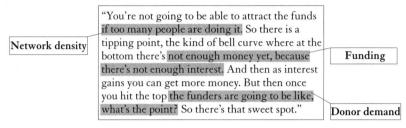

Figure 8. Example of a coded passage.

problem must be amenable to data-gathering and empirical evidence; or that the availability of data or evidence impacts advocacy attention." This code was attached, for example, to the following string of text from the transcripts: "Institutions, organizations, are more likely to give attention to things that can be measured as opposed to other things that are perhaps more important but cannot be measured or we don't have measures for them or to set up measures, it will imply to set up systems that they're not willing to organize."

Because we coded at the paragraph level, multiple codes might be applied to the same passage of text. For example, the passage in Figure 8 received the "network density" code (from the Network Effects cluster); the "funding" code (from the Adopter Attributes cluster), and the "donor demand" code (from the Broader Context cluster).

The students worked in iterated pretests, learning the initial code definitions, attempting to apply them to the raw data independently, examining the (lack of) inter-rater reliability together in a group, modifying the code/the coders' understanding, and recoding to improve the reliability of the codes. Network effects codes were especially challenging. For example, we discovered that coders could not distinguish easily between "issue competition" (the notion that advocacy space is zero sum) and "issue conflicts" (the notion that some issues conflicted politically with others) as these narratives manifested in the transcripts, so these two codes were collapsed.

Despite up to three pretests for each code, some codes were easier to apply than others due to the complexity of the dataset and the coding scheme. We found many concepts that make sense in the abstract to scholars are hard to observe empirically in conversational dynamics. Some codes were fairly straightforward for coders to apply reliably, others were harder; and mismatches mattered mathematically more for codes applied infrequently than for those appearing often. For example, the "entrepreneur credentials" code, meant to capture passages where participants stated that appropriate credentials increased entrepreneurs' credibility, was applied twelve times and reliable at a kappa score of 0.75 percent. The "chance" code—designed to capture statements about the idiosyncrasy of decision making—was applied only twice (and determined by the principal investigator to be valid) but no *two* coders ever applied it in the same place so it had a kappa score of 0.

We achieved an average inter-rater reliability score of 0.47 for the entire dataset of focus group transcripts.[29] Although some investigators will drop out any codes (such as "chance") that could not be applied reliably in order to increase their average inter-rater reliability score, my goal was to identify valid codes with coders' help, and to use kappa scores as an indicator of the presence or absence of intersubjective agreement rather than as a basis for eliminating analytical categories. We also used reliability scores to determine which set of coding would be retained as a baseline (for each code we defaulted to the annotations by the pair of coders with the highest kappa score). I adjudicated remaining disagreements among these pairs of annotations using the Coding Analysis Toolkit to arrive at a single annotated dataset and frequency distribution.[30] Content analysis from these transcripts is drawn on throughout the book, as are specific quotations from focus group participants, whose identities remain anonymous.

The analysis in chapter 3 details the descriptive statistical findings from the resulting aggregate annotations, whose frequencies are visualized in plate 5. For this methods appendix, it is enough to comment on the value added of coding with large teams of undergraduates rather than simply interpreting the data myself—the standard practice in international relations scholarship for dealing with large quantities of interview/focus group or ethnographic data. I found that this approach, at least for the focus group data, had several advantages.

One intellectual advantage was the synergy created by integrating teaching and research. Working with students to examine the observable implications of theory in a coding lab is a uniquely rewarding way to understand one's data, check one's assumptions, and document the dance between theory, data, and interpretation.

Second, particularly because this was the dataset from which I was attempting to extrapolate a "generalizable" argument about agenda setting, it seemed only right that the findings be, if not strictly replicable, then at least as self-evident to as many other individuals as possible. Coding with students is certainly less easy and far more time-consuming than simply interpreting the data oneself; at the same time, since in the end the principal investigator must apply an interpretive lens to resolve discrepancies, and since the coding itself is subject to interpretation by coders, complete validity and reliability is an illusion. What coding allows, however, is a detailed genealogy of the interpretation process, and a quantitative measure of its successes and limitations. It is an effort to render interpretation more systematic, more open to public criticism, and hence more broadly scientific.

Exploring the Dialectic between Entrepreneurs and Gatekeepers: Case Studies

My case studies, of course, would not be subject to the same sort of process as they relied on a more ethnographic approach and made no pretense at replicability or generalization. Rather, here I sought to explore as closely as possible how those findings—the balance between concerns about issue attributes, environmental factors, organizational factors, and network relations—manifested in the historiography of issue emergence around specific social problems. In Jackson's terms, as I understand them, I used a (mostly) critical-realist approach to cases, comparing them not to test hypotheses but to show the "various ways that dispositional properties manifest themselves in the world."[31]

As noted in chapter 1, I chose case studies where a plausible human security argument had already been proposed and formulated by an issue entrepreneur with an organizational platform, but had not yet (at the time of the research) gained salience within the human security network. I then traced the development of these issues throughout some portion of the life of the project, between April 2008 and April 2013. I derived my conclusions from a combination of iterated interviews with stakeholders, participant-observation at focusing events where these issues were pitched to advocacy elites, and by carefully following advocacy discourse around the issues in question as it gradually made inroads in the media and in policy documents.

In each case, I began by gathering oral histories from the entrepreneurs whose ideas and efforts I wanted to study, and then checked back with them at regular intervals over the course of the time that I was studying the circulation of their ideas throughout global policy networks. Initial conversations took place by phone or in person; later conversations sometimes occurred face to face but sometimes took the form of long e-mail correspondences.[32]

The initial task was to establish an ongoing relationship with entrepreneurs conducive to observing their efforts. My inroads and precise relationship with entrepreneurs were different in each case. In the autonomous weapons case, I visited Noel Sharkey at his home near the start of my project, when his own efforts to engage the media and governments were just beginning. In the circumcision case, I interviewed Marilyn Milos and many of her colleagues by phone some thirty years after their initial efforts began. Much of these interviews were more historical in nature, gathering recollections of efforts over the years. In the CIVIC case, NGO staffers contacted me based on my earlier work in civilian protection and agenda setting, and this early set of conversations turned into a dialectical collaboration in which they provided ongoing insights in interviews, personal conversations, and e-mails designed to help me capture the story of their work, in exchange for scholarly insight on norm development strategies.

At the start, I asked all my entrepreneurs a generic set of questions: Tell me about yourself. How did you get involved in advocating for this issue? What is the nature of the problem that concerns you and why should the international community pay attention to it? What is the solution you propose? Who agrees with you? Who do you feel you need to convince? What kind of reaction do you get from them? (As needed and appropriate, I would probe specifically about reactions from the media, NGOs, military, governments, the United Nations, scientists, and the public.) What do you think are the greatest obstacles you face in getting the global community to take this seriously? What are your future plans? Who else should I talk to?

In the course of interviews with entrepreneurs I was able to identify key advocacy elites whom I approached with a different set of interview questions. Tell me about yourself and your work for organization X. How did you get involved in [human rights/humanitarian/disarmament] advocacy? How does your organization decide which [human rights/humanitarian/ disarmament] issues to work on? What issues are now on your agenda? What is percolating within your organization but not yet formally a part of your work? What issues has your organization specifically avoided working on?

Then, if I knew they had already been approached by an entrepreneur, I would ask my respondent to talk to me about the specific case I was working on—either collateral damage compensation, or infant circumcision, or autonomous weapons. They could comment as candidly as they were able about what they thought of the issue, of the entrepreneur, of the framing strategies being used, and the extent to which their organization could or could not get involved and why. Often I went back to the same "gatekeeper" multiple times during a case study to follow up on the campaign in question and gauge how their organizational stance was evolving or shifting and why.

Finally, I also approached individuals in organizations that I knew were logical advocacy targets for issue entrepreneurs, whether or not I expected them to even be aware of a specific entrepreneur or advocacy campaign. Then, I would begin with the same set of general questions but instead of asking my informant to give their opinion of a specific entrepreneur or campaign, I would ask my advocacy elites to "think aloud" about different issues in the abstract—similar to the focus groups, only in a one-on-one confidential setting rather than in front of colleagues.[33]

In each of these interviews I included the relevant case study alongside other "neglected issues" in that issue cluster. For example, for the infant circumcision case, I also asked respondents about water rights, forced conscription, sexual orientation rights; for the autonomous weapons cases, I also asked respondents about pain weapons, depleted uranium, psychotropic weapons, explosive weapons, and so forth. This not only enabled me to see how the type of conversational setting might influence answers and narratives (I expected greater candor in interviews than in focus groups) but it also enabled me to see how the case I was following was perceived to be similar or different from other "neglected" and "nonneglected" issues in the eyes of my informants.

These interviews provided both another set of data I could use on the substance of my specific cases and a basis for checking or substantiating the conclusions I was drawing about generalities from my focus group transcripts. They also helped me understand organizational cultures in the human security network as they influenced agenda setting, and by triangulating the narratives of both various advocacy elites and entrepreneurs

I was able to trace the percolation of new normative ideas through global issue networks.

Finally, a component of the case study research involved what might be described as participant-observation: interacting with activists and stakeholders at specific focusing events where problems were articulated as issues among various audiences. For example, these included side events at a disarmament conference; a meeting between CIVIC staff and NGO representatives in Washington; a workshop on emerging technologies organized by CETMONS; a Genital Integrity symposium in Helsinki; and the NGO conference preceding the launch of the Campaign to Stop Killer Robots.

My approach in these formal settings was more observation than participation. Unlike my earlier project on children of rape, when I involved myself as a consultant on an agenda-setting project to understand the process from within, on this project I situated myself as an observer of events, and a participant only in the socializing around them.[34] I used these movement settings as an opportunity to gather data, to learn from off-the-record interactions that helped me interpret my formal data, and to observe conversations and social dynamics as they unfolded in transnational spaces. But to the largest degree I avoided attempting to influence the direction of the discussion until the study period was over. In no case during field work did I attempt an explicitly participatory approach or involve myself openly in advocating for specific issues.[35] Rather, my access to and rapport with entrepreneurs, counterentrepreneurs, and gatekeepers depended to some degree on a cultivated neutrality about the merit of issues or specific issue frames. Only at the conclusion of each case study did I openly begin to take positions regarding the merit of advocacy claims whose circulation through global civil society I had been documenting.

Hanging Out on the Theory/Policy Divide: A Methodological Stance

That last said, it is certain that my very presence in and around these campaigns, as an observer of advocacy settings, as an interviewer and correspondent, and as an educator and blogger/commentator, constituted participation in this world of global issue construction in some respects no matter how I aimed to minimize it. Consistent with the quantum social theory proposed by Wendt, simply observing politics can affect what is being observed. Mentioning a neglected issue in conversation with an advocacy "gatekeeper" affects their understanding of their menu of options. Asking them to justify inattention to such an issue is a cognitive and communicative exercise with political effects as well as intellectual value. The iterated back and forth of dialogues with entrepreneurs thinking aloud about their strategies constituted a cross-fertilization of ideas and insights about campaign dynamics.

As an educator, I taught about these issues and campaigns in my classes, and some of my students went on to intern at NGOs I canvassed during my field research. The emphasis in my classes is always on the social construction of political claims rather than the moral merit of those claims themselves, but simply teaching about CIVIC's work or that of NOCIRC also constitutes an agenda-setting exercise. One semester, a team of my students produced a strategy paper for CIVIC on branding the Making Amends Campaign.[36] Although the ideas in the paper were my students', and although CIVIC didn't enact many of them, collaboration with informants in my capacity as an educator constituted a two-way transmission belt of ideas.

In addition, I wore a different hat as a blogger and commentator throughout the study period. At Duck of Minerva, Lawyers Guns and Money, and Complex Terrain Lab I wrote a combination of posts combining research, pedagogy, opinions, and analysis of human rights and human security issues, among other things. I was also writing op-eds and analytical pieces for newspapers and Beltway journals, and sometimes I referenced or acknowledged the cases I was working on for my book project or wrote analytical pieces about the relevant humanitarian law issues.

In a 2008 blog post, I ruminated about this dynamic and what it meant for my research on global agenda setting.[37] I concluded, following a point made by Stephen Krasner on an International Studies Association panel, that a different set of guidelines was needed for scholars interfacing with agenda-setting dynamics than for those simply seeking to influence policy debates. Since academics do in factual terms and as a matter of course contribute to the "policy soup" that John Kingdon describes, the best researchers of that soup can do is to acknowledge ways in which that occurs, and be transparent about the ways in which they minimize its undue effects on their research design.[38]

So how did I accept the inevitability of my small role in barking softly about these neglected issues while preventing my "scientific" project from bleeding into partisan advocacy? How did I leverage this "participation" in the circulation of global ideas around the edges with my role as a neutral observer of those processes?[39] I handled this dilemma by setting very clear boundaries with myself and with my informants during the course of my fieldwork. I was open about my sympathy for entrepreneurs' efforts, but made it clear that I could see both sides of any argument about the merit and framing of issues, and that my book would be a work of social science, not an advocacy treatise. I willingly shared explanatory insights I had as a social scientist with my informants, but I kept my political opinions to myself. I rarely blogged openly about the issues I was studying until the fieldwork was done, and when I did I limited myself to describing the work and the political dynamics of agenda setting, rather than endorsing campaigns or advocacy strategies themselves. And I refused requests from entrepreneurs to use my role as an educator, blogger, or public intellectual to openly advocate for them or against their opponents—I declined, for example, to allow entrepreneurs to guest post at the Duck of Minerva in reply to their detractors, or to write advocacy pieces for intactivist newsletters.[40]

At the same time, I did feel a moral responsibility to give something back to these activists who had shared so much of their time and trust with me. One way that I did so was by sharing my research findings in a publicly accessible format. In addition to publishing this book and various scholarly offshoots in journals and edited volumes, I worked with several graduate students to produce a sleek, colorful write-up of the focus group results, which was sent to all the focus group participants and published on the World Wide Web.[41] And at the conclusion of my case study fieldwork, I covered the campaigns on my academic blog or constructed applied projects helpful to campaigners. In support of the Making Amends Campaign, I began to write more openly at the conclusion of fieldwork about the rise of collateral damage as a proportion of all civilian war casualties, the value of filling that legal gap for collateral damage victims, and CIVIC's efforts as a leader in these areas.[42] For the genital integrity movement "giving back" involved constructing and collecting a web survey of the movement that helped them understand movement demographics and respond to some of their critics.[43] For killer robot campaigners, this meant consulting with disarmament NGOs about norm-building dynamics, conducting a

U.S. public opinion poll that turned out to confirm an important claim in their early rhetoric, and writing a series of blog posts using social science to address the claims of some of their opponents.[44]

These efforts are quite distinct from what I was willing to do publicly while conducting fieldwork. Though I blogged and even published scholarly articles about autonomous weapons earlier, it was usually through a detached analytical frame describing various points of debate, rather than taking sides in the discussion.[45] After the book project, I took much clearer positions. Even so, I continued to intervene primarily as a "Weberian activist"—a social scientist whose values may guide where to invest consulting energy, and whose work as a public intellectual may include an honesty about those values, but whose analytical arguments must remain in the realm of and based on facts, and whose policy interventions must primarily include educating stakeholders and the public about the relevant empirical relationships underlying pressing policy decisions and global processes. In that sense, I agree with Jackson and Kaufman about the appropriate stance for public intellectuals, even as I agree with Robert Keohane that we have a responsibility to ask questions and do research "that might conceivably matter in the real world."[46]

Where does this leave us in terms of an understanding of the truth claims in this book and the method(ologie)s by which I arrived at them? Patrick Jackson suggests four ideal types of research methodology in international relations and proposes a pluralist acceptance of all four as scientific. Scientific approaches differ, writes Jackson, based on how they view the relationship of the researcher to her subject matter, and what kind of knowledge it is possible to access. From these two axes Jackson derives four sets of analytical positions (see figure 9).[47]

The structure of this inquiry into global issue networks suggests that rather than situating oneself in these kinds of boxes, methodological pluralism can involve crafting specific configurations of those four methodologies in ways tailored to specific projects. Not only might different researchers position themselves differently within this type of grid, but the same researcher might construct different projects differently depending on the demands of social inquiry itself. My first book on gender and humanitarian action was probably firmly located between the neopositivist and critical-realist boxes. My second book on children born of war was a single case involving a participatory methodology, probably located between analyticism and reflectivism. On this project, I would imagine

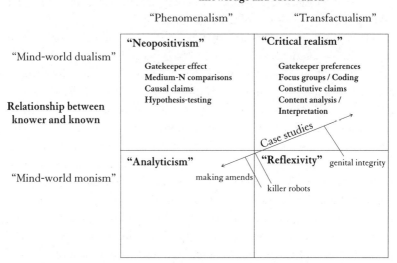

Figure 9. Pluralist method(ologies)s in *Lost Causes.*

a much more complicated relationship between my research design and these big questions of how the knower "hooks up" to the world.

If I were to describe my methods and methodological approach in a way consistent with Jackson's typology, I would place them not in a single box but in different boxes depending on the specific phase of research (see figure 9); in many ways the project involved hanging out uncomfortably at intersections. My argument about the "gatekeeper" effect was derived using neopositivist medium-N case comparisons using data constructed at a high level of abstraction, solely from a desk review, with minimal direct hookup to the social world under observation, in the service of exploring falsifiable causal claims.[48] However, my exploration of elite preferences through focus groups is constitutive analysis that I associate with middle road constructivism and which Jackson characterizes as "critical realism."[49] That is, it is still conducted as systematically as possible, with a commitment to the empirical study of social facts in an effort to establish explanatory relationships. But the type of facts under study are not necessarily brute observables such as "treaties" but rather facts whose existence must be detected or inferred through narratives or behaviors, such as "preferences" or "norms" or "identities." And the types of explanations are better described as "causal/constitutive complexes," accounting for the complex interaction of various factors in specific contexts, rather than as X > Y statements.

My case studies also included elements of critical realism more than neopositivism. Comparisons among and within the cases were leveraged to illustrate (rather than test) the general argument but more specifically to highlight the distinctive configurations within which these general tendencies about networks manifest in combination with other key factors affecting agenda setting. But the cases also bleed somewhat into an analyticist approach in their distinctiveness as individuated accounts of agenda vetting and agenda setting in action: each story is as much a genealogy of a specific campaign as it is an effort to illustrate a broader argument about campaigns in general.

And finally, though I do not claim to have adopted a reflexivist stance in this project, because my single case studies (unlike the earlier medium-N comparison) relied on methods in which I interfaced with and around the social relations under study, an honest account could not help but at least draw on insights of the reflexivist school. This means at minimum acknowledging and noting the partiality of truth claims here as mediated through a researcher who also occupies a specific structural location in these wider networks of meaning. I chose to use a methodology that notes and corrects for this as much as possible rather than one where dwelling on it is central to the project. But acknowledging the fuzzy boundaries between knower and known is an imperative that I at minimum remained conscious of throughout my fieldwork. And in studying the circulation of ideas through globalized spaces, "the field" is anywhere that ideas are touched and bumped—including when scholars think and write and blog and speak about them. So I encourage students of international politics to adopt this stance as well—acknowledging and controlling for if not embracing their situatedness in the worlds we study, regardless of methodological approach—for we too are networked beings, agents as well as travelers through these webs of meanings.

Notes

Preface

1. Such children face a variety of adverse social circumstances in war's aftermath, including infanticide, discrimination, stigma, statelessness, and denial of the means to track their birth fathers or establish their biological identities. See Grieg 2001.

2. Field notes, Cologne, Germany, December 2006. His remarks echoed the position of other leading child rights organizations, none of which deal explicitly with stigma against children born as a result of militarized sex in conflict zones. See Carpenter 2010b.

3. Carpenter 2006.

1. Agenda Vetting and Agenda Setting in Global Governance

1. Carpenter 2011b.

2. Kellenberger 2011.

3. Human Rights Watch 2012a.

4. Finnemore 1996; Finnemore and Sikkink 1998.

5. By this I mean "policymaking activities that produced coordinated action in the absence of global government." See Avant, Finnemore, and Sell 2010, 14.

6. Schmitz, 2006.

7. Thompson 2002.

8. Carpenter 2007b.

9. Hubert 2000.

10. Forman and Segaar 2006

11. Schiffman and Smith 2007.

12. For example, in UN circles and among the foreign policy establishment of once-norm leaders such as Canada, the term has all but disappeared since the mid-2000s. See Martin and Owen 2010.

13. Paris 2001; Carpenter et al. 2014.

14. I use the term "human security network" to describe the empirically measurable relational ties between these organizations, and not to refer to the Human Security Network as such (a former group of like-minded states). On the history and fate of the Human Security Network, see Martin and Owen 2010. On the wider meaning of "human security," see Paris 2001.

15. Murdie and Davis 2012.

16. It may therefore be most appropriate to think of this as a "global policy network" encompassing a variety of distinct though interlinked "issue networks."

17. Keck and Sikkink 1998; Joachim 2007; Khagram, Riker, and Sikkink 2002.

18. For example, in their groundbreaking study on transnational advocacy networks, Keck and Sikkink (1998) emphasized the importance of *issue attributes* in explaining the success of specific campaigns, an argument that might also be applicable to the construction of particular problems as issues in the first place. Price (1998) suggests that issues succeed depending on whether advocates can link a new set of intersubjective understandings to preexisting applicable moral standards. According to a third line of thinking, international advocacy is best pictured as a *marketplace* for short-term contracts (Cooley and Ron 2002), in which the public visibility of a problem generates pressure to appear to be addressing it (Bob 2005), and in which savvy advocates gravitate toward "hot" issues likely to draw donor funding and good media coverage for their organizations (Dale 1996). The empirical research from which these hypotheses were derived consists largely of inductive case studies, but it has rarely been tested across many cases or cases of norm failure.

19. See also Checkel 2012.

20. Joachim 2007.

21. Bob 2005.

22. The concept of an "issue" is ill-defined and contested within the literature on agenda setting, and ill-defined in the transnational advocacy networks literature. For the purposes of this project, an issue is "an identifiable problem or category of concern on an official agenda." It is somewhat broader than definitions requiring a problem to be linked to a policy solution, and narrower than definitions that include any problem identified by anyone, regardless of their connection to some sort of official platform. It also includes both thematic problems ("human trafficking") and categories of concerns, including countries ("Darfur") and populations ("internally displaced persons"). This roughly corresponds to the way in which advocacy organizations themselves define issues on their web pages.

23. Transnational advocacy networks are composed of a variety of nongovernmental organizations, international organizations, governments, and myriad individuals located within these bureaucracies and other levers of symbolic power in world affairs, including academia and the media.

24. Keck and Sikkink 1998.

25. Price 2003.

26. This is widely recognized, for example, within the agenda-setting literature on domestic U.S. politics (e.g., Kingdon 1994), and the sociology literature on the construction of social problems (e.g., Spector and Kituse 1977; Hilgartner and Bosk 1988).

27. I am grateful to Michael Goodhart for this analytical insight.

28. Finnemore 1996.

29. Keck and Sikkink 1998, 19.

30. I thank Betcy Jose-Thota, Ben Rubin, and Rebecca Wall for discussions that helped to clarify this distinction for me.

31. Lord 2009.

32. Shiffman 2009.

33. Rapp and Carpenter 2012.

34. To some extent this example proves the point about the importance of international norms, however: CIVIC changed its strategy precisely because states would not construe this type of case-by-case policy change as a precedent and therefore could not be counted on to do the same in the future.

35. Early bans on exploding and flattening bullets, for example, were promoted not by transnational norm entrepreneurs but by the Russian government, whose military establishment

opposed the use of such inhumane weapons but could ill afford to ban their production in the absence of assurances from neighboring governments.

36. Inal 2013.

37. Hubert 2007.

38. I follow Avant, Finnemore, and Sell (2010, 2) in defining governors as "authorities who exercise power across borders for the purposes of affecting policy."

39. Barnett and Duvall 2005.

40. Barnett and Finnemore 2004.

41. Lake and Wong 2009, 2.

42. Bob 2005, 6.

43. Barnett and Finnemore 2004; Holzscheiter 2005; Lipschutz 2005.

44. For example, as Bob (2005) notes in appendix 1 of his book, organizations as diverse as Human Rights Watch, the Sierra Club, and the Worker's Rights Consortium have internal documents outlining the criteria they use in sifting among the various requests they receive from civil society for assistance.

45. Barnett and Duvall 2005, 21.

46. This does not necessarily ensure that new norms will be implemented or that governance will be effective, as Karen Mundy's analysis of the Education for All campaign demonstrates (2010). However, had there been no consensus among organizations associated with child rights and education, such as UNICEF (United Nations Children's Emergency Fund) and UNESCO (the United Nations Educational, Scientific and Cultural Organization), that education for children was a human right, implementation of such a right would have been impossible: the adoption of education as an issue for these organizations provided a permissive context in which a discussion of governance was made possible.

47. Holzscheiter 2005, 731.

48. Bachrach and Baratz 1963, 641, 632.

49. Wendt and Duvall 2008.

50. Avant, Finnemore, and Sell 2008, 11.

51. Thompson 20025.

52. Bob 2009.

53. Price 1998.

54. I am grateful to Erin Baines for this insight.

55. For example, the Campaign for Innocent Victims in Conflict was once encouraged to emphasize women and children as victims, which would draw donor attention but constitute a significant narrowing of their vision. So far the organization has refused. This principled stand has affected CIVIC's ability to spread its message.

56. My emphasis on a Canadian conception of human security that focuses on humanitarian issues and bodily integrity rights stems largely from the logistical feasibility of gathering data on those issues, given my preexisting research in these areas and the ease of making contacts within organizations working on those issues. It should not be interpreted as a defense of what is an admittedly limited view of "human security"—I could have chosen to cast a much wider net to examine myriad environmental and economic security issues as well, but this would have increased the complexity and methodological difficulty of completing the research.

57. Anonymity in the focus groups was protected by assigning each participant a number. Some quotations in this book by these individuals are identified by the participant's number, others simply as "focus group participant." All unattributed quotations in this book are by focus group participants.

58. Interviewees are quoted by name only if they have signed a release form permitting this; they also had the opportunity to stipulate conditions. Respondents who were quoted by name were permitted to review and approve, edit, or veto quotes. Interviewees wishing to remain anonymous are identified by a number.

59. As Wendt (2006) describes, this "measurement problem" is consistent with a quantum view of the study of social processes.

60. Indeed, I specifically avoided issues where I felt *strongly* in favor of a specific policy position. This both reduced the likelihood of slipping into action research and enabled dispassionate conversations both with proponents and dismissers of new ideas.

61. For example, I considered but declined to study the movement for a global right to bear arms. Even though I think this claim may have merit from a rights-based perspective, and while it certainly constitutes a conceptually useful case of human rights agenda denial, it was not clear to me whether the goals of gun advocates, if achieved, would contribute to the general security of human beings. Although gun advocates make an important claim that the right to self-defense can prevent genocides and state-perpetrated atrocity, I know of no study that has weighed the gains for human security against the well-documented threats posed by the presence of light arms among civilian populations, so I remain agnostic on this point.

62. For example, economic and social rights are a major concern of local actors in the developing world, but they are not covered at length in this study.

2. Networks, Centrality, and Global Issue Creation

1. On norm entrepreneurs, see Finnemore 1996; on gatekeepers, see Bob 2005 and Mertus 2009. On issue attributes, see Keck and Sikkink 1998 and Carpenter 2005. On political opportunity structures, see Burgerman 2001, Joachim 2007, and Davies 2007.

2. Keck and Sikkink 1998, 2, 8.

3. Hertel 2006; Bob 2010.

4. Cooley and Ron 2002; Sell and Prakash 2004.

5. As Holton has observed, this is a problem with literature on global networks generally, which "has seldom set out to measure network features; rather to provide in-depth understanding from a single case or small number of cases." See Holton 2008, 49.

6. Hafner-Burton, Kahler, and Montgomery 2009, 561.

7. Ibid., 562. In social network theory, a link can be anything: an interaction, a joint membership, a hyperlink, or a citation, to give a few examples. The definition of a "node" too, can be used to characterize many different types of "social sites." See Nexon 2009.

8. Ingram, Robinson, and Busch 2005; Hafner-Burton and Montgomery 2006; Kahler 2009, 103.

9. For a clearer demarcation of these types, see Murdie and Davis 2012. Using the concept of "global public policy networks," Reinicke and Deng (2000, 28) argue that the activities of such networks are best understood in terms of the policy cycle: agenda setting, negotiation, implementation, and policy reformulation.

10. Rogers and Ben-David 2008.

11. See "Small Glossary of Terms" at issuenetwork.org, the workshop website of govcom.org, University of Amsterdam, http://www.issuenetwork.org/node.php?id = 21#13; and Richard Rogers 2012. See also Castells 2011.

12. Nexon 2009, 25; Hafner-Burton, Kahler, and Montgomery 2009, 562.

13. Holton 2008, 80.

14. Keck and Sikkink began this trend when they wrote that although advocacy networks can include many types of organizations, "NGOs play a central role in all advocacy networks" (1998, 9). See also Joachim 2007. For a critique of this understanding of NGOs, see DeMars 2005.

15. Joachim, 2007.

16. Stone 2001. For example, the process by which the Guiding Principles on Internal Displacement took place in UN circles was spearheaded by the Brookings Institution. See Cohen 2006.

17. Donors: Berkovitch and Gordon 2008; academic experts: Haas 1992, Adler 1992; media organizations: Ron, Ramos, and Rodgers 2005; powerful individuals: Huliaras and Tzifakis 2010; government agencies: Slaughter 2004; private firms: Haufler 2010.

18. I follow Rogers and Ben-David (2008) in defining an "issue" as a "claim that has been constructed or 'formatted' in such a way as to circulate and attract actors to network around it, turning 'it' into a collective cause of concern." This is distinct from "problem construction," which involves articulating a social condition as a political concern. Activists may name problems without causing them to emerge as issues, as issue emergence has a more intersubjective component: entrepreneurs must format them into frames that appeal to other actors before the issues "emerge" in political space.

19. Schrad 2010.

20. This analysis was rendered using Issuecrawler, a co-link analysis tool developed by gov-com.org. The visualization shows hyperlinking practices between organizational websites that appear at the top of a Google search for "human security" and demonstrates the centrality of certain organizations online. Although this map represents linking practices on the web rather than physical ties between organizations, similar findings were obtained by surveying professionals associated with the human security network for "organizations that come to mind when you think about human security." For more on this method, see the appendix.

21. In particular: United Nations Development Program (UNDP), United Nations High Commissioner for Refugees (UNHCR), United Nations High Commissioner for Human Rights (UNHCHR), the UN Office for the Coordination of Humanitarian Affairs (OCHA), the World Health Organization (WHO), and the UN Children's Emergency Fund (UNICEF).

22. The former include Canada and Japan; an example of the latter is the United Kingdom. The so-called Human Security Network, a coalition of like-minded governments, is actually a single hub within the broader advocacy network around human security. See Brysk 2009.

23. These include the Human Security Report Project at Simon Fraser University, the Liu Institute at the University of British Columbia, and the Institute for Human Security at the Fletcher School of Tufts University.

24. The most prominent NGOs in the human security area are Human Rights Watch, the International Crisis Group, and the International Committee of the Red Cross.

25. This population of organizations is confirmed by surveying individuals associated with the "human security network" about the "organizations that come to mind when you think of human security."

26. White 1992.

27. Riles 2001.

28. In fact, very little of the literature on advocacy networks does this, although the literature on terrorist networks does so. See Williams 2011.

29. Wendt 1992; Maoz 2001.

30. Nexon 2009, 52–61.

31. Wong 2012.

32. Mathiason 2007.

33. Such networks are said to follow a "power law," in which the vast majority of network activity engages a very few nodes within the network. Information flows in such networks function less like road systems and more like airlines, where the route between any two small cities generally depends on passing through a major hub; or like the World Wide Web, where hubs such as Google and Yahoo are necessary to direct attention to the myriad yet largely invisible "nodes" (websites) online. See Barabasi 2002, 67.

34. Freeman 1979.

35. Keck and Sikkink 1998, 29.

36. Bob 2009a, 6

37. Duygulu and Carpenter 2013; Busby 2010.

38. See Duygulu and Carpenter 2013.

39. In network theory, a link can be anything: an interaction, a joint membership, a hyperlink, or a citation. In the human security network, I measured network centrality through hyperlinks and through citations in survey data. The organizations receiving the most hyperlinks on their websites from the members of the network, and those most often mentioned when survey respondents were asked to list "organizations that come to mind when you think of human security," correspond to the same central players in the human security network.

40. Hafner-Burton, Kahler, and Montgomery 2009, 19.

41. Murdie 2013.

42. Hafner-Burton, Kahler, and Montgomery 2009, 571–72. For example, Dan Nexon's work on empires suggests that much of their power was derived by positioning themselves as exclusive access points between nodes on the periphery.

43. Goddard 2009.

44. Even among NGOs that earn consultative status there is a hierarchy that affects such matters as the word limit for statements that may be submitted to government delegates at UN conferences. The most privileged status is reserved for the older and larger NGOs. See Merry 2006, 53.

45. Murdie 2013.

46. Finnemore 1996.

47. Carpenter 2011b.

48. Murdie and Davis 2012, 198; Mische 2003.

49. Respondent #25, personal interview, Washington, DC, May 2010.

50. Nexon 2009, 49.

51. Bob 2010, 6.

52. Wong 2012.

53. As Wong writes, "First-movers in building the network often have an easier time constructing incentives in their favor, so that it is easier to control what principles become norms." Wong 2012, 19.

54. A survey of subscribers to two "Women, Peace and Security" Listservs in 2007 found that WILPF was the NGO most often mentioned when respondents were asked to list "organizations that come to mind when you think of 'women, peace and security.'" See Carpenter and Jose 2012.

55. Snyder 2003.

56. Global Witness launched its original report on the problem in 1998, and began pitching it to the news media, industry, and governments as early as 1999, but only after Amnesty International picked up the issue and launched its media campaign in 2000 did the issue proliferate into a large-scale transnational campaign in 2001. Grant and Taylor 2004.

57. Indeed, Global Witness's minimal attention to coltan (a rare earth ore used in electronic devices and mined in conflict zones) as an analogous problem may explain the lack of a campaign or strong governance in this area, alluded to by Haufler 2010.

58. Lake and Wong 2009.

59. Joachim 2007, 37.

60. Merry 2006, 54.

61. For example, more central organizations are likelier to receive opportunities for professional experience, which then confers additional recognition and connections. But these experiences also lead to skill sets and attributes requisite for effective future multilateral diplomacy, skill sets that peripheral organizations may not develop as easily.

62. Wendy Wong (2012) has demonstrated how this privileged position allowed Amnesty International to control international understandings of human rights for much of the second half of the twentieth century.

63. Respondent #38, phone interview, May 2008.

64. Carpenter and Jose 2012.

65. When asked to brainstorm, the same professionals can easily identify a long list of "neglected" issues seldom discussed by human security gatekeepers. For example: "gender imbalances in births because of gender bias in fetus selection, or what practitioners refer to as the 'proliferation of small men' problem"; "complicity of Western consumer choices on a broad scale...much more than a fair trade issue"; "safe passage for destabilized refugee populations traveling to and from conflict zones"; "liberation of hostages, famous or not"; "people don't see the plight of the poor, the mentally ill, the homeless in the U.S. and other rich countries"; "countries like Canada where there are absolutely no restrictions on abortion leading to the abuse/killing of children in the womb right up until the moment of their birth. If that isn't a human security problem, then I don't know what is!" For a complete list of "neglected" issues culled from this survey, see table 1. As chapter 3 shows, the contagion effect of issue adoption or nonadoption by hubs is an important reason given for this variation.

66. Barnett and Duvall 2005.

67. It can also vary by the life cycle of an issue and the goal of the norm entrepreneur. Carpenter 2010a.

68. Indeed, my interviews within the human security network suggest that staff within human security "hubs" are likelier to see themselves as entrepreneurs in a relatively weak position relative to their own targets of influence (usually states) than as powerful actors in a position to block ideas from below, foregrounding the importance of network power as relational. Personal interviews, New York and Washington, DC, 2008–09.

69. Goddard 2009.

70. Bob uses this term to refer to middle power NGOs or individuals who aid new organizations in fitting their cause to the interests of network gatekeepers. Bob 2005, 19.

3. A Network Theory of Advocacy "Gatekeeper" Decision Making

1. Keck and Sikkink 1998; Carpenter 2005.

2. Finnemore and Sikkink 1998.

3. Carpenter 2010b.

4. Stone (2006, 130) suggests that causal stories must describe the problem as "amenable to human action" rather than being "mere accidents or fate." See also Keck and Sikkink 1998, 27.

5. Carpenter 2007a.

6. Sometimes entrepreneurs come from within gatekeeper organizations (Oestreich 2007). However, actors outside established networks such as prominent individuals (Finnemore 1996), small NGOs (Keck and Sikkink 1998), states (Hubert 2007), celebrities (Huliaras and Tzifakis 2010), epistemic communities (Haas 1992; Parson 2003) or think tanks (Stone 2001) can also play this role.

7. Busby 2010, 169.

8. Bob 2005, 28.

9. Busby 2010, 34.

10. See Prakash and Gugerty 2010.

11. Bloodgood 2011.

12. Bob 2005, 2009a.

13. Cooley and Ron 2002, 6.

14. Joachim 2007, 23.

15. This concept, originating in the social movement literature, is increasingly applied to transnational advocacy networks. See Tarrow 2005.

16. Joachim 2007; Shawki 2010.

17. Hertel 2006; Bob 2012.

18. Hadden 2008.

19. Carpenter 2005, 2010a.

20. This chapter draws on findings detailed in Carpenter, Duygulu, Montgomery, and Rapp 2014.

21. We considered incoming hyperlinks as well as survey citations to be indicators of in-degree centrality and we averaged organizations' rankings from these two measures to arrive at their overall centrality score.

22. These are drawn from a combination of grounded theory and the earlier survey data. The moderator provided brief descriptions of issues for which individuals or small organizations are attempting to gain global attention. Participants were asked to discuss reasons why advocacy might not have been successful as of yet, whether or not it was likely to ever be successful, and whether or not they thought it *should* succeed.

23. See appendix for a discussion of coding methods.

24. Some of these factors are related to chance: participants suggested that the actual geographical location of the entrepreneur matters; it is easier to advocate for an international issue in Geneva than it is in Auckland, New Zealand.

25. Another example is the embrace of the Jubilee 2000 campaign by former foreign-aid skeptic Jesse Helms, as documented in Busby 2010.

26. Carpenter 2010a.

27. One participant said: "If there are bad people who are to blame for something by their individual behavior and you can point to the bastards and suggest that they ought to stop being such bad people, then your chances are dramatically higher."

28. This echoes Joachim's claims that "testimonial knowledge" must be combined with "scientific knowledge." The campaign against domestic violence in the European Union and the use of detailed aggregate statistics in the child soldiers campaign provide examples of such a use of information. On violence against women, see Joachim 2007 and Keck and Sikkink 1998. On child soldiers, see Heckel 2005 and Rapp and Carpenter 2012. Similarly, key actors did not sign on to the ozone campaign until scientists provided evidence proving the existence of an ozone hole: see Haas 1992; Parson 2003.

29. Participants stressed the importance of credible data on problems as an important element in the recipe for agenda-setting success.

30. The sudden end of the Cold War, for instance, is frequently said to have opened up the political space for various issues ranging from women's rights to genocide prevention to find a place on the political agenda; likewise, the global war on terror narrowed the international community's focus. Joachim 2007.

31. Adler 1991, 55

32. Kingdon 1984, 177. See Inal 2013 on activists' role in constructing trigger events as "normative shocks."

33. On these dynamics, see Berkovitch and Gordon 2008 and Reinmann 2006. We heard both references to donors as actors and references to the facilitating/inhibiting effect of the general state of the economy.

34. Hubert 2007.

35. It was mentioned that academics and experts can lend both credibility to an issue and empirical evidence that helps to define the extent and severity of the problem. On experts and agenda setting, see Haas 1992. On celebrities and agenda setting, see Drezner 2007; Huliaras and Tzifakis 2010; Tsakali, Frangonikolopoulos, and Huliaras 2011.

36. The same was true of some actor effects: practitioners discussed the characteristics of entrepreneurs in the abstract but stressed them less in evaluating candidate issues (although the importance of adopter organizational interests remained constant).

37. It is likely that when asked about issue neglect in the abstract, practitioners think about issues they *want* to see on the agenda, and so place the blame for their absence on external factors.

However, in the thought experiments section many of the practitioners were actually skeptical about the merit of the issues in question, and therefore explained their exclusion from the network agenda by downplaying the broader context. I am grateful to Andrew Cockrell for this insight. On attribution theory generally, see Pettigrew 1979; on attribution theory as applied to international relations, see Mercer 1996.

38. Focus group participant.

39. Mische 2003.

40. Carpenter 2011a.

41. An issue can also end up "belonging" to a particular venue as a result of norm entrepreneurs' preferences, foreclosing alternative frames later on. Praelle 2003.

42. Goddard 2009.

43. Jones and Baumgartner 2005; Carpenter 2010b.

44. This relates to a distinction between "perspective diversity" and "identity diversity" described by Borrie and Thornton 2008.

45. For example, how closely tied the entrepreneur is to the claimant community on whose behalf they are advocating matters to elites in constructing "credibility." See Carpenter 2009.

46. Oestreich 2007.

4. "You Harm, You Help"

1. Slim 2010; Grimsley and Rogers 2008.

2. Chuter 2003.

3. Byers 2005; Gross 2010.

4. Carpenter 2010c.

5. Downes 2009; Hicks et al. 2011.

6. Thomas 2002; Kahl 2007.

7. Analysts at the New America Foundation published a dataset of casualty reports in 2009 that shows that at least one-third of those killed in "surgical" drone strikes in Pakistan's Federally Administered Tribal Areas are civilians. See Bergen and Tiedeman 2009.

8. Herrold 2009.

9. Campaign for Innocent Victims in War website, http://www.civicworldwide.org/about-us/our-history. It should be noted that the Making Amends Campaign is only one component of CIVIC's work, which includes documenting civilian harm, policy advocacy, and military training.

10. Golzar Kheiltash, phone interview, February 17, 2012.

11. Chaulia 2011.

12. Cooley and Ron 2002.

13. Weiss and Collins 2000.

14. Minear and Smillie 2004.

15. Yael Ronen provides a detailed overview about how the concept of liability for incidental harms fits conceptually into existing legal regimes. See Ronen 2008.

16. Holewinski 2012.

17. In other words, CIVIC's strategy was to reconstitute the nature of network ties between civilians, warring parties, and humanitarian organizations. Under the conventional humanitarian system, Government A might send Military A to carry out operations causing civilian harm in the territory of Government B. Government A might simultaneously provide funding to UN agencies and humanitarian organizations to carry out independent, impartial, and neutral civilian relief activities in the territory of Government B, though there is no obligation under international law for it to do so. What CIVIC proposed was that Government A feel socially obligated to have Military A directly make amends to civilians in the territory of Government B, irrespective of and in addition to the support Government A might also provide to the civilian humanitarian sector.

18. Walzer 2006.

19. Personal interview, January 2009.

20. According to Abrahamson, "On February 13, Marla led a group of these victims in a demonstration outside the US Embassy. . . . Marla demanded that the United States create a twenty-million dollar fund to compensate civilian war victims. . . . She had recruited much of Kabul's international press corps to attend the show. [One] later said that was the moment when Marla's real fame began." Abrahamson 2006, 105–6. By April 2002, Ruzicka was referred to by *Newsweek* as "arguably the best-known foreign figure in Kabul." Abrahamson 2006, 118.

21. Abrahamson 2006, 135.

22. Jennifer Abrahamson, who wrote Ruzicka's biography, describes in her book the fan-like attitude of those in the field who introduced her to Ruzicka: "My colleagues in Islamabad told me to keep an eye out for a Californian woman called Marla with 'wild blond hair. . . .' I pressed further. Did she have a last name? Smiling secretively, they simply assured me that she was a good person to talk to" (Abramson, 2006, 6–7).

23. Peter Bergen later described what he called "the Marla treatment": "Phase one: 'Everyone says you're great!' Phase two: 'You're great. In fact, you're the most amazing person on this Earth.' Phase three: 'Let me tell you about my work.' Phase four: 'How can you help?'" Quoted in Abrahamson 2006, 252.

24. Abrahamson 2006, 176.

25. See *Portraits of Grief*, http://peacefultomorrows.org/downloads/apogreport.pdf.

26. According to interviews with those familiar with the transition, the original board included practitioners with field experience but no one with experience running an NGO.

27. Heather Hamilton, personal interview, May 2009.

28. Sarah Holewinski, personal interview, April 2008.

29. For example, Pederson recruited Marc Garlasco, Human Rights Watch's arms expert.

30. A significant portion of CIVIC's staff time remained focused on traveling to war zones to collect video interviews with civilians, document civilian harms, and liaise with generals and lawyers on both sides of conflicts about the concept of amends.

31. The site read: "[We] believe that no warring party should walk away from the harm it has caused ordinary people caught up in fighting, no matter how unintentional." See http://www.civicworldwide.org/index.php?option = com_content&task = view&id = 162&Itemid = 99.

32. CIVIC web archive, on file with author.

33. Holewinski 2008. When I first spoke with Holewinski that year, she had just returned from a trip to Europe enthused by the Netherlands' success in convincing NATO countries to establish a Post-Operations Humanitarian Relief Fund. The U.S. condolence payment program had not until then been replicated by other International Security Assistance Force countries, leaving the amends civilians could expect in Afghanistan contingent on which troops happened to shoot them: those countries with condolence programs would give payments, but some didn't have any. "That's morally wrong," Holewinski said. "Compensation should be given uniformly; everyone deserves some sort of recognition and aid. So I said, 'You guys have to get on board with this, the U.S. does it, you can do it.' The NATO Secretary General Chief of Staff has been a great supporter of this and now we're pitching it to every single NATO country."

34. See Tracy 2007. Similarly, in summer of that year CIVIC staff spent weeks in Israel and Lebanon documenting harms to civilians in the 2006 war.

35. Sarah Holewinski, personal interview, February 2008.

36. Holewinski described the many quandaries stakeholders perceived in implementing the new standard: "Should you compensate someone who's a civilian by day but planted an IED [improvised explosive device] at night if they are harmed during the daytime? Well, were they a civilian during the time they were engaging in hostilities?" Personal interview, April 2008.

37. Marla Keenan, personal interview, January 2009.

38. Byers 1999.

39. Sarah Holewinski, e-mail correspondence, March 2012.

40. Georgia established a compensation program for civilians harmed in the 2008 August War after lobbying by CIVIC; Pakistan established a program to compensate civilians harmed in the Federally Administered Tribal Areas; numerous North Atlantic Treaty Organization (NATO) countries established programs as well. Yet few admitted this was a moral requirement; most saw it as a pragmatic move at their own discretion.

41. Even so, CIVIC operated on a shoestring.

42. Bob 2009a.

43. Jessi Schimmel, personal interview, September 2008. Similarly, another CIVIC staff person told me in 2012: "What we want most from big organizations, existing norm entrepreneurs like Human Rights Watch, is regular and forceful validation. Norms are like neural connections: the more you use them, the stronger they become. So an organization like HRW, who other people pay attention to, weighing in and calling on someone to make amends is actually a really big deal. It not only builds momentum among advocates, it helps reinforce the norm itself."

44. Respondent #25, personal interview, May 2010.

45. Respondent #19, personal interview, April 2009.

46. In focus groups, participants brought up the difficulty in distinguishing unintentional harms due to combat operations from secondary victimization: "For every person that gets killed on the battlefield, ten, twenty, fifty people die of disease and malnutrition. You cannot compensate those people because people also die of diarrheal disease, respiratory infections, in peacetime. So you can say there's been a 20 percent increase in deaths, but you can never say which are the ones that would have died or wouldn't have died otherwise."

47. Joachim 2007, 181–82. According to Holewinski, CIVIC's job was harder precisely because of the lack of statistical measurability: "The need for amends is clear in any given conflict, but difficult to measure with precision. . . . Successful civil society initiatives in the past have generally addressed problems that feel more tangible and definable in quantitative terms." Holewinski 2012, 327.

48. Focus group participant, December 2009.

49. Focus group participant, December 2009.

50. Respondent #22, phone interview, October 2009.

51. Price 1998.

52. Ron, Ramos, and Rodgers 2005.

53. Brett 2004; see also Oestreich 2004.

54. Orchard 2010.

55. Sarah Holewinski, personal interview, February 2008. The importance of existing network ties in early coalition building as a signal of credibility and do-ability is suggested by this quote from one early supporter: "We were attracted to it initially because we had worked with CIVIC, worked with some of the other groups involved in the campaign, so it wasn't that far of an extension from work that was already done, relationships that were already developed." Respondent #24, personal interview, June 2009.

56. Carpenter 2010b, 168–69.

57. Respondent #18, personal interview, September 2009.

58. Respondent #67, personal interview, June 2010.

59. Sarah Holewinski, personal interview, February 2008.

60. Matthew and Rutherford 2003.

61. Grant and Taylor 2004.

62. Ingenkamp 2008.

63. Abrahamson 2006, 146.

64. Focus group participant #1, December 2009. Although CIVIC never suggested that money could entirely compensate for the loss of life or that amends were necessarily limited to monetary compensation, it was the "blood money" narrative that critics would frequently push back with.

65. Respondent #25, personal interview, May 2010.

66. Minear and Smillie 2004.

67. ICRC staffer, personal interview, April 2009.

68. Sarah Holewinski, personal interview, February 2008.

69. It must be noted that CIVIC had never asked ICRC to sign on (they understood from the start that ICRC would not join the coalition or do direct advocacy), but they asked them not to push back and considered them an ally. Author's field notes, April 2007.

70. Students in my UMass-Amherst class on Global Agenda Setting studied CIVIC for a semester, wrote a strategy paper, and conducted a briefing in Washington in December 2008. See Tillmann et al. 2009. At Harvard University, Bonnie Docherty and a team of law students worked on an analysis of how the concept of "amends" might draw on humanitarian and human rights law.

71. A particular point of discussion was whether or not having the United States as an ally would be useful or not given the change in administrations. Just prior to Barack Obama's inauguration, it was still unclear to Washington advocacy elites what sort of approach he might take toward humanitarian issues. As one NGO staffer said, "We might want to see what those coattails look like first."

72. Heather Hamilton, CIVIC board member, May 2009.

73. In September 2009, the campaign membership included four NGOs from the global South (Control Arms Foundation of India, Egyptian Initiative for Personal Rights, the War Legacies Project, and the National Alliance for Human Rights and Social Justice–Nepal); one faith-based group (the United Methodist Church); two women's groups (Mothers Acting Up and Women for Women International); two major human rights groups (Human Rights Watch and Physicians for Human Rights); one environmental group (Global Green USA); and one multi-issue NGO (Citizens for Global Solutions).

74. NGOs mobilized in 2005 to prevent the neoconservative Bush administration official John Bolton from becoming U.S. ambassador to the United Nations.

75. Heather Hamilton, personal interview, May 2009.

76. Sarah Holewinski, personal correspondence, April 2012.

77. "We can't call it a 'missing law of war,' which is a shame 'cause I really loved that phrase, but we could call it a 'gap'—not in IHL, but in international law broadly. When you put human rights law and humanitarian law together, there's a gap between the dignity and respect afforded every individual civilian and what happens to them in war." Sarah Holewinski, informal conversation, April 2009.

78. According to Keiltash, whose background included Human Rights Watch and the Arms Trade Treaty, in human security practitioner circles the term "norm" connotes legal obligations, rather than extralegal social pressures as political scientists understand it.

79. At the Interaction Protection Working Group that Keenan attended in 2008, her sense was that "protection was already a very full topic. It means so many things and varies depending on the mission of each organization. So, for example, children's organizations would use it to talk about protection of children from trafficking, which had very little connection to what we were working on." Marla Keenan, personal interview, January 2009.

80. Scott Paul, personal e-mail, July 29, 2009.

81. Scott Paul, e-mail correspondence, December 23, 2011.

82. For a detailed exploration of this "securitization" of global social problems, see Hudson 2009.

83. True-Frost 2007.

84. See Making Amends Campaign website archive, on file with author.

85. In particular, the operational refugee and relief NGOs continued to express skepticism through this same period in the idea that there even was a gap: "We have heard this a couple of times now: that warring parties have all sort of obligations, human rights obligations, IHL obligations, refugee law obligations, IDP[internally displaced persons]-related obligations, so really there is not that much of a gap.... But from our perspective only the warring party that does damage to a civilian victim is really capable of repairing the dignity that is injured through a combat act." Scott Paul, phone interview, February 2010.

86. See True-Frost 2007. For example, in autumn 2010 the Security Council dealt with such topics as peacekeeping operations in Nepal, Darfur and Burundi, instability in Afghanistan, maritime piracy off Somalia, and the question of Palestine.

87. Ibid.

88. Similarly, in another meeting with a Quaker UN Office representative, Paul was reminded that the concept of liability for incidental harm was already reflected in one specific treaty: the Fifth Additional Protocol to the Geneva Conventions on Explosive Remnants of War, which puts the onus on warring parties to clean up their mess when they go to war.

89. This shift in CIVIC's lexicon—and in the emphasis on the United States and NATO as examples of emerging practice—was also an attempt to move away from compensation as a legal concept, implying that money could adequately compensate for losses, to focus instead on the wider symbolic purpose of "tangible assistance," and frame both of these as one of many strategies to signal respect and regret for causing harm.

90. UN Security Council 2010.

91. Through Paul, CIVIC learned how important it was to present amends as complementary or supplementary to the reparations issue, which was the key focus of the "accountability" discourse within protection of civilians' circles at this time. Doing so effectively had been a process of trial and error. By November 2009, many delegates were still unsure about this, and OCHA had not endorsed amends.

92. See Scott Paul, "United Nations: Uganda Steps Up in Security Council Debate," *Civic Field Reports*, November 16, 2009. Available online at http://civicfieldreports.wordpress.com/2009/11/16/united-nations-uganda-steps-up-in-security-council-debate/.

93. One of these was the OHCHR officer in charge of the body's Expert Seminar on Human Rights of Civilians in Armed Conflict, who was much more sympathetic in January 2010 than his colleague had been the previous year. OHCHR invited Paul to send him all the information he could on the amends concept in case he could get it on the agenda for the seminar. Scott Paul, e-mail correspondence, January 14, 2010.

94. OCHA representative, personal interview, June 2010.

95. Scott Paul, e-mail correspondence, February 24, 2010.

96. UN Security Council 2010a. The language read: "I note the emerging practice of several States, one that other parties to armed conflict might consider, of acknowledging the harm they cause to civilians and compensating victims. The practice of making amends may range from public apologies to financial payments and livelihood assistance provided to individuals, families and communities. This practice must not be seen, however, as an alternative to prosecuting those responsible for violations of international humanitarian and human rights law and delivering justice to the victims and their families and communities."

97. UN Security Council 2010b, 3.

98. By July 2011, the Making Amends website read: "Protection of civilians is built into the laws of war. But when these protections fail, warring parties have no formal responsibility to help. The Making Amends Campaign is a call to all warring parties to help the civilians they harm in armed conflict. It seeks to set a new standard where none currently exists." See Making Amends Campaign web archive on file with author.

99. In an exit interview in May 2011, Holewinski told me: "We now don't talk about compensation at all. . . . Compensation raises a lot of legal issues with policymakers and their lawyers, not to mention international NGOs and institutions focused on legal accountability for human rights violations. . . . What we have come to mean by 'amends' is investigations, recognition of harm, public apologies, and assistance." Sarah Holewinski, personal interview, May 2011.

100. Sarah Holewinski, personal interview, May 2011.

5. From "Stop the Robot Wars!" to "Ban Killer Robots"

1. Two excellent overviews of these developments are Singer 2009 and Krishnan 2010.

2. As far back as 2005, Joint Forces Command fielded a concept paper entitled "Unmanned Effects: Taking the Human Out of the Loop." See Singer 2009, chapter 6. In December 2008, the U.S. Navy released a report presenting "the presumptive case for the use of autonomous military robotics." Lin, Bekey, and Abney 2008.

3. For descriptions of existing systems, as well as an enthusiastic appraisal of their potential fit with the laws of war, see Arkin 2009.

4. See, for example, Sharkey 2007.

5. Sparrow 2007. Sparrow wonders whether the use of robots is any different ethically from the arming of child soldiers who too cannot be entirely held responsible for the war crimes they may commit.

6. Borenstein 2008; Singer 2009. In a series of blog posts, Kenneth Anderson has gone even farther to argue that the use of military robotics in fact problematizes the structure of humanitarian law itself, insofar as it blurs the distinction between "weapons" and "soldiers."

7. For example, the targeting of Iran Air Flight 655 by the Aegis system on the U.S.S. *Vincennes* in 1988 lends credence to concerns over whether unmanned systems can accurately distinguish civilian from hostile targets. In 2007, a fully automated MK5 antiaircraft system, in use by the 10th Anti-Aircraft regiment as a part of a South African military training exercise, accidentally killed nine friendly soldiers, injuring fourteen (though observers disagree over whether this was a hardware or software glitch). See Schactman 2007 and Simonite 2007. Industrial statistics suggest a record of routine safety problems with automated systems: according to Peter Singer, 4 percent of American factories in which robots are present have "major robotic accidents," in which human workers end up dead. See Singer 2009, 195.

8. Garcia 2012.

9. Singer 2009, 385.

10. Haas 1992.

11. For example, see Peterson 2010 on the role of anthropologists in indigenous human rights agenda setting.

12. These include Martin Dent, a political scientist who came up with the idea of Jubilee 2000 (Busby 2010, 71) and public health professors Allan Rosenfield and Deborah Maine, whose presentations to the World Health Organization are credited with putting the issue of maternal mortality on the international health agenda (Shiffman 2007).

13. Adler 1992.

14. Garcia 2006.

15. Knopf 2012.

16. Avant, Finnemore, and Sell 2010, 12.

17. Stone 2001.

18. See Altmann and Gubrud 2004, 39: "Autonomous killer robots should be prohibited: a human should be the decision maker when a target is to be attacked." Gubrud had in fact raised concerns of this sort even earlier in a 1997 paper on nanotechnology while a doctoral student in physics at the University of Maryland. See Gubrud 1997.

19. Minkel 2008.

20. Noel Sharkey, personal interview, Sheffield, May 2008.

21. For example, on February 10, 2009, roboticist Noel Sharkey was featured on *The Daily Show* with Jon Stewart for a segment entitled "Roombas of Doom."

22. Personal interview, May 2008.

23. Personal interview, May 2008

24. Sparrow 2009.

25. Peter Asaro, phone interview, June 2011.

26. ICRAC website, http://www.icrac.net.

27. Jürgen Altmann, phone interview, July 2011.

28. These included Mark Avrum Gubrud, Altmann's coauthor on the paper calling for an AWS ban, who was now doing doctoral work in physics at the University of Maryland; Colin Allen and Wendell Wallach, coauthors of *Moral Machines;* and German researchers Niklas Schornig of the Frankfurt Peace Research Institute and Frank Sauer of Universitat der Bundeswehr.

29. Altmann described reaching out to "landmines and cluster organizations, human rights groups, humanitarian law groups." Representatives from Human Rights Watch, the ICRC, and Landmine Action attended; Amnesty International did not. Phone interview, June 2011.

30. Few active duty military representatives responded, but an Air Force reserve colonel from the U.S. Naval Academy, Edward Barrett, did attend.

31. "Arms Control for Robots Workshop Agenda," September 20–22, 2010, Berlin Germany. Document on file with author.

32. Respondent #55, Skype interview, July 2011.

33. Respondent #70, e-mail correspondence, July 2011.

34. Respondent #57, phone interview, July 2011; respondent #56, phone interview, July 2011.

35. "Berlin Statement," September 2010, Outcome Document for the International, Interdisciplinary Expert Workshop on "Arms Control for Robots—Limited Armed Teleoperated and Autonomous Systems," September 20–22, 2010, Berlin. Available online at http://icrac.net/statements/.

36. Arkin 2004.

37. As Arkin later wrote in the preface to his book, these connections to many transnational communities played an important role in shaping his thought: "Follow-up meetings in similar symposia continued to broaden my view, introducing me to the ethical perspectives of pacifists, philosophers, social scientists, ethicists and many others through numerous enriching talks, debates and discussions." Arkin 2009, xv.

38. Ron Arkin, personal interview, December 2011.

39. Arkin 2011.

40. Arkin 2009, xv.

41. Arkin 2009.

42. Arkin 2010.

43. Rothman 2007.

44. Arkin 2011.

45. Indeed, Arkin acknowledges this, emphasizing that such systems would not be advisable in counterinsurgencies or military operations other than war, but only in conventional combat situations where battle spaces took place away from civilian areas.

46. For example, in the *Journal of Military Ethics'* 2010 special issue on "Emerging Technologies," Arkin's piece was titled "The Case for Ethical Autonomy in Unmanned Systems," and Sharkey's was titled "Saying 'No!' to Lethal Autonomous Targeting."

47. CETMONS website, "Thrust Group 2: International Law, Ethics and Governance on Robotics and National Security." See http://cetmons.org/thrust2_robotic.

48. Some individuals were recruited into the network through fellowships at the Stockdale Ethics Center at the U.S. Naval Postgraduate Institute, which as a founding member of the consortium restructured its fellowship program in 2010 to reflect the thematic interests of the consortium. Field notes, Chautauqua Council meeting, Chautauqua, New York, July 2012.

49. This contrasts with the ICRAC membership, which includes no direct ties to militaries but several of whose members do have backgrounds in the peace, humanitarian, human rights, and NGO sector.

50. Brad Allenby, phone interview, October 9, 2012.

51. Other CETMONS members describe the differences between the groups in this way, saying they are more focused on reason/ethics/logic vs. emotion: "ICRAC is more 'pathos-oriented,'" one told me.

52. Marchant et al. 2011.

53. Ibid., 274.

54. "While ICRAC's work has raised the issue of limited lethal autonomous robots through an international arms control agreement, the wisdom of such a course of action is far from clear." Ibid., 299.

55. According to conversations with some of the authors, this article was "cobbled together" after discussions at a meeting of CETMONS and the authors in fact had varying opinions on the value of different governance options. The published language was thus a compromise position emphasizing the need for international discussion to commence, but shying away from any specific prescriptions.

56. Similarly, the outcome document of the 2012 Chautauqua Council meeting of CETMONS emphasized not whether but "how should robots be designed to be ethical?...If militaries keep moving forward towards the deployment of intelligent autonomous weaponized robots at its current rapid pace, these systems should be deployed ethically, in a manner consistent with both standing and mission-specific Rules of Engagement (ROEs) and other legal and ethical constraints." See Lincoln Center 2012.

57. Forsythe 2005.

58. Human Rights Watch, established in 1993 as a successor organization to Helsinki Watch, is headquartered in New York with regional offices globally and three thematic divisions: women, children, and arms (based in Washington). For a discussion of its role in the human rights movement, see Brown 2001 and Welch 2001.

59. On HRW's role in spearheading the fusion of human rights and humanitarian law through its arms work, see Wong 2012, 150. In interviews, campaigners often referenced the political significance of HRW's involvement on weapons campaigns. One former cluster munitions campaigner said, "When HRW joined the campaign, that was a critical moment." A former landmine advocate told me, "HRW has a lot of credibility in arms-related areas: certainly external government audiences will notice if HRW is engaging on an issue and take it as a sign that something's going to happen in that area." Respondent #38, phone interview, 2008, and respondent #54, phone interview, 2011.

60. Of the organizations identified by web analysis and surveys as being prominent in the human security network, twenty-five are actively involved in disarmament, arms control, or weapons issues. Of these twenty-five "core organizations" doing weapons work in the broader area of "human security," just five organizations receive nearly half of all the citations from the network. Of these five, two are information portals rather than advocacy organizations (Small Arms Survey and Human Security Report Project); one is an international organization interested predominantly in biological weapons, the World Health Organization; and the two advocacy NGOs are the International Committee of the Red Cross and Human Rights Watch's Arms Division. Drilling down more thoroughly into online networks specifically around the issues

of arms control, disarmament, and the humanitarian effects of weapons (which are somewhat distinct issue areas), ICRC and HRW are also among the most prominent actors across these adjacent networks.

61. Carpenter 2011b.

62. In the napalm case, one former ICRC official told me, "In hindsight, it would have taken only a very slight effort from the ICRC to push that through. The time was ripe, public pressure was extraordinary. We held back because we had been burned in the 1950s lobbying for a nuclear ban, and as a result napalm is still legal." Respondent #47, personal interview, Geneva, 2011.

63. Personal interview, May 2008.

64. For example, a network analysis of websites addressing the issue of autonomous weapons or battlefield robots includes military and media sources as well as science magazines, but relatively few .orgs, and none from the human rights and humanitarian law advocacy community. By contrast, landmines, cluster munitions, and small arms discourse online is dominated by advocacy positions from networks of civil society organizations.

65. The Arms Unit at the ICRC was not oblivious to ICRAC's concerns. In my first meetings with representatives of the ICRC's Arms Unit in 2009, I asked about the key issues percolating on ICRC's agenda before I ever mentioned autonomous weapons, and several individuals raised the issue unprompted alongside a welter of other "new" weapons. However, this level of understanding had not proliferated throughout the organization beyond the Arms Unit—personnel I interviewed in the Legal Division, for example, had given little thought to the issue. And even the Arms Unit had a relatively conservative posture toward these developments.

66. Mariner 2010.

67. Moyes explained the analogy between robots and cluster munitions in a 2008 interview: "Our concern is that humans, not sensors, should make targeting decisions. So similarly, we don't want to move towards robots that make decisions about combatants and noncombatants." See Marks 2008.

68. Quoted in Singer 2009, 385.

69. Like landmines that sense targets and detonate according to preprogrammed criteria, autonomous weapons are designed to identify targets independent of a human in the loop. And like landmines, whose effects were deemed indiscriminate and uncontrollable after being deployed precisely because one could not be certain whom they might hit after a war ended, autonomous weapons cannot be reliably programmed to distinguish civilian from combatant targets with any certainty; and given their capacity to "go haywire," cannot necessarily be controlled once deployed. See Singer 2009.

70. Focus group participant. All unattributed quotations in this chapter are by focus group participants.

71. As Singer's work (2009) details, this perception that lethal military robots are largely "lab weapons" was incorrect even at this time, but it was the perception that mattered.

72. Respondent #3, personal interview, Washington, DC, 2009.

73. Respondent #9, personal interview, Geneva, 2009.

74. One campaigner said in 2008, "These are fundamentally different issues, in the sense that robots aren't killing huge numbers of people around the world like landmines and clusters. . . . It's very difficult to get people to engage on an issue where the humanitarian cost hasn't been realized." Respondent #54, phone interview, June 2011.

75. Indeed, while humanitarian disarmament types were slow to openly acknowledge the issue, it was acknowledged in a UN report as early as 2010 under Human Rights Council auspices: Philip Alston, the UN special rapporteur on extrajudicial executions, discussed the "very important ramifications in terms of the right to life" and called on the international community to "urgently address the legal, political, ethical and moral implications of the development of lethal

robotic technologies." But the same report noted a "general lack of international attention to this issue" and mentioned that the human rights as well as disarmament community "continued to see advances in robotics as an exotic topic that does not need to be addressed until the relevant technologies are actually in use." See Alston 2010.

76. Gross 2010.

77. Blinding laser weapons are defined in Protocol IV to the Convention on Conventional Weapons as laser weapons "specifically designed, as their sole combat function or as one of their combat functions, to cause permanent blindness to unenhanced vision." On the history of the ban, see Carnahan and Robertson 1996.

78. Anderberg, Bring, and Wolbarsht 1992.

79. Doswald Beck 1996; Peters 1996.

80. Carpenter 2011b.

81. The ICRAC statement refers to "pressing dangers posed to peace and international security and to civilians in war" by developments in military robotics, stressing "their potential to lower the threshold of armed conflict; machines should not be allowed to make the decision to kill people; limitations on the range and weapons carried by 'man in the loop' unmanned systems and on their deployment in postures threatening to other states; a ban on arming unmanned systems with nuclear weapons; the prohibition of the development, deployment and use of robot space weapons." See ICRAC Mission Statement, http://www.icrac.net.

82. According to one member of ICRAC, donors reacted the same way: CS Fund reportedly declined to support a 2010 proposed anti-AWS campaign because "they didn't want to get into peace and security work."

83. Respondent #54, phone interview, June 2011.

84. One official told me that "it's very unlikely that we would join a well-established campaign led by others." Even the group's choice of an acronym troubled some ICRC practitioners, as it was too similar to their own: "The fact that they're already established and they've picked the acronym ICRAC leaves us less room to maneuver.... They're far more political than we would ever be." Respondent #7, personal interview, Geneva, 2009.

85. Respondent #7, personal interview, Geneva, 2009.

86. Personal interview, HRW, Washington, DC, 2008.

87. Sharkey and Arkin were both invited to brief the ICRC at various points during the period of this study.

88. Arkin quickly learned to emphasize, in meetings with ICRC officials, that he didn't believe ending war was possible, that mitigating its effects was a priority, and that he thought autonomous systems could help.

89. Kellenberger 2011.

90. The frame soup problem was not just an issue for Human Rights Watch and the ICRC: it was a problem for all civil society organizations thinking about robotic weapons in this period. One cluster munitions advocate from another organization told me: "It's hard to pin down: ICRAC is still conflating drones and AWS...so it's hard to tell what the problem is, whether it's about revolutions in military robotics, or limiting collateral damage or extrajudicial execution. That would all have to be unpacked a bit."

91. Indeed, Human Rights Watch's subsequent report went far beyond the standard "humanitarian law" frame, questioning the entire ethics of removing humans from the loop.

92. Human Rights Watch 2012c.

93. HRW consultant Mary Wareham linked to the HRW press release with a tweet that read: "Concern @ development of fully autonomous weapons that select + engage targets w/out human intervention" using the hashtag #killerrobots. See https://twitter.com/marywareham/status/261124227971813376.

94. The ICRAC statement proposes both that "machines should not be allowed to make the decision to kill people" and "limitations on the range and weapons carried by 'man in the loop' unmanned systems and on their deployment in postures threatening to other states." See ICRAC Mission Statement, http://www.icrac.net.

95. My student Lina Shaikhouni and I documented these conflations in the public debate in our *Foreign Policy* article "Don't Fear the Reaper" in 2011 (http://www.foreignpolicy.com/articles/2011/06/07/dont_fear_the_reaper). The analysis of op-eds on which this article is based is explained in our companion blog post at Duck of Minerva, "Unpacking the Anti-Drone Debate," http://duckofminerva.blogspot.com/2011/06/unpacking-drone-debate.html#disqus_thread.

96. As Noel Sharkey said, "Momentum on AWS began to pick up around the time of San Remo." Personal interview, September 2012, Oslo.

97. Examples include the New America Foundation dataset developed by Peter Bergen and Katherine Tiedeman, http://counterterrorism.newamerica.net/drones; Pakistan Body Count, maintained by Pakistani computer scientist Zeeshan-ul-hassan Usmani, http://www.pakistanbodycount.org/index.html; Jamestown Foundation data published by Brian Glyn Williams, Matthew Fricker, and Avery Plaw: http://www.jamestown.org/single/?no_cache = 1&tx_ttnews%5btt_news%5d = 37165; and a dataset from the Bureau of Investigative Journalism, http://www.thebureauinvestigates.com/2012/01/11/obama-2012-strikes/.

98. Quotations from field notes, 3rd Meeting of States Parties to the Cluster Munitions Convention, Oslo, Norway, September 2012.

99. Personal interview, Washington, DC, February 20, 2013.

100. Issues addressed by the report regarding targeted killings broadly included whether armed attacks inside a state's territory absent a state of war were legal; whether a civilian intelligence agency could lawfully engage in these attacks; and whether it was lawful to target "rebel suspects" with lethal force rather than arresting them for trial.

101. BBC 2012.

102. Bergen 2012.

103. See "US: Transfer CIA Drone Strikes to Military," April 20, 2012, http://www.hrw.org/news/2012/04/20/us-transfer-cia-drone-strikes-military; and "US: Targeted Killing Policy Disregards Human Rights Law," May 1, 2012, http://www.hrw.org/news/2012/05/01/us-targeted-killing-policy-disregards-human-rights-law.

104. Respondent #52, phone interview, June 2011.

105. As Noel Sharkey put it in a presentation to the cluster munitions community in 2012, "Discrimination is more than just saying 'this is a combatant, this is not.' There are an extremely large number of circumstances in which it is inappropriate to kill an insurgent."

106. Price 1998; Borrie 2009.

107. This did not mean that this was the only moral argument against AWS. Underlying the distinction question for some was a deeper revulsion about the possibility of machines killing. Both Mark Avrum Gubrud and Robert Sparrow had previously articulated a "human right to be killed only by humans," and humanitarian disarmament expert Richard Moyes perhaps tapped into a similar sentiment in his remarks at a side event at the Cluster Munitions Convention in Oslo in 2012: "To be killed by a machine that had decided to kill me itself I would find, in moral terms, extremely disappointing."

108. According to its website, Article 36 "operates from a principle that practical, policy and legal controls over weapons should be founded on publicly transparent and evidence-based analysis. Such controls should aim for prevention of unintended, unnecessary or unacceptable harm, and should be open to ongoing review. The standards of analysis should be the same whether the population likely to be put at risk by specific weapons is domestic or foreign and whether the weapons are intended to be lethal or for coercion." See http://www.article36.org/about.

109. This work is conducted on behalf of the International Network on Explosive Weapons, a new civil society partnership that includes NGO heavyweights Oxfam, Save the Children, and Human Rights Watch with Article36 as coordinator; and that seeks to limit the use of all types of explosive weapons in populated areas.

110. The landmine, cluster, and small arms communities enjoyed close ties to human security organizations partly because their causes have attracted the support of human security "superpowers" such as Human Rights Watch and the ICRC. But the nuclear and anti-DU community had historically enjoyed ties with the peace and environmental networks instead. Widespread networks around pain weapons, nonlethal weapons, psychotropic weapons, or autonomous weapons had yet to emerge at this point.

111. In 2011, as the project was just emerging, Moyes told me: "We're responding a bit to thinking, 'Hmm, there isn't really any organization with a focus just on weapons-related policy and law. There are plenty of organizations, obviously, that work on weapons stuff, but none that can choose to work flexibly across different weapon issues.'" Phone interview, June 2011.

112. In this capacity, whether by joining networks as individual members (as with ICRAC) or by endorsing and linking to others' campaigns without officially joining (as with the International Coalition to Ban Uranium Weapons and the International Network Against Small Arms), Moyes and Nash both engaged with and aimed to support members of these more marginalized movements.

113. Examples of this "brokering" role played by Article36 staff include introducing ICRAC members to Human Rights Watch contacts, encouraging members of the uranium weapons coalition to attend multilateral conferences where they could network with other civil society groups, or organizing a dinner at the 2012 Cluster Munitions Conference to connect the increasingly professionalizing nuclear abolitionists to the landmines/cluster munitions crowd to exchange ideas and campaign strategies.

114. Recall Goddard 2009 on the significance of brokers as entrepreneurs.

115. Only Pax Christi is more highly connected, largely because of its formal affiliation with the uranium weapons campaign, an otherwise marginalized network in humanitarian disarmament (see Carpenter 2011). By contrast, Article36.org intentionally remained formally aloof from this particular campaign, which had widely been associated with the far-left environmentalist movement, positioning itself as slightly more within the human security mainstream while offering informal advice, encouragement, and ideas to anti-DU campaigners. Thus, the early adoption of the AWS issue by Article36 meant the "killer robot" problem was conceptually linked to the landmines/cluster munitions community more than to the antinuclear side of the humanitarian disarmament sector.

116. Clifford Bob refers to this role by middle-power NGOs as "matchmaking." See Bob 2005.

117. One of Moyes's and Nash's early projects together had been authoring a handbook on global campaign coalition work, and much of their work as members of Article36 seemed to be mentoring issue entrepreneurs outside mainstream networks on how to professionalize in order to promote their agenda.

118. Moyes took a very practical view as a campaigner experienced in marketing concepts through civil society: for example, he thought the term "robot arms" was likely to mislead the public, conjuring images of factory robots rather than robotic weapons. ICRAC's "frame soup" problem was also very clear to Moyes from early on. He encouraged Sharkey to focus on the autonomous weapons ban and leave aside "distracting" aspects such as nuclear weapons, drones, or the possibility that AWS might increase war. But he also suggested that the key would be to focus broadly on the underlying principle that made the weapons problematic, rather than just the weapons themselves—a similar strategy he and IKV Pax Christi staff advocated for with the depleted uranium community as they developed a framing around "toxic remnants of war." See http://www.toxicremnantsofwar.info.

119. Noel Sharkey and Peter Asaro did a lot of speaking and media spots, but generally as individuals rather than as ICRAC representatives. When Sharkey became the point person for Human Rights Watch's interest in the campaign, it aroused some jealousy within the group and Sharkey himself expressed discomfort with this role.

120. Wong 2012.

121. At the Third Meeting of States Parties of the Cluster Munitions Convention, considerable effort was spent by the International Campaign to Abolish Nuclear Weapons to cultivate professional connections to the mainstream humanitarian disarmament movement; some talk centered around the importance of the DU community following suit. In fact, IKV Pax Christi, another middle-power NGO with unusually high "betweenness" in humanitarian disarmament, was already engaged in the same process with respect to the depleted uranium issue.

122. John Borrie, personal interview, UNIDIR, June 2011.

123. Personal interview, Washington, DC, February 20, 2013; e-mail correspondence, May 1, 2013.

124. Steve Goose, personal interview, Washington, DC, February 2013.

125. Jody Williams, personal conversation, April 2013, London. See also Jody Williams 2012.

126. Williams 2011.

127. The Humanitarian Disarmament Summit in fall 2012 included remarks by Jody Williams calling for a complete prohibition on autonomous weapons. Bolton 2012.

128. The Heyns report, which called not for a ban but for a moratorium, was presented to the UN four months after the release of the HRW report. See Heyns 2013.

129. Ron, Ramos, and Rodgers 2005.

130. At the NGO conference that preceded the formal campaign launch in April 2013, much discussion centered on how campaign messaging might counteract the media imagery of Terminators, which was helpful in capturing public attention but unhelpful in describing real-life autonomous weapons.

6. "His Body, His Choice"

1. World Health Organization 2007. The most common version of the practice involves immobilizing an infant boy, tearing the foreskin away from his glans, then either slicing or burning the foreskin off, leaving the glans (normally an internal organ) exposed. Rarer and more extreme versions involve peeling back the entire skin of the shaft (sometimes including the skin on the scrotum and pubis); or subincision of the urinary tube from the scrotum to the glans.

2. In 1971, the American Academy of Pediatrics stopped endorsing the routine circumcision of males, stating that there was "no absolute medical indication" for doing so. Their 1989 statement modified this view slightly, mentioning potential benefits as well as risks; a 1999 revised statement took note of new studies linking circumcision to HIV-AIDS reduction but described them as too inconclusive to justify routine circumcision of babies. The 2012 updated guidelines acknowledge the potential benefits are great enough to allow parents to continue choosing the practice but continue to stop short of recommending circumcision.

3. See Abu-Sahlieh 2001.

4. DeLaet 2009.

5. See the International Coalition for Genital Integrity website for a listing of affiliated groups and advocacy statements: http://www.icgi.org/. On pain in the neonate, see Anand 1987.

6. Negative side effects of *successful* circumcision include disfiguration and desensitization, effects on the neonate's brain development, and (according to some studies) a higher risk of STDs. One in 476 routine circumcisions in the United States results in complications including hemorrhage, infections, urinary retention, heart attack, amputation of the penis, and, in rare cases, death. See Weiss et al. 2010

7. Somerville 2000.

8. Svoboda 1999.

9. DeLaet 2009, 8.

10. Glick 2005.

11. Marilyn Milos, phone interview, June 2010.

12. Marilyn Milos, phone interview, June 2010.

13. Wallerstein 1980; see also Gollagher 2001.

14. One early movement participant told me: "Marilyn might have been the norm entrepreneur for the anti-circumcision movement but she was able to play that role because of this sort of permissive context where men were already receptive, and sort of rethinking cultural notions of masculinity, and there was sympathy for this position among many more fragmented groups." Phone interview, June 2010.

15. See Van Howe 1999.

16. At the 2012 Symposium in Helsinki, for example, presentations included "One Mother's Sad Story" featuring a Finnish woman whose Nigerian husband had circumcised their son without her consent, and testimonies from Finnish intersex individuals who provided oral and photographic evidence of the physical and psychosocial sequelae to painful childhood surgeries they had endured.

17. Nonetheless, some intactivists from more activist backgrounds criticize the Symposiums for being unduly scientific in their organization and content. Everyone speaks in plenary: there are no breakout groups. One participant told me the movement would benefit from equivalent yearly meetings structured more like activist caucuses, where the emphasis was less on presenting scientific papers and more about skill-building and brainstorming for grassroots activism.

18. See "Declaration of the First International Symposium on Circumcision," http://www.nocirc.org/declare.php. This statement in whole has been adopted as the charter for the International Coalition of Genital Integrity's "Declaration of Genital Integrity."

19. These efforts have been largely unsuccessful to date and *Foreskin Man* has drawn criticism from the Jewish community for playing on ethnic and gender caricatures.

20. Letter to the editor, *Los Angeles Times*, March 19, 1989. Emphasis in the original. Cited in Laura Carpenter 2009, 519.

21. Tim Hammond, personal interview, Helsinki, October 2012.

22. U.S. Jewish intactivist groups included Jews Opposing Circumcision, the Jewish Circumcision Resource Center, and Jews for the Rights of the Child. Similar groups sprung up in Israel, including Kahal, Gonnen, and the Israeli Association Against Genital Mutilation. Books written during this period by prominent Jewish intactivists included Ron Goldman's *Questioning Circumcision: A Jewish Perspective* and Leonard Glick's *Marked in Your Flesh: Circumcision from Ancient Judea to Modern America*. The documentary film *Cut!* chronicles the quest of an Orthodox Jewish father to understand circumcision.

23. Field notes, September 2012. This is consistent with Debbi Avant, Martha Finnemore, and Susan Sell's (2010) emphasis on "expert authority." By contrast, mainstream media coverage of the movement typically portrayed intactivists as a nonexpert community relative to the procircumcision medical establishment. Although the movement includes numerous scientists and doctors, an analysis of fifty *New York Times* articles covering the circumcision debate from 1985 to 2012 shows news articles generally include quotations from doctors, scientists, or religious leaders on the procircumcision side but primarily nonmedical personnel from the intactivist side. See figure 6.

24. Personal correspondence, Matthew Hess, October 2012.

25. See Murdie 2013; Kindornay, Ron, and Carpenter 2012.

26. DeLaet 2009.

27. In 1994, a UN Commission of Experts submitted a report to the UN Security Council on human rights abuses in the former Yugoslavia. In the section on "Rape and Other Forms of Sexual Assault," the report makes mention of circumcision: "Men are also subject to sexual assault. They are forced to rape women and to perform sex acts on guards or each other. They have also been subjected to castration, circumcision or other sexual mutilation." See United Nations Security Council 1992.

28. United Nations 2006.

29. Tina Kimmel, personal interview, September 2012.

30. Tim Hammond, personal interview, Helsinki, September 2012.

31. Ron Goldman, phone interview, October 5, 2012.

32. Tina Kimmel, personal interview, Helsinki, September 2012.

33. According to Goldman, these included modifications to proposed resolutions and statements by board members and the chair against resolutions prior to a vote. Several eyewitnesses at the 1995 meeting wrote the chapter afterward protesting what appeared to them to be violations of chapter protocol. Primary documents on file with author.

34. In media coverage of a Canadian film, *Intact*, Junos later described her reaction when faced with videos of circumcisions: "I remember gripping the edge of my seat. I was twisting and turning. It was as if it was actually happening in front of me. I wanted to say, 'Stop! Stop him from doing that!' I wanted to protect the child." See http://archives.lists.indymedia.org/imc-editorial/2000-October/000908.html.

35. Svoboda 1999, 460.

36. Amnesty International Bermuda 1998.

37. Leonard Glick, personal interview, June 2010.

38. Field notes, Helsinki, October 2012.

39. J. Steven Svoboda, personal interview, September 2012.

40. Matthew Hess, e-mail correspondence, October 5, 2012. MGMBill.org advocates legislative bans of circumcision at a state level. See Hess 2009.

41. Primary documents on file with author.

42. Respondent #5, personal interview, May 2008.

43. Warzazi made note of this correspondence in her 1997 report on human traditional practices to the UN Sub-Commission: "Certain universities are beginning to take a closer look at the problem [of infant male circumcision]. In early January 1997, for example, a lecturer from the Swiss Institute of Comparative Law sent the Special Rapporteur a questionnaire that was to serve as a basis for a book on male and female circumcision. In her reply, the Special Rapporteur made a point of mentioning that circumcision of male children did not concern the United Nations, as only female circumcision was deemed a harmful practice to be eradicated.... It would seem inappropriate to consider together both female circumcision, which is harmful to health, and male circumcision, which has no undesirable effect and is even considered to be beneficial." See United Nations 1997a.

44. Immediately following the June 1997 report, Sub-Commission documents began referring instead to "Traditional Practices Affecting the Health of Women and the Girl Child." See the November 1997 report summarizing the 49th Session of the Sub-commission in August 1997 (United Nations 1997b).

45. In her 2001 report, the special rapporteur included the following paragraph: "The Special Rapporteur...continues to receive occasional letters condemning male circumcision. She would like to recall that her mandate, as defined by the Sub-Commission on the Promotion and Protection of Human Rights, concerns traditional practices affecting the health of women and the girl child. The same mandate applies with regard to the General Assembly or other United Nations bodies. By restricting herself to female circumcision, the Special Rapporteur is there only

keeping to her terms of reference. Furthermore, she considers that the harmful effects of male circumcision cannot in any way be compared to equated with the violence, danger and risk faced by girl children and women." See United Nations 2001.

46. The Commission, like the Human Rights Council that succeeded it, was composed of delegates from member states; the Sub-Commission is composed of experts whose job is to produce and disseminate reports.

47. The written version of this statement is available on the UN website at http://www.unhchr.ch/Huridocda/Huridoca.nsf/%28Symbol%29/E.CN.4.Sub.2.2002.NGO.1.En. Notes on the oral version appear on the Attorneys for the Rights of the Child website at http://arclaw.org/our-work/presentations/oral-intervention-united-nations-regarding-male-circumcision.

48. Steven Svoboda, personal interview, June 2010.

49. In a follow-up document available on the Attorneys for the Rights of the Child website, Svoboda recounted the experience: "The United Nations bureaucracy and the Sub-Commission members and employees always treated us with respect. But clearly they talked among themselves and learned what our issue was. Evidently they were not—with some exceptions—seriously considering our claims. Eventually Sub-Commissioners and their staff members started to regularly avoid scheduled meetings with us, without canceling the meetings or contacting us in any way, not even in response to our follow-up contacts." See Svoboda 2001.

50. Auvert et al. 2005. Several studies have confirmed this correlation between circumcision and lower female-to-male HIV-AIDS transmission rates. A comparable effect on transmission from men to women, or from men to men, has not been found. See Millet et al. 2008. Some in-tactivists have disputed the findings; others accept them but argue that neonatal circumcision is not necessary to protect from STDs since infants are not sexually active, and that other preventive measures for HIV-AIDS are available to adult men.

51. Dan Bollinger, phone interview, May 2010.

52. Personal conversation, David Smith, Genital Autonomy, Helsinki, September 2012.

53. See NOCIRC, "International Symposia," for primary documents, http://www.nocirc.org/symposia/.

54. Respondent #6, personal interview, January 2009.

55. Keck and Sikkink 1998.

56. In the United Kingdom, the removal of routine circumcision from the national health plan resulted in the near-eradication of the practice within a generation after World War II. See Gollagher 2001.

57. Wong 2012.

58. Hopgood documents the ongoing dialectic within the Secretariat about what constitutes an issue falling within the AI mandate (Hopgood 2006, 92–96). For example, regarding sexual orientation rights: "The question was: "Could someone imprisoned for being gay be a prisoner of conscience? Could someone advocating gay rights, versus being gay as such, be a prisoner of conscience? The Research Department had reservations. There would be mandate problems over national differences in ages of consent and rules for heterosexual behavior. There was little international legal support for the proposed position, and fact-finding would be hard. And AI's image might suffer" (Hopgood 2006, 117). But "the true challenge of sexual orientation rights was that some members and some sections did not think it should be part of AI's mandate. One senior researcher at the time described the African, Middle Eastern and Latin American sections as saying, 'Oh my God no, you'll destroy us." See Hopgood 2006, 119.

59. Thompson 2008.

60. Routine circumcision in U.S. hospitals costs about $400 on average. Estimate based on $2 million boys born per year and a 56 percent circumcision rate in 2010.

61. See Robbins 2012; Deasy 2012.

62. However, a few respondents also pointed out that religion should not trump bodily integrity rights. One focus group participant said: "I personally don't care about this issue, but the argument about culture or sovereignty or religion, that doesn't cut much wood with me. The whole point of human rights is precisely to go beyond sovereignty and culture, right?" Another said, "There are places where we legitimately intrude on religious practices for the sake of civil and political rights."

63. Focus group participant. All unattributed quotations in this chapter are by focus group participants.

64. Anne Lindboe, remarks at the 12th International Symposium on Genital Autonomy, Helsinki, Finland, October 1, 2012.

65. Laura Carpenter 2009.

66. For example, anthropologist Eric Silverman (2009) writes that "opposition to male circumcision, widely hailed by the mytho-poetic men's movement, also has revealed an enduring and disturbing anti-Semitism."

67. An activist told me in 2011: "We've been greeted with deafening silence.... We have not been successful at engaging people about it as a human rights issue, which is I think a result of people being afraid of being accused of being anti-Semitic." Phone interview, June 2011.

68. For example, Sami Aldeeb Abu-Sahlieh, who authored an important early treatise on circumcision, described the reaction of a WHO family planning specialist in 1993 when during the course of his research he asked her to defend the organization's policy on medical grounds. According to Abu-Sahlieh: "She replied: 'Circumcision is in the Bible. Do you want us to get in trouble with the Jews?'" Personal interview, Helsinki, October 2012.

69. Keck and Sikkink 1998.

70. In my earlier work on the absence of attention to children born of wartime rape, for example, I found an inhibiting factor was the perception that the abuses they suffered came at the hands of other victim groups—genocide or rape survivors—and that therefore a naming and shaming strategy was politically inadvisable. See Carpenter 2010b.

71. Bouris 2007, chap. 4

72. Respondent #85, phone interview, October 2012.

73. See Busby 2010 and Oestriech 2007. Indeed, as plate 8 shows, global health hubs constitute a vital set of connectors between the development, humanitarian, and human rights organizations in the wider human rights network, enjoying a brokerage position between advocacy groups such as Human Rights Watch and Amnesty International and service-oriented groups such as UNDP or UNHCR. Indeed, several key hubs in the child rights movement have mandates that cut across these three areas simultaneously—health, human rights, and development.

74. Respondent #4, personal interview, Human Rights Watch, May 2008.

75. World Health Organization 2006.

76. UNICEF/WHO/UNAIDS 2006.

77. Respondent #2, personal interview, Human Rights Watch, May 2008.

78. Brysk 2005.

79. Indeed, to some extent both were the case: the FGM issue had been championed by health organizations before being adopted by human rights groups, so human rights groups may have been particularly primed to follow the lead of the health sector on circumcision in general. See Duygulu and Carpenter 2013.

80. Quoted in Carpenter 2010b, 183–84.

81. On comparisons between the practices, see Abu-Sahlieh 2001 and DeLaet 2009. On comparisons between the discourses, see Lightfoot-Klein 1997, 131–35.

82. See Bell 2005.

83. See Laura Carpenter 2009.

84. For example, the World Health Organization discussed the issue at its 1979 Seminar on Harmful Traditional Practices Affecting the Health of Women and Children; both WHO and UNICEF funded civil society efforts to eradicate FGM in the 1980s; whereas Amnesty and HRW did not begin working on FGM until the late 1990s.

85. See Baer and Brysk 2009.

86. Carpenter 2003; Jones 1996.

87. Winter, Thompson, and Jeffreys 2002.

88. This perception may have been reinforced by some intactivists' ties to men's movement organizations.

89. Georgeanne Chapin told me in 2012 that since our first interview the concept that boys have a human right to an intact body was beginning to resonate with parents: "I think people are beginning to understand that circumcision violates boys' rights to an intact body. The rates of circumcision are plummeting as parents listen to their instincts... and both physician organizations and courts in European countries are beginning to take the position that circumcision is a violation of children's basic human rights, or even a crime." E-mail correspondence, October 2012.

90. It should be noted, however, that while the movement may not succeed in creating a norm, it does seem to have had some influence on the practice, which has declined in the United States from 80 percent to 56 percent in the last two decades.

Appendix

1. Carpenter 2012.

2. According to Jackson (2011, 25), citing Sartori (1970), methodology is "a concern with the logical structure and procedure of scientific enquiry" whereas methods are "techniques for gathering and analyzing bits of data."

3. Hafner-Burton and Ron 2009.

4. King, Keohane, and Verba 1994.

5. Smith and Zalewski 1996.

6. Jackson and Kaufman 2007.

7. This process was replicated on several more discrete subnetworks (human rights and disarmament) to draw inferences about network structure relevant to the case studies.

8. This survey went out to over six thousand individuals in global civil society, who were encouraged to pass it along to others whose insights they thought we should include. In total, we received 290 survey responses.

9. Social network analysis relies on data organized as links between nodes. Citations to organizations by survey respondents represent a type of prestige measurement but do not themselves imply structural ties between organizations. On network analysis, see Wasserman and Faust 1994.

10. Barabasi 2002, 5; Henzinger 2001, 45; Park, Kim, and Barnett 2004.

11. Adamic and Adar 2001; Park and Thelwall 2003.

12. See Issuecrawler, "Instructions of Use," at http://www.govcom.org/Issuecrawler_instructions.htm. For additional information, see Rogers 2012.

13. Butts 2013. Node radius is proportional to the log of in-degree centrality, because in-degree varies from 4 to 506 (UNDP) and is highly skewed.

14. The human rights hyperlink network was identified by Issuecrawler by triangulating crawls from three separate sets of starting points—Amnesty International's directory, the Choike Human Rights Directory, and the UDHR-60 website, identifying the overlapping organizations and using those as starting points for a single crawl. An equivalent human rights survey was disseminated through multiple human rights Listservs, collecting 351 answers. Fifty-five global South activists answered the Montreal survey, providing an additional set of information on perceptions of the actors and issues that constitute the network.

15. See Kindornay, Ron, and Carpenter 2012.

16. Fleiss 1971.

17. This finding suggests the official network agenda as measured by aggregating network websites either reflects or constructs the understandings of individuals who identify themselves closely with a transnational network. Indeed, 82 percent of the survey respondents reported they got either "some" or "a lot" of their information on the human security network from websites. Also see Carpenter and Jose 2012.

18. We considered in-coming hyperlinks as well as survey citations to be indicators of in-degree centrality and we averaged organizations' rankings from these two measures to arrive at their overall centrality score.

19. Barbour and Kitzinger 1999, 5.

20. We follow John Borrie and Ashley Thornton (2008) in treating these multilateral practitioners as members of a "community of practice."

21. Hafner-Burton, Kahler, and Montgomery 2009.

22. Bob 2005; Carpenter 2007a, 2007b; Wong 2008.

23. However, participants in the focus groups were more alike than they were different. Over 75 percent of the participants held graduate degrees, and over 70 percent held senior-level positions in their organizations. All were fluent in English. Although our sample included participants currently based in Africa, South America, Asia, and the Middle East, over 80 percent of our respondents were currently based in North America or Western Europe.

24. Glaser and Strauss 1967.

25. See Mische (2003) for a discussion of how to code conversational dynamics in network settings.

26. Fleiss 1971.

27. Master codes for "issue attributes," "adopter attributes," "entrepreneur attributes," "broader context," and "network effects" were applied to the entire set of transcripts. More detailed codes regarding different types of subexplanations for issue adoption were applied in the pre-coffee-break and "conclusion" sections of each transcript; an additional set of codes captured affect, including "enthusiasm" and "nay-saying" as well as conversational dynamics (e.g., "buck-passing" and "finger-pointing" were applied to the section where participants discussed candidate issues).

28. Joachim 2007.

29. Complete appendices for the coding scheme and kappa scores are available from http://www.people.umass.edu/charli/networks.

30. Lu and Shulman 2008.

31. Jackson 2011.

32. Entrepreneurs whose individual work is dealt with at length were asked to provide feedback on sections of the manuscript in which their work is described. I am thankful to those who took the time to do so.

33. Interviewees are quoted by name only if they have signed a release form permitting this; they also had the opportunity to stipulate conditions. Respondents who were quoted by name were permitted to review and approve, edit, or veto quotes. Interviewees wishing to remain anonymous are identified by a number.

34. For a discussion of epistemological issues related to that earlier project, see Carpenter 2012.

35. In this sense, I drew different boundaries on this project than on my earlier book, *Forgetting Children Born of War*. That project adopted a participatory methodology to examine the pitfalls of agenda-setting projects as an insider. Here, I limited my role to observing the efforts of others with minimal intervention on what those projects should look like until after the conclusion of the field research. See Carpenter 2010b.

36. See Tillmann et al. 2009.

37. See Carpenter 2008.

38. See Kingdon 1994.

39. I am frequently asked this question by graduate students at invited talks, and it is a very important one particularly given that blogging and social media is breaking down conventional boundaries between academics as experts and as citizens with their own political agendas. See Carpenter and Drezner 2010.

40. This stance of neutrality coupled with wide-ranging writings on adjacent issues bothered some of my informants. A long e-mail exchange ensued when an anti-AWS campaigner viewed my satirical ISA presentation "Cyborg Zombies," developed for an academic audience but posted on YouTube. Unable to easily ascertain my actual political opinion on the merits of anti-killer-robot campaigning, this viewer mistook the mixture of empirical fact and satirical international relations theory argument in the video for a mockery of the cause and stated that he was worried about my intentions in studying their movement.

41. Tomaskovic-Devey, Brownlie, and Carpenter 2011.

42. Carpenter 2011a.

43. Carpenter, in progress.

44. Carpenter 2013a, 2013b, 2013c.

45. Carpenter 2011b; Carpenter and Shaikhouni 2011.

46. Keohane 2009.

47. Jackson 2011, 197

48. On fuzzy-sets, see Ragin 2000.

49. On constitutive claims in international relations constructivism, see Wendt 1999.

REFERENCES

Abrahamson, Jennifer. 2006. *Sweet Relief: The Marla Ruzicka Story*. New York: Simon Spotlight Entertainment.

Abu-Sahlieh, Sami Aldeeb. 2001. *Male and Female Circumcision among Jews, Christians, and Muslims: Religious, Medical, Social, and Legal Debate*. Warren Center, PA: Shangri La Publications.

Adamic, Lada, and Eytan Adar. 2001. "You Are What You Link." Presented at the 10th Annual International World Wide Web Conference, Hong Kong. http://www10.org/program/society/yawyl/YouAreWhatYouLink.htm.

Adler, Emanuel. 1991. "Cognitive Evolution: A Dynamic Approach for the Study of International Relations and Their Progress." In *Progress in Postwar International Relations*, edited by Emanuel Adler and Beverly Crawford. New York: Columbia University Press.

———. 1992. "The Emergence of Cooperation: National Epistemic Communities and the International Evolution of the Idea of Nuclear Arms Control." *International Organization* 46 (1): 101–45.

Alston, Philip. 2010. "Interim Report of the Special Rapporteur on Extrajudicial, Summary or Arbitrary Executions." UN Document A/65/321.

Altmann, Jürgen, and Mark Avrum Gubrud. 2004. "Anticipating Military Nanotechnology." *IEEE Technology and Society Magazine* 39.

Amnesty International Bermuda. 1998. *Bodily Integrity for Both: The Obligation of Amnesty International to Recognize All Forms of Genital Mutilation of Males as Human Rights Violations.* Hamilton, Bermuda: AI Bermuda.

Anand, K. 1987. "Pain and Its Effects in the Human Neonate and Fetus." *New England Journal of Medicine* 317:1321–29.

Anderberg, Bengt, Ove Bring, and Myron Wolbarsht. 1992. "Blinding Laser Weapons and International Humanitarian Law." *Journal of Peace Research* 29 (3): 287–97.

Arkin, Ronald. 2004. "Bombs, Bonding, and Bondage: Human-Robot Interaction and Related Ethical Issues." Presented at the First International Symposium on Roboethics. January 30–31, Villa Nobel, San Remo, Italy. http://www.roboethics.org/sanremo2004/.

———. 2009. *Governing Lethal Behavior in Autonomous Robots.* New York: Chapman and Hall.

———. 2010. "The Case for Ethical Autonomy in Unmanned Systems." *Journal of Military Ethics* 9 (4): 332–41.

———. 2011. "Governing Lethal Behavior in Autonomous Combat Robots." Remarks presented at the University of Massachusetts Department of Computer Science Distinguished Lecture Series, December 2011, Amherst.

Auvert, B., D. Taljaard, E. Lagarde, J. Sobngwi-Tambekou, R. Sitta, and A. Puren. 2005. "Randomized, Controlled Intervention Trial of Male Circumcision for Reduction of HIV Infection Risk: The ANRS 1265 Trial. "*PLoS Medicine* 2 (11): 1112–22.

Avant, Deborah D., Martha Finnemore, and Susan Sell, eds. 2010. *Who Governs the Globe?* New York: Cambridge University Press.

Bachrach, Peter, and Morton S. Baratz. 1963. "Decisions and Nondecisions: An Analytical Framework." *American Political Science Review* 57 (3): 632–42.

Baer, Madeline, and Alyson Brysk. 2009. "Female Genital Mutilation." In *The International Struggle for New Human Rights*, edited by Clifford Bob, 93–107. Philadelphia: University of Pennsylvania Press.

Barabasi, Alberto. 2002. *Linked: The New Science of Networks.* New York: Basic Books.

Barbour, Rosaline, and Jenny Kitzinger. 1999. *Developing Focus Group Research.* London: Sage.

Barnett, Michael, and Raymond Duvall, eds. 2005. *Power in Global Governance.* New York: Cambridge University Press.

Barnett, Michael, and Martha Finnemore. 2004. *Rules for the World: International Organizations in Global Politics.* Ithaca: Cornell University Press.

BBC. 2012. "UN Drone Strikes Raise Questions: Navi Pillay." June 8. http://www.bbc.co.uk/news/world-asia-18363003.

Bell, Kristen. 2005. "Genital Cutting and Western Discourses of Sexuality." *Medical Anthropology Quarterly* 19 (2): 125–48.

Bergen, Peter. 2012. "A Dangerous New World of Drones." CNN National Security analyst, and Jennifer Rowland, October 2. http://www.cnn.com/2012/10/01/opinion/bergen-world-of-drones/index.html.

Bergen, Peter, and Katherine Tiedeman. 2009. "Revenge of the Drones." *New America Foundation*, October 19. http://www.newamerica.net/publications/policy/revenge_of_the_drones.

Berkovitch, Nitza, and Neve Gordon. 2008. "The Political Economy of Transnational Regimes: The Case of Human Rights." *International Studies Quarterly* 52 (4): 881–904.

Bloodgood, Elisabeth. 2011. "The Interest-Group Analogy: International Non-Governmental Organizations in International Politics." *Review of International Studies* 37 (1): 93–120.

Bob, Clifford. 2005. *The Marketing of Rebellion: Insurgents, Media, and International Activism.* New York: Cambridge.

———. 2009a. Introduction to *The International Struggle for New Human Rights*, edited by Clifford Bob, 30–51. Philadelphia: University of Pennsylvania Press.

———. 2009b. "Dalit Rights Are Human Rights: Caste Discrimination, International Activism, and the Construction of a New Human Rights Issue." In *The International Struggle for New Human Rights*, edited by Clifford Bob, 30–51. Philadelphia: University of Pennsylvania Press.

———. 2010. "Packing Heat: Pro-Gun Groups and the Governance of Small Arms." In *Who Governs the Globe?* edited by Deborah D. Avant, Martha Finnemore, and Susan Sell. New York: Cambridge University Press.

———. 2012. *The Global Right Wing and the Clash of World Politics.* Cambridge: Cambridge University Press.

Bolton, Matthew. 2012. "Nobel Peace Laureate Jody Williams Backs Campaign to Ban Killer Robots." Political Minefield blog, October 21. http://politicalminefields.com/2012/10/21/nobel-peace-laureate-jody-williams-backs-campaign-to-ban-killer-robots/.

Borenstein, Jason. 2008. "The Ethics of Autonomous Military Robots." *Studies in Ethics, Law, and Technology* 2 (1).

Borrie, John. 2009. *Unacceptable Harm: A History of How the Treaty to Ban Cluster Munitions Was Won.* New York: United Nations.

Borrie, John, and Ashley Thornton. 2008. *The Value of Diversity in Multilateral Disarmament Work.* New York: United Nations Institute for Disarmament Research.

Bouris, Erica. 2007. *Complex Political Victims.* San Francisco: Kumarian Press.

Brett, Derek. 2004. "How Many Child Soldiers: Is the 300,000 Still Valid?" *Child Soldier Newsletter*, May.

Brown, Wendy. 2001. "Human Rights Watch: An Overview." In *Human Rights NGOs: Promise and Performance*, edited by Claude Welch Jr., 72–84. Philadelphia: University of Pennsylvania Press.

Brysk, Alison. 2005. *Human Rights and Private Wrongs: Constructing Global Civil Society.* New York: Routledge.

———. 2009. *Global Good Samaritans: Human Rights as Foreign Policy.* Oxford: Oxford University Press.

Burgerman, Susan. 2001. *Moral Victories: How Activists Provoke Multilateral Action.* Ithaca: Cornell University Press.

Busby, Joshua W. 2010. *Moral Movements and Foreign Policy.* Cambridge: Cambridge University Press.

Butts, Carter T. 2013. *Sna: Tools for Social Network Analysis. R package version 2.3-1.* http://CRAN.R-project.org/package=sna.

Byers, Michael. 1999. *Custom, Power and the Power of Rules: International Relations and Customary Law.* Cambridge: Cambridge University Press.

———. 2005. *War Law.* New York: Grove Press.

Carnahan, Burrus M., and Marjorie Robertson. 1996. "The Protocol on Blinding Laser Weapons." *American Journal of International Law* 90 (3): 484–90.

Carpenter, Charli. 2003. "Women and Children First: Gender, Norms and Humanitarian Evacuation in the Balkans, 1991–1995." *International Organization* 57 (4): 661–694.

———. 2005. "Women, Children and Other Vulnerable Groups: Gender, Strategic Frames and the Protection of Civilians as a Transnational Issue." *International Studies Quarterly* 49:295–334.

———. 2006. *Innocent Women and Children: Gender, Norms and the Protection of Civilians.* London: Ashgate.

———. 2007a. "Studying Issue (Non)-Adoption in Transnational Advocacy Networks." *International Organization* 61 (Summer): 643–67.

———. 2007b. "Setting the Advocacy Agenda: Theorizing Issue Emergence and Nonemergence in Transnational Advocacy Networks." *International Studies Quarterly* 51:99–120.

———. 2008. "Kingdonian Activism?" Duck of Minerva blog. http://www.whiteoliphaunt.com/duckofminerva/2008/03/kingdonian-activism_31.html.

———. 2009. "Orphaned Again? Children Born of Wartime Rape as a Non-Issue for the Human Rights Movement." In *The International Struggle for New Human Rights*, edited by Clifford Bob, 14–29. Philadelphia: University of Pennsylvania Press.

———. 2010a. "Governing the Global Agenda: 'Gatekeepers' and 'Issue Adoption' in Transnational Advocacy Networks." In *Who Governs the Globe?* edited by Deborah D. Avant, Martha Finnemore, and Susan K. Sell. New York: Cambridge University Press.

———. 2010b. *Forgetting Children Born of War: Setting the Human Rights Agenda in Bosnia and Beyond.* New York: Columbia University Press.

———. 2010c. "Collateral Damage Control." *New York Times*, August 11.

———. 2011a. "Fighting the Laws of War." *Foreign Affairs* (March/April).

———. 2011b. "Vetting the Advocacy Agenda: Networks, Centrality and the Paradox of Weapons Norms." *International Organization* 65 (1).

———. 2012. "'You Talk Of Terrible Things So Matter-of-Factly in This Language of Science': Constructing Human Rights in the Academy." *Perspectives on Politics* 10 (2): 363–83.

———. 2013a. "The Fear Factor in Killer Robot Campaigning." Duck of Minerva blog. http://www.whiteoliphaunt.com/duckofminerva/2013/06/the-fear-factor-in-killer-robot-campaigning.html.

———. 2013b. "How Scared Are People of 'Killer Robots' and Why Does It Matter?" OpenDemocracy.org. July. http://www.opendemocracy.net/charli-carpenter/how-scared-are-people-of-%E2%80%9Ckiller-robots%E2%80%9D-and-why-does-it-matter.

———. 2013c. "Why Human Security Campaigners Are Winning the Killer Robot Debate." *Foreign Affairs*, July.

———. In progress. "The Global Intactivist Movement: Survey Findings." Presenting to the 13th International Symposium on Genital Autonomy and Children's Rights, to be held at the University of Colorado, Boulder, CO, July 24–26, 2014.

Carpenter, Charli, and Daniel Drezner. 2010. "IR 2.0: The Implications of New Media for an Old Profession." *International Studies Perspectives* 11: 255–72.

Carpenter, Charli, Sirin Duygulu, Alexander Montgomery, and Anna Rapp. Forthcoming. "Explaining the Advocacy Agenda: Insights from Human Security Practitioners." *International Organization* 68 (2).

Carpenter, Charli, and Betcy Jose. 2012. "Transnational Issue Networks in Real and Virtual Space: The Case of Women, Peace and Security." *Global Networks* 12 (4): 525–43.

Carpenter, Charli, and Lina Shaikhouni. 2011. "Don't Fear the Reaper." *Foreign Policy.* http://www.foreignpolicy.com/articles/2011/06/07/dont_fear_the_reaper?page=full.

Carpenter, Laura. 2009. "Influencing Health Debates through Letters to the Editor: The Case of Male Circumcision." *Qualitative Health Research* 19.

Castells, Manuel. 2011. "A Network Theory of Power." *International Journal of Communication* 5: 773–87.

CETMONS. 2011. "Thrust Group 2: International Law, Ethics and Governance on Robotics and National Security." http://cetmons.org/thrust2_robotic.

Chaulia, Sreeram. 2011. *International Organizations and Civilian Protection.* London: I.B. Tauris.

Checkel, Jeffrey T. 2012. "Norm Entrepreneurship: Theoretical and Methodological Challenges." Working paper presented at the workshop, "The Evolution of International Norms and 'Norm Entrepreneurship': The Council of Europe in Comparative Perspective," Wolfson College, Oxford University, January 2012. http://www.sfu.ca/content/dam/sfu/internationalstudies/checkel/Oxford-NormWorkshop-Paper.0112.pdf

Chuter, David. 2003. *War Crimes: Confronting Atrocity in the Modern World.* Boulder, CO: Lynne Rienner.

Cohen, Roberta. 2006. "Developing an International System for Internally Displaced Persons." *International Studies Perspectives* 7: 87–101.

Cooley, Alexander, and James Ron. 2002. "The NGO Scramble: Organizational Insecurity and the Political Economy of Transnational Action." *International Security* 27:5–39.

Dale, Stephen. 1996. *McLuhan's Children: The Greenpeace Message and the Media.* Toronto: Between the Lines.

Davies, Thomas Richard. 2007. *The Possibilities of Transnational Activism: The Campaign for Disarmament between the Two World Wars.* Leiden: Martinus Nifjhof.

Deasy, Kristen. 2012. "German Parliament Defends Faith-Based Circumcision amid Controversy." *Global Post*, July 20. http://www.globalpost.com/dispatch/news/regions/europe/germany/120720/german-parliament-defends-faith-based-circumcision-amid-.

DeLaet, Debra. 2009. "Framing Male Circumcision as a Human Rights Issue? Contributions to the Debate over the Universality of Human Rights." *Journal of Human Rights* 8:405–26.

DeMars, William. 2005. *NGOs and Transnational Networks.* London: Pluto Press.

Doswald-Beck, Louise. 1996. "New Protocol on Blinding Laser Weapons." *International Review of the Red Cross* 312: 272–99.

Downes, Alexander. 2009. *Targeting Civilians in War.* Ithaca: Cornell University Press.

Drezner, Dan. 2007. "Foreign Policy Goes Glam." *National Interest*, November 1.

Duygulu, Sirin, and Charli Carpenter. 2013. "Issue Adoption in Transnational Networks." Manuscript in progress, University of Massachusetts.

Finnemore, Martha. 1996. *National Interests in International Society.* New York: Cornell University Press.

Finnemore, Martha, and Kathryn Sikkink. 1998. "International Norm Dynamics and Political Change." *International Organization* 52:887–918.

Fleiss, Joseph L. 1971. "Measuring Nominal Scale Agreement among Many Raters." *Psychological Bulletin* 76 (5): 378–82.

Forman, Shepard, and Derk Segaar. 2006. "New Coalitions for Global Governance: The Changing Dynamics of Multilateralism." *Global Governance* 12 (2): 205–25.

Forsythe, 2005. *The Humanitarians: The International Committee of the Red Cross.* Cambridge: Cambridge University Press.

Freeman, Linton. 1979. "Centrality in Social Networks: Conceptual Clarification." *Social Networks* 1:215–39.

Garcia, Denise. 2006. *Small Arms and Security: New Emerging International Norms.* London: Routledge.

———. 2012. *Disarmament Diplomacy and Human Security: Regimes, Norms and Moral Progress in International Relations.* London: Routledge.

Glaser, Barney, and Anselm Strauss. 1967. *The Discovery of Grounded Theory: Strategies for Qualitative Research.* Chicago: Aldine Publishing Company.

Glick, Leonard. 2005. *Marked in Your Flesh.* Oxford: Oxford University Press.

Goddard, Stacie E. 2009. "Brokering Change: Networks and Entrepreneurs in International Politics." *International Theory* 1 (2): 249–81.

Gollagher, David. 2001. *Circumcision: A History of the World's Most Controversial Surgery.* New York: Basic Books.

Gourevitch, Peter, David Lake, and Janice Stein. 2012. *The Credibility of Transnational NGOs: When Virtue Is Not Enough.* Cambridge: Cambridge University Press.

Grant, J. Andrew, and Ian Taylor. 2004. "Global Governance and Conflict Diamonds: The Kimberley Process and the Quest for Clean Gems." *Round Table* 93 (37): 385–401.

Grieg, Kai. 2001. *War Children of the World.* Bergen: War and Children Identity Project.

Grimsley, Marc, and Clifford Rogers, eds. 2008. *Civilians in the Path of War.* Lincoln: University of Nebraska Press.

Gross, Michael. 2010. *Moral Dilemmas of Modern War.* Cambridge: Cambridge University Press.

Gruenbaum, Ellen. 1996. *The Female Circumcision Controversy.* Philadelphia: University of Pennsylvania Press.

Gubrud, Mark Avrum. 1997. "Nanotechnology and International Security." Archive of the Fifth Foresight Conference on Molecular Nanotechnology. http://www.foresight.org/Conferences/MNT05/Papers/Gubrud/index.html.

Haas, Peter. 1992. "Introduction: Epistemic Communities and International Policy Coordination." *International Organization* 46 (1): 1–35.

Hadden, Jennifer. 2008. "Society Spillover(s) in EU Climate Change and Labor Politics." Transatlantic Graduate Workshop Hanse Wissenschaftskolleg, Delmenhorst, Germany, May 9–11.

Hafner-Burton, Emilie, Miles Kahler, and Alexander Montgomery. 2009. "Network Analysis for International Relations." *International Organization* 63 (3): 559–92.

Hafner-Burton, Emilie, and Alexander Montgomery. 2006. "Power Positions, International Organizations, Social Networks and Conflict." *Journal of Conflict Resolution* 50 (1): 3–27.

Hafner-Burton, Emilie, and James Ron. 2009. "Seeing Double: Human Rights Impact through Qualitative and Quantitative Eyes." *World Politics* 61:360–401.

Haufler, Virginia. 2010. "Corporations in Zones of Conflict." In *Who Governs the Globe?*, edited by Deborah D. Avant, Martha Finnemore, and Susan Sell, 102–30. Cambridge University Press.

Hay, Iain. 2005. *Qualitative Research Methods in Human Geography*. 2nd ed. Oxford: Oxford University Press.

Heckel, Heather. 2005. "Transnational Advocacy against the Use of Child Soldiers." In *Subcontracting Peace: The Challenges of NGO Peacebuilding*, edited by Oliver P. Richmond and Henry F. Carey. London: Ashgate.

Henzinger, Monika. 2001. "Hyperlink Analysis for the Web." *IEEE Internet Computing* 5 (1): 45–50.

Herrold, Marc. 2009. "Unworthy Afghan Bodies: 'Smarter' US Weapons Kill More Innocents." In *Inventing Collateral Damage*, edited by Stephen Rockel and Rick Halpern, 303–28. Toronto: Between the Lines Press.

Hertel, Shareen. 2006. *Unexpected Power: Conflict and Change among Transnational Activists*. Ithaca: Cornell University Press.

Hess, Matthew. 2009. "The MGM Bill: A Legislative Strategy for Protecting US Boys from Circumcision." In *Circumcision and Human Rights*, edited by George Denniston, Frederick Hodges, and Marilyn Fayre Milos. New York: Springer.

Heyns, Christof. 2013. "Report of the Special Rapporteur on Extrajudicial, Summary or Arbitrary Executions." UN Doc. A/HRC/23/47.

Hicks, M. H.-R., U. R. Lee, R. Sundberg, and M. Spagat. 2011. "Global Comparison of Warring Groups in 2002–2007: Fatalities from Targeting Civilians vs. Fighting Battles." *PLoS ONE* 6 (9): e23976.

Hilgartner, Stephen and Charles Bosk. 1988. "The Rise and Fall of Social Problems." *American Journal of Sociology* 94 (1): 53–78.

Holewinski, Sarah. 2012. "Making Amends." In *Civilians and Modern War: Armed Conflict and the Ideology of Violence*, edited by Daniel Rothbart, Karina Korostelina, and Mohammed Cherkaoui. London: Routledge.

Holton, Robert J. 2008. *Global Networks*. New York: Palgrave Macmillan.

Holzscheiter, Anna. 2005. "Discourse as Capability: Non-State Actors' Capital in Global Governance." *Millennium* 33 (3): 723–46.

Hopgood, Stephen. 2006. *Keepers of the Flame: Understanding Amnesty International*. Ithaca: Cornell University Press.

Hosken, Graeme, Michale Schmidt, and Johan du Plessis. 2007. "Nine Killed in Army Horror." *Independent Online*. http://www.iol.co.za/news/south-africa/9-killed-in-army-horror-1.374838#.UpUhW8RDsWE.

Hubert, Don. 2000. *The Landmine Ban: A Case Study in Humanitarian Advocacy*. Occasional Paper #42. Providence: Watson Institute for International Studies.

——. 2007. "Humanitarian Advocacy Campaigns: Lessons on Government–Civil Society Collaboration." In *Joint Action for Prevention: Civil Society and Government Cooperation on Conflict Prevention and Peace Building*. Issue Paper 4, edited by Paul van Tongeren and Christine van Empel, 79–86. Den Haag, the Netherlands: Global Partnership for the Prevention of Armed Conflict.

Hudson, Natalie Florea. 2009. "Securitizing Women's Human Rights and Gender Equality." *Journal of Human Rights* 8 (1): 53–70.

Huliaras, Asteris, and Nikolaos Tzifakis. 2010. "Celebrity Activism in International Relations: In Search of Framework for Analysis." *Global Society* 24 (2): 255–74.

Human Rights Watch/International Human Rights Clinic. 2012a. *Losing Humanity: The Case against Killer Robots*. New York: Human Rights Watch.

——. 2012b. "US: Transfer CIA Drone Strikes to Military." April 20. http://www.hrw.org/news/2012/04/20/us-transfer-cia-drone-strikes-military.

——.2012c."US:TargetedKillingPolicyDisregardsHumanRightsLaw."May1.http://www.hrw.org/news/2012/05/01/us-targeted-killing-policy-disregards-human-rights-law.

——. 2012d. "Nations Should Step Up Humanitarian Disarmament." October 24. http://www.hrw.org/news/2012/10/24/nations-should-step-humanitarian-disarmament.

Inal, Tuba. 2013. *Looting and Rape in Wartime: Law and Change in International Relations*. Philadelphia: University of Pennsylvania Press.

Ingenkamp, Nina. 2008. *How HIV-AIDS Has Made It: An Analysis of Global HIV-AIDS Agenda-Setting between 1981 and 2002*. Saarbrücken, Germany: VDM Verlag Dr. Muller.

Ingram, Paul, Jeffrey Robinson, and Marc Busch. 2005. "The Intergovernmental Network of World Trade: IGO Connectedness, Governance and Embeddedness." *American Journal of Sociology* 111 (3): 824–58.

Jackson, Patrick. 2011. *The Conduct of Inquiry in International Relations*. London: Routledge.

Jackson, Patrick, and Stuart Kaufman. 2007. "Security Scholars for a Sensible Foreign Policy: A Study in Weberian Activism." *Perspectives on Politics* 5 (1): 95–103.

Joachim, Jutta. 2007. *Agenda Setting, the UN, and NGOs: Gender Violence and Reproductive Rights*. Washington, DC: Georgetown University Press.

Jones, Adam. 1996. "Does Gender Make the World Go Round?" *Review of International Studies* 22 (4): 405–29.

Jones, Bryan, and Frank Baumgartner. 2005. *The Politics of Attention: How Governments Prioritize Issues*. Chicago: University of Chicago Press.

Kahl, Colin. 2007. "In the Crosshairs or Crossfire?" *International Security* 32 (1): 7–46.

Kahler, Miles. 2009. *Networked Politics: Agency, Power, and Governance*. Ithaca: Cornell University Press.

Keck, Margaret, and Kathryn Sikkink. 1998. *Activists beyond Borders: Advocacy Networks in International Politics*. Ithaca: Cornell University Press.

Kellenberger, Jakob. 2011. "Keynote Address." 34th Round Table on Current Issues of International Humanitarian Law, San Remo, September 9.

Keohane, Robert. 2009. "Political Science as a Vocation." *Political Science and Politics* 42 (2): 359–63.

Khagram, Sanjeev, James Riker, and Kathryn Sikkink, eds. 2002. *Restructuring World Politics: Transnational Social Movements, Networks, and Norms*. Minneapolis: University of Minnesota Press.

Kindornay, Shannon, James Ron, and Charli Carpenter. 2012. "Rights-Based Approaches to Development: Implications for NGOs." *Human Rights Quarterly* 34 (2): 472–506.

King, Gary, Robert Keohane, and Sidney Verba. 1994. *Designing Social Inquiry*. Princeton: Princeton University Press.

Kingdon, John W. 1994. *Agendas, Alternatives, and Public Policies*, 2nd ed. New York: HarperCollins.

Knopf, Jeffrey. 2012. "NGOs, Social Movements, and Arms Control." In *Arms Control: History, Theory, and Policy*, vol. 1, edited by Robert E. Williams and Paul R. Viotti, 169–94. New York: Praeger.

Krishnan, Armin. 2010. *Killer Robots: Legality and Ethicality of Autonomous Weapons*. London: Ashgate Press.

Lake, David, and Wendy Wong. 2009. "The Politics and Power of Networks." In *Networked Politics: Agency, Power, and Governance*, edited by Miles Kahler. Ithaca: Cornell University Press.

Lightfoot-Klein, Hanny. 1997. "Similarities in Attitudes and Misconceptions toward Infant Male Circumcision in North America and Ritual Female Genital Mutilation in Africa." In *Sexual Mutilations: A Human Tragedy*, edited by George C. Denniston and Marilyn Fayre Milos. New York: Plenum Press.

Lin, Patrick, George Bekey, and Keith Abney. 2008. *Autonomous Military Robots: Risk, Ethics, and Design*. San Luis Obispo: California Polytechnic University.

Lincoln Center. 2012. Chautauqua Council Final Report. September. http://lincoln-center-dev.asu.edu/ChautauquaCouncil/chautauqa-council-2012-final-report?q=ChautauquaCouncil/chautauqa-council-2012-final-report.

Lipschutz, Ronnie. 2005. "Power, Politics and Global Civil Society." *Millennium: Journal of International Studies* 33 (3): 747–69.

Lord, Janet. 2009. "Disability Rights and the Human Rights Mainstream: Reluctant Gate-Crashers." In *The International Struggle for New Human Rights*, edited by Clifford Bob. Philadelphia: University of Pennsylvania Press.

Lu, Chi-Jung, and Stuart Shulman. 2008. "Rigor and Flexibility in Computer-Based Qualitative Research: Introducing the Coding Analysis Toolkit." *International Journal of Multiple Research Approaches* 2:105–17.

Maoz, Zeev. 2001. *Networks of Nations*. New York: Cambridge University Press.

Marchant, Gary, Braden Allenby, Ronald Arkin, Edward T. Barrett, Jason Borenstein, Lyn M. Gaudet, Orde Kittrie, Patrick Lin, George R. Lucas, Richard O'Meara, and Jared Silberman. 2011. "International Governance of Lethal Autonomous Robots." *Columbia Science and Technology Law Review* 12:272.

Mariner, Joanne. 2010. "When Machines Kill." FindLaw, September 22. http://writ.news.findlaw.com/mariner/20100922.html.

Marks, Paul. 2008. "Anti-Landmine Campaigners Turn Sights on War Robots." *New Scientist*, March. http://www.newscientist.com/article/dn13550-antilandmine-campaigners-turn-sights-on-war-robots.html.

Martin, Mary, and Taylor Owen. 2010. "The Second Generation of Human Security: Lessons from the UN and EU Experience." *International Affairs* 86 (1): 211–24.

Mathiason, John. 2007. *Invisible Governance: International Secretariats in Global Politics.* San Francisco: Kumarian Press.

Matthew, Richard, and Kenneth Rutherford. 2003. "The Evolutionary Dynamics of the Movement to Ban Landmines." *Alternatives* 28:29–56.

Mercer, Jon. 1996. *Reputation in International Politics.* Ithaca: Cornell University Press.

Merry, Sally. 2006. *Human Rights and Gender Violence: Translating International Law into Local Justice.* Chicago: University of Chicago Press.

Mertus, Julie. 2009. "Applying the Gatekeeper Model of Human Rights Activism: The U.S.-Based Movement for LGBT Rights." In *The International Struggle for New Human Rights*, edited by Clifford Bob. Philadelphia: University of Pennsylvania Press.

Millett, G. A., S. A. Flores, G. Marks, J. B. Reed, and J. H. Herbst. 2008. "Circumcision Status and Risk of HIV and Sexually Transmitted Infections among Men Who Have Sex with Men." *JAMA* 300 (14): 1674–84.

Minear, Larry, and Ian Smillie. 2004. *The Charity of Nations: Humanitarian Action in a Calculating World.* Bloomfield, CT: Kumarian Press.

Minkel, J. R. 2008. "Robotics Professor Sees Threat in Military Robots." *Scientific American*, August 15.

Mische, Ann. 2003. "Cross-Talk in Movements: Reconceiving the Culture Network Link." In *Social Movements and Networks: Relational Approaches to Collective Action*, edited by Mario Diani and Doug McAdam. New York: Oxford University Press.

Mundy, Karen. 2010. "Education for All and the Global Governors." In *Who Governs the Globe?*, edited by Deborah D. Avant, Martha Finnemore, and Susan Sell. Cambridge: Cambridge University Press.

Murdie, Amanda. 2013. "The Ties That Bind: A Network Analysis of Human Rights International Nongovernmental Organizations." *British Journal of Political Science* 44 (1): 1–27. doi:10.1017/S0007123412000683.

Murdie, Amanda, and David Davis. 2012. "Looking in the Mirror: Comparing INGO Networks across Issue Areas." *Review of International Organizations* 77 (2): 177–202.

Nexon, Daniel. 2009. *The Struggle for Power in Early Modern Europe: Religious Conflict, Dynastic Empires, and International Change.* Princeton: Princeton University Press.

Oestreich, Joel. 2004. "The Impact of War on Children: What Can We Know and How Can We Know It?" Working paper, prepared for presentation at the "Children and War: Impact" Conference, Edmonton, Canada.

———. 2007. *Power and Principle: Human Rights Programming in International Organizations.* Washington: Georgetown University Press.

Orchard, Phil. 2010. "The Guiding Principles on Internal Displacement: Soft Law as a Norm-Generating Mechanism." *Review of International Studies* 36: 281–303.

Paris, Roland. 2001. "Human Security: Paradigm Shift or Hot Air?" *International Security* 26 (2): 87–102.

Park, Han Woo, Chun-Suk Kim, and George A. Barnett. 2004. "Socio-communicational Structure among Political Actors on the Web in South Korea." *New Media and Society* 6 (3).

Park, Han Woo, and Mike Thelwall. 2003. "Hyperlink Analyses of the World Wide Web: A Review." *Journal of Computer-Mediated Communications* 8 (4). http://www.ascusc.org/jcmc/vol8/issue4/park.html.

Parson, Edward. 2003. *Protecting the Ozone Layer: Science and Strategy.* New York: Oxford University Press.

Peters, Ann. 1996. "Blinding Laser Weapons." *Conflict and Survival* 12:107–13.

Peterson, M. J. 2010. "How the Indigenous Got Seats at the UN Table." *Review of International Organizations* 5:197–225.

Pettigrew, Thomas. 1979. "The Ultimate Attribution Error." *Personality and Social Psychology* 5 (4): 461–76.

Praelle, Sarah. 2003. "Venue Shopping, Political Strategy, and Policy Change: The Internationalization of Canadian Forest Advocacy." *Journal of Public Policy* 23 (3): 233–60.

Prakash, Aseem, and Mary Kay Gugerty, eds. 2010. *Advocacy Organizations and Collective Action.* New York: Cambridge University Press.

Price, Richard. 1998. "Reversing the Gun Sights: Transnational Civil Society Targets Land Mines." *International Organization* 52:613–44.

———. 2003. "Transnational Civil Society and Advocacy in World Politics." *World Politics* 55 (July): 579–606.

Ragin, Charles. 2000. *Fuzzy-Set Social Science.* Chicago: University of Chicago Press.

Rapp, Anna, and Charli Carpenter. 2012. "Agenda Re-Setting: Issue Creation, Norm Life-Cycles, and the Child Soldiers Campaign." Working paper, University of Massachusetts.

Reinicke, Wolfgang, and Francis Deng. 2000. *Critical Choices: The United Nations Networks and the Future of Global Governance.* Ottawa: International Development Research Center.

Reinmann, Kim D. 2006. "A View from the Top: International Politics, Norms and Worldwide Growth of NGOs." *International Studies Quarterly* 50 (1): 45–67.

Riles, Annelise. 2001. *The Network Inside Out.* Ann Arbor: University of Michigan Press.

Robbins, Liz. 2012. "Baby's Death Renews Debate over a Circumcision Ritual." *New York Times*, March 13, A26.

Rogers, Richard. 2012. *Digital Methods.* Cambridge: MIT Press.

Rogers, Richard, and Anat Ben-David. 2008. "The Palestinian-Israeli Peace Process and Transnational Issue Networks: The Complicated Place of the Israeli NGO." *New Media and Society* 10 (3): 497–528.

Ron, James, Howard Ramos, and Kathleen Rodgers. 2005. "Transnational Informational Politics." *International Studies Quarterly* 49 (3): 557–88.

Ronen, Yael. 2008. "Avoid or Compensate? Liability for Incidental Injury for Incidental Injury to Civilians during Armed Conflict." Research Paper No. 04–08. International Law Forum of the Hebrew University of Jerusalem Law Faculty.

Rothman, Wilson. 2008. "Autonomous Robots: Suicide Bombers or Ethical Combatants?" Gizmodo, February 27. http://gizmodo.com/361400/autonomous-robots-ethical-combatants-or-suicide-bombers.

Sartori, Giovanni. 1970. "Concept Misformation in Comparative Politics." *American Political Science Review* 64 (4): 1033–53.

Schmitz, H. 2006. *When Networks Blind: Human Rights and Politics in Kenya*. Cornell University Workshop on Network Contention Working Paper #2001–06.

Schrad, Mark Lawrence. 2010. *The Political Power of Bad Ideas*. Oxford: Oxford University Press.

Sell, Susan K., and Aseem Prakash. 2004. "Using Ideas Strategically: The Contest between Business and NGO Networks in Intellectual Property Rights." *International Studies Quarterly* 48:143–75.

Shachtman, Noel. 2007. "Robot Cannon Kills 9, Wounds 14." Danger Room blog. http://www.wired.com/dangerroom/2007/10/robot-cannon-ki/.

Sharkey, Noel. 2007. "Automated Killers and the Computing Profession." *Computer* 40 (11).

Shawki, Noha. 2010. "Political Opportunity Structures and the Outcomes of Transnational Campaigns: A Comparison of Two Transnational Advocacy Networks." *Peace and Change* 35 (3): 381–411.

Shiffman, Jeremy. 2009. "A Social Explanation for the Rise and Fall of Global Health Issues." *Bulletin of the World Health Organization* 87 (8): 608–13.

Shiffman, Jeremy, and Stephanie Smith. 2007. "Generation of Political Priority for Global Health Initiatives: A Framework and Case Study of Maternal Mortality." *Lancet* 370 (9595): 1370–79.

Silverman, Eric. 2009. "Anthropology and Circumcision." *Annual Review of Anthropology* 33:419–45.

Simonite, T. 2007. "Robot Rampage Unlikely Reason for Deaths." New Scientist.com. http://www.newscientist.com/article/dn12812-robotic-rampage-unlikely-reason-for-deaths.html.

Singer, Peter. 2009. *Wired for War: The Robotics Revolution and Conflict in the 21st Century*. New York: Penguin.

Slaughter, Anne Marie. 2004. *A New World Order*. Princeton: Princeton University Press.

Slim, Hugo. 2010. *Killing Civilians: Methods, Madness, and Morality in War*. New York: Columbia University Press.

Smith, Steve, and Marysia Zalewski. 1996. *International Theory: Positivism and Beyond*. New York: Cambridge University Press.

Snyder, A. 2003. *Setting the Agenda for Global Peace: Conflict and Consensus Building*. Burlington, VT: Ashgate.

Somerville, M. 2000. "Altering Baby Boys' Bodies: The Ethics of Infant Male Circumcision." In *The Ethical Canary: Science, Society and the Human Spirit*, edited by Margaret Somerville, 202–19. Toronto: Viking.

Sparrow, Robert. 2007. "Killer Robots." *Journal of Applied Philosophy* 24 (1).

———. 2009. "Predators or Plowshares? Time to Consider Arms Control of Robotic Weapons?" *IEEE Technology and Society* 28 (1): 25–29.

Spector, Malcolm, and John Kitsuse. 1977. *Constructing Social Problems*. Menlo Park, CA: Cummings.

Stone, Deborah. 2006. "Reframing the Racial Disparities Issue for State Governments." *Journal of Health Politics, Policy and Law* 31 (1): 127–52.

Stone, Diane. 2001. "Think-tanks, Global Lesson-Drawing and Networking Social Policy Ideas." *Global Social Policy* 1 (3): 338–60.

Svoboda, J. Steven. 1999. "Attaining International Acknowledgment of Male Genital Mutilation as a Human Rights Violation." In *Male and Female Circumcision*, edited by George Denniston, Frances Hodges, and Marilyn Milos, 455–64. New York: Springer.

———. 2001. "UN Criticized for Sex Discrimination against Males." http://arclaw.org/resources/articles/united-nations-criticized-sex-discrimination-against-males-0.

Tarrow, Sidney. 2005. *The New Transnational Activism*. New York: Cambridge University Press.

Thomas, Ward. 2002. *The Ethics of Destruction*. Ithaca: Cornell University Press.

Thompson, Andrew. 2008. "Beyond Expression: Amnesty International's Decision to Oppose Capital Punishment, 1973." *Journal of Human Rights* 7:327–40.

Thompson, Karen Brown. 2002. "Women's Rights Are Human Rights." In *Restructuring World Politics: Transnational Social Movements, Networks, and Norms*, edited by Sanjeev Khagram, James Riker, and Kathryn Sikkink, 96–122. Minneapolis: University of Minnesota Press.

Tillmann, Patricia, Anna Tomaskovic-Devey, Stephanie Boucher, Mandy Brule, Sirin Duygulu, Amy Fleig, and Daniel Scarnecchia. 2009. "Changing the Rules: Strategies for Creating an International Standard for the Compensation of Civilians Harmed Unintentionally in Armed Conflict." Working paper, University of Massachusetts.

Tomaskovic-Devey, Anna, Kyle Brownlie, and Charli Carpenter. 2011. *Agenda-Setting in Transnational Networks: Findings from Consultations with Human Security Practitioners*. Amherst: University of Massachusetts Center for Public Policy and Administration.

Tracy, Jonathan. 2007. "Responsibility to Pay: Compensating the Civilian Casualties of War." *Human Rights Brief* 15 (1): 16–19.

True-Frost, Cora. 2007. "The Security Council and Norm Consumption." *International Law and Politics* 40:115–217.

Tsaliki, Liza, Christos A. Frangonikolopoulos, and Asertis Huliaris. 2011. *Transnational Celebrity Activism in Global Politics: Changing the World?* Chicago: University of Chicago Press.

United Nations Economic and Social Council. 1997a. "The Implementation of the Human Rights of Women: Traditional Practices Affecting the Health of Women and Children." June 25. E/CN.4/Sub.2/1997/10.

———.1997b. "Report of the Sub-Commission on Prevention of Discrimination and Protection of Minorities on Its Forty-Ninth Session." Geneva, Switzerland. E/CN.4/1998/2; E/CN.4/Sub.2/1997/50.

———. 2001. "Traditional Practices Affecting the Health of Women and the Girl Child." July 4. E/CN.4/Sub.2/2001/27.

United Nations General Assembly. 2006. "Rights of the Child. Report of the Independent Expert for the United Nations Study on Violence against Children." A/61/299.

United Nations Security Council. 1992. "Final Report of the Commission of Experts Established Pursuant to Security Council Resolution 780." S/1994/674.

———. 2010a. "Report of the Secretary General on the Protection of Civilians in Armed Conflict." November 11. S/2010/579.

———. 2010b. "Statement by the President of the Security Council." November 22, 3. S/PRST/2010/25.

Van Howe, Robert. 1999. "Peer Review Bias Regarding Circumcision in American Medical Publishing: Subverting the Dominant Paradigm." In *Male and Female Circumcision*, edited by George Denniston, Frances Hodges, and Marilyn Milos. New York: Kluwer.

Wallerstein, Edward. 1980. *Circumcision: A Public Health Fallacy.* New York: Springer.

Walzer, Michael. 2006. *Just and Unjust Wars*, 2nd ed. New York: Basic Books.

Wasserman, Stanley, and Katherine Faust. 1994. *Social Network Analysis: Methods and Applications.* Cambridge: Cambridge University Press.

Weiss, Helen, Natasha Larke, Daniel Halperin, and Inon Schenker. 2010. "Complications of Circumcision in Male Neonates, Infants and Children: A Systematic Review." *BMC Urology* 10 (2): 1–13.

Weiss, Thomas, and Cindy Collins. 2000. *Humanitarian Challenges and Intervention*, 2nd ed. Boulder, CO: Westview Press.

Welch, Claude, Jr. 2000. "Amnesty International and HRW: A Comparison." In *Human Rights NGOs: Promise and Performance*, edited by Claude Welch Jr., 85–118. Philadelphia: University of Pennsylvania Press.

Wendt, Alexander. 1992. "Anarchy Is What States Make of It." *International Organization* 46 (2): 391–425.

———. 1999. *Social Theory of International Politics.* Cambridge: Cambridge University Press.

———. 2006. "Social Theory as Cartesian Science: An Auto-Critique from a Quantum Perspective." In *Constructivism and International Relations: Alexander Wendt and His Critics*, edited by Stefano Guzzini and Anna Leande, 178–216. New York: Routledge.

Wendt, Alexander, and Robert Duvall. 2008. "Sovereignty and the UFO." *Political Theory* 36 (4): 607–33.

Williams, Jody. 2011. "Borderless Battlefield: The CIA, the U.S. Military and Drones." *International Journal of Intelligence Ethics* 2 (1): 2–23.

———. 2012. Remarks on NPR Radio, WBEZ Chicago. http://llnw.wbez.org/WV20121003.mp3.

———. 2013. *My Name Is Jody Williams: A Vermont Girl's Winding Path to the Nobel Peace Prize.* Berkeley: University of California Press.

Williams, Phil. 2001. "Transnational Criminal Networks." In *Networks and Netwars*, edited by David Arquila and John Ronfeldt, 61–98. Washington, DC: Rand Corporation.

Winter, Bronwyn, Denise Thompson, and Sheila Jeffreys. 2002. "The UN's Approach to Harmful Traditional Practices: Some Conceptual Problems." *International Feminist Journal of Politics* 4 (1): 72–94.

Wong, Wendy H. 2008. "Centralizing Principles: How Amnesty Shaped Human Rights Policies through Its Transnational Network." PhD diss., University of California, San Diego.

———. 2012. *Internal Affairs: How the Structure of NGOs Transforms Human Rights.* Ithaca: Cornell University Press.

World Health Organization. 2006. *WHO Meeting Report: Strategies and Approaches for Male Circumcision Programming.* Geneva: WHO.

———. 2007. *Male Circumcision: Global Trends and Determinants of Prevalence, Safety, and Acceptability.* Geneva: WHO.

Index